Toward a Society of Leisure

Joffre Dumazedier

TOWARD
A SOCIETY
OF LEISURE

Translated from the French by
Stewart E. McClure

Foreword by David Riesman

THE FREE PRESS, *New York*
COLLIER-MACMILLAN LIMITED, *London*

Collier-Macmillan Canada, Ltd., Toronto, Ontario

Library of Congress Catalog Card Number: 67-12513

Originally published as *Vers une civilisation du loisir?* by
Editions du Seuil, Paris, 1962

Foreword

ONE SUMMER A FEW YEARS AGO, JOFFRE DUMAZEDIER PAID HIS
first visit to America, a country where he, like other French sociologists, had already lived in his imagination. He had at that time
completed a meticulous study of leisure-time behavior among the
residents of Annecy—work which is reflected in this volume. He
had hoped to find in the United States sociologists and economists
and planners who, recognizing the importance of mass leisure in
post-industrial society, would be working together to consider how
it might be made more emancipating and fruitful, while its evils
would be anticipated and warded off. But he was disappointed to
discover that neither governmental agencies nor private or academic
researchers were pursuing such questions systematically. I, at least,
he had thought, would have around me a team of social scientists
surveying all aspects of leisure, perhaps even beginning to plan for
its future. What he discovered instead was that the Center for the
Study of Leisure which I had briefly headed at the University of
Chicago had been dissolved, and that so far as I knew there was
no such center anywhere in America. Even with work diminishing
in emotional importance for millions, there were still centers of

labor and industrial relations and of industrial sociology, but none for the investigation of play and leisure.

Perhaps the economists would be better prepared, M. Dumazedier thought. I introduced him to my colleague, John Kenneth Galbraith; but although he wrote brilliantly about the maldistribution of affluence, he too directed no center, supervised no team, and, at that time, planned no futures.

American sociology is by no means monolithic in its attitude toward policy-oriented research, and concern with social problems and prospects varies within subfields and over time. It has often been charged that American academicians prefer to avoid controversial issues, but the fear of controversy may be less important than the attraction of the conceptual and methodological infrastructure of a newly elaborating discipline, and of the manageable as well as exhilirating problems provided by the discipline's autonomous development. Moreover, while the industries and services catering to free time and money wanted market researchers to help discover and expand markets, no large public client was commissioning studies of the Annecy sort.

For one thing, America is decentralized to the point of anarchy compared with France. There is no national broadcasting system, no national educational system (though the rudiments of this may be discerned), no national vacation policy (though there are the national parks, which have their problems with public leisure). In the absence of all-inclusive researches on a national scale, American researchers have tackled more manageable items: the effect of television on children's attitudes towards violence; the actualities and possibilities of adult education; and many specific studies of reading, viewing, listening, visiting, and sociability. (M. Dumazedier treats some of this work in his Appendix A, browsing through *Mass Leisure, Mass Culture,* and *Leisure in America*.) M. Dumazedier went home again with the realization that, while America is munificent in the production of social scientists compared with

Europe, these social scientists may be more peripheral than those of a country more given to conscious planning.

Of course, we do plan and did so even in the Eisenhower years: we plan fiscally and militarily; we exhort nationally even if we administer locally, but we do not call it planning. We do study and collect figures on unemployment and on saving and spending, on television-watching, book-buying, and movie-attendance; but we do not study or collect figures on the overall problems of leisure, for it is somehow still not serious with us, in the sense of having a bureau or department of its own, or even a section meeting at the American Sociological Association annual meetings. This seems to me one reason why a book almost entirely devoted to French data and interpretations may be a useful import.

I do not mean by these remarks to suggest that French academic life makes it easy to study leisure and to plan for its future. Certainly, French schooling, either in the lycée or in the university, is not at all geared to preparation for leisure. M. Dumazedier is an activist and an organizer of research who has worked hard to overcome the biases of French cultural formation and of contempt for how "the masses" spend the free time thought to be undeserved. In this, he has the support of a minority tradition in French intellectual life concerned with popular culture: a tradition that helped to discover American jazz for the high-brows in both countries and that has brought to the movies the kind of attentive criticism of Edgar Morin.

Thus, neither the problems of leisure in an industrial society nor the problems of research in this area are bounded by national lines. The American reader will nod with recognition at the discussions of the French do-it-yourself cult, of active and spectator sports, or of the "action" orientation of French workers, such as the man quoted herein who liked *War and Peace* because "there is plenty of action." There is also a discussion of moonlighting, about which Dumazedier remarks that "time off from one's regular job is [often] used for doing other paid work. . . ." If this is so, then the French are as much—or even more—driven than the Americans who employ leisure to absorb the signals demanding a still more expensive style of life, which in turn demands another job. The annual summer hegira which takes nearly three-quarters of the population of Paris out of the city is part of a vacation cult more concentrated in time and space than anything we know in the United States. Centralization has an impact on this phenomenon in providing a national labor policy and, to back it up in some measure, national efforts at rail transport and the provision of camping facilities. Friends of mine tell a nice story to illustrate the prevalence of this cult: they went with their three-year-old daughter to visit a couple with a recent baby, but on arrival they were told that the newborn was away; my friends' little girl asked, "Away on vacation?"

In addition to reporting studies done by himself and others, M. Dumazedier seeks in his book to respond to the criticisms of contemporary popular culture and mass leisure made by those who look back to an earlier day of supposedly more strenuous and less dehydrated pleasures. In part, this nostalgia reflects, as it does in the United States, the disappointment of the intellectual Left with the uses the working class has made of its new-found freedoms and amenities. To rebut such a picture, he points out that the working class even in the nineteenth century was already disappointing its middle-class friends by its low tastes and frequent drunkenness on Sundays and the ensuing Mondays. Moreover, he insists, from a study of best-sellers, that taste has actually risen with increments of schooling and much more free time, although not in the ways that socialist prophets hoped for who were too romantic about the oppressed. Instead, the Annecy study revealed that the greatly increased free time of the working class lures them away from unions and political activities into familistic and private pursuits; he declares that 80 per cent of the workers are wholly indifferent to any problems, whether of the company or of the union: what matters to them is their paycheck and the non-work life it enables them to create. But the author insists that that life is not necessarily passive because it is spent watching television or the movies, for activity and passivity are states of mind and cannot be inferred from behavior itself. Thus, 20 per cent of the Annecy moviegoers belong to cinema clubs and take movies seriously, experiencing them as "waking dreams" and making an effort to evaluate them.

At the same time, M. Dumazedier differs from a good many American defenders of the present against the past by being unashamedly eager for improvement. He wants much more planning for leisure. He points out that the country-dweller is still a substantial fraction of the French population and is badly served by television (backward in France compared with England or America) and by other services for leisure time. He sees that adults read geography and history, while in school they study mathematics and French; he would like to see the schools anticipate the later voluntary activities in order to intensify them. He would like to see vacation time-off better distributed throughout the year, and more facilities built for internal tourism rather than for American big spenders. He wonders whether do-it-yourself should take so much time of the worker away from the solidarity of the union into what he calls the daily trifling in the family workshop, although he does not here suggest how this balance of energies could be voluntarily altered. Indeed, he approaches leisure with a moralism more characteristic of Soviet than American scholarship.* He argues, at least by implication, that the housewife is the most underprivileged person in the leisure economy, besieged by tiny distractions and only recently able to use American-style appliances to shorten her "porous" workday.

It would seem that the hopes of the socialist still live in chastened form in the empirical sociologist. Jean Jaurès declared that "the workers have fought for a reduction in their workday. . . . All the while, they have made it clear that it is not only to conserve their strength that they need this shorter day, but in order to be

* Cf. Paul Hollander, "Leisure as an American and Soviet Value," paper read at the annual ASA meetings in Chicago, August, 1965.

able to live more of a family life, to read, to educate themselves, to become, truly, men" (quoted on page 48). In 1936, under the Léon Blum government, a Ministry of Leisure was established which sought to organize workers' universities and Houses of Culture; Youth Hostels and the People's Theater also grew up—a theater increasingly active. Yet it was not until 1950 that standard minimum family budgets, as set forth by the government, included items for leisure. However, if I read M. Dumazedier correctly, there is presently no overall French policy about how to distribute the increasing supply of "free" time. Should it be spent to give more schooling to the young, earlier retirement for the old, more time or more money to the workers? *Toward a Society of Leisure* raises questions here but does not pursue them. Written for a French audience, it sheds only oblique light on an American's query as to whether the French suffer from "fun morality" and are surrounded, as we Americans are, by an ideology which makes people feel guilty if they are not young, peppy, appropriately happy, and relaxed. Perhaps, having suffered only mild inroads of Puritanism, they will escape the twin threat of being unhappy and being blamed for that state; indeed, French families may still be sufficiently solipsistic to pretend to the outside world that they are too miserable to be envied.

In these introductory remarks, I am suggesting that *Toward a Society of Leisure* be read with a double vision: on the surface, for what it has to say about its topic, and on a second level, for what it has to say about the state of French social science in the person of a dedicated and energetic spokesman.

DAVID RIESMAN

Cambridge, Mass.

Contents

xi

Part I

Leisure

and the

Social System

Chapter 1

The Chips
Are Not
Down

LEISURE TODAY IS A FAMILIAR REALITY IN OUR ADVANCED societies. Yet the concept of leisure has yet to gain full admittance into the systems of thought that guide the thinking of intellectuals and the action of activists, be they of the Left or the Right, supporters or adversaries of capitalism or socialism. Some good minds reason about society as if the notion of leisure didn't exist at all. Some audacious intellectuals even deliberately omit it from their search for new systems that they hope will be a more faithful reflection of the reality of our day.

Now a theoretical system that neglects to take full account of leisure risks being maimed, from inception, as we propose to show.

In order to comprehend the general nature of leisure as it bears on our contemporary culture, it will not be enough to investigate the effects on our lives of movies or sports or theatre or television. Seen in the complex of its multiple relations to the other aspects of our mechanized and democratic civilization, leisure is no longer a minor item, postscript to the major ones, to be studied or not, depending on whether there is time or money left. . . . Leisure is, on the contrary, the very central element in the *life*-culture of

3

millions upon millions of workers. It has a deep-going, intricate relatedness to the largest questions of work, family, and politics, and these, therefore, must now be re-examined and reformulated. No theorizing about our basic social realities can be valid, in the mid-twentieth century, without consideration of the relevancy of leisure to them. If the futility of leisure so alarmed the poet Valéry in his day, for us now the moment has come to investigate its—utility.

Inversely, there is the danger of being bedazzled by a leisure looming large, reaching into every sector of society. Essayists and poets have been misled by the spectacle into thinking that leisure plays an even more autonomous and preponderant role in daily life than it does. Denis de Rougemont, for one, has described our "era of leisure" as a new Golden Age which will witness the magical vanishing of all social problems (1).[1] And Roger Caillois ends his brilliant essay *Les Jeux et les Hommes* with a proposal for a new sociology, not just of play, but of society as characterized fundamentally by its play (2). Finally, the "mass leisure" of certain American sociologists soon went from a fashionable cliché to a total perspective, whether dark or rosy, on man's future. If all these writers—their analyses often exceedingly keen—have performed the service of establishing the growing importance of the factor of leisure in contemporary life, they have at the same time frequently simplified, distorted, even perverted its true nature. They forget too often the heterogeneous pattern of a leisure that has evolved from work in many different social contexts, and forget, therefore, the disparities and inequalities of its distribution in the life of city and country. Forgetting all this, our writers have fallen from the "work" myth straight into the "idleness" myth.

The leisure of today is in its essence ambiguous, appearing in various and contradictory guises. If, in speaking about it, we refrain from Aesopian phrases, it is perhaps because these have lost their point through overuse. Nevertheless, beware of the a priori defini-

[1] Numbers in parentheses refer to the bibliography arranged by chapters beginning on page 289.

tion, the too hasty generalization, and the premature synthesis. It is well to observe, take one's bearings, then philosophize. Over the past thirty years, bit by bit, the body of social science studies of leisure has grown—granted; but the general sociology of leisure is still, I maintain, in its infancy. In the United States and in Europe— here in France—various global-historical investigations are under way or projected. Until their results are in, we reserve decision— stay this side of what we know for certain, and meanwhile take as guide an inflexible principle: Before embarking on research or theory or action of any kind, pose the problem in terms indisputably inherent in the advanced social and cultural context of our own day. It will be no small gain if we succeed in throwing light on whatever fundamental changes have taken place in the phenomenon of leisure since the time when those well-known major ideologies were elaborated which our present society, barring some few isolated attempts, has still scarcely bothered to reconsider, or lay open to question. The chips are not down . . .

At the time that Marx lumped together all respite from work as, simply, "reproduction of the labor force," there was no law limiting the duration of the industrial work day to twelve hours. A member of the Academy of Moral and Political Sciences of that day, Louis-René Villermé, noted that the workday averaged thirteen hours, six days a week (3). The number of holidays was about the same as now—the increase in secular holidays having compensated for reduction in the old religious ones. Thus the average work week came to about seventy-five hours. Today, it is about forty-five hours—a gain of thirty hours nonwork time. And subtracting three weeks annually—thanks to the law making vacation with pay compulsory—we see that, in a little over one hundred years, the industrial worker has enlarged the total of his yearly free time to approximately fifteen hundred hours, working now no more than about twenty-two hundred hours a year.

What proportion of hours released from work is given over to leisure activity? It remains a controversial figure. On the basis of findings of the French Institute of Public Opinion gathered between 1945 and 1958, Jean Stoetzel estimated the average urban family enjoys about two hours of leisure during the evenings (4). To which should be added some time following the noon meal and some preceding the evening supper—perhaps another whole hour, at least for the man of the house (5).

Average daily leisure of the "adult worker of 1950" was put by Jean Fourastié (6) at three hours, a figure which would seem to be contradicted by the results of Henri Chombart de Lauwe's systematic sampling of 120 working-class families of the Paris region, which showed the average daily leisure to be somewhere between one and one half and two hours. Here, however, "puttering around" was excluded, which Chombart de Lauwe noted, accounted for a daily average of another hour and a half to two hours. Actually, "a part of puttering around may be regarded as leisure" (7). A detailed analysis of what this puttering is for and about would, we think, show that among the large majority of the industrial workers more than half their quasileisure puttering is in fact leisure, since it is pursued neither as domestic obligation nor from financial necessity. The results of our own study of the inhabitants of Annecy (pop. 60,000) revealed that 60 per cent of the workers regard puttering as part of leisure, 25 per cent as work, and 15 per cent as an admixture of the two. We may conclude that the average daily leisure of the industrial worker is two and one half hours, adding up to twelve and one half for the five-day week.

From these same studies, we learn that, generally, about two thirds of the free weekend goes to leisure; for more than one third of the Annecy workers, all day Saturday is leisure time; and for practically all of them, in any case, Saturday afternoon plus all Sunday spells leisure. Results of certain statistical studies in progress are still not in; but we can estimate that, on the average, urban industrial workers enjoy twenty to thirty hours of leisure a week; to which, again, we must not forget to add the 225 hours, approximately, of the three-week annual legal holiday. (For professionals and executives in every field, overwork makes accurate leisure figures difficult to arrive at.) Still, the actual amount of leisure does not parallel the ever-growing need of escape from the job. The work of production in the industrial plant of to-day, more fragmentized and mechanized, and geared to a greater speed than in the nineteenth century, is also far more exhausting to the nerves of workers, so that they feel all the more a deep-seated need for rest and escape from the job. Farther on, we shall examine how and when leisure becomes dissipated, reduced, erased even, by supplementary jobs, lack of means for enjoyment, distance from the place of work, and the like. Nevertheless, consideration of differences in leisure ought not distract sociologists from seeing how this universal phenomenon shapes group attitudes in all classes and layers of society today.

The important fact now is that work is not the whole activity; the day, no longer filled to the brim with work, allows two or even three hours for leisure pursuits. The work week tends to be reduced to five days, ending in the "two Sundays," and the work years do not, as in the past, follow one after the other without surcease. Between them fall three weeks of holiday. Nor must a worker's life inevitably finish in sickness or death; it has a legal termination now—an assured right to some repose at the end. We see that the rise in the worker's standard of living has been paralleled by a growing rise in the number of his free hours. Even if his place in the production process is still that of the wage-slave it was a hundred years ago, the possibilities available, his daily, monthly, and yearly prospects, have changed. A new era has arrived for him, for doing and dreaming.

Ever more alluring, as we know, are the activities, actual and potential, that this new era holds for the worker. It is a commonplace to observe that amusements have multiplied, thick and fast, into a complexity far greater than a hundred, even fifty, years ago. The industry serving leisure activities is overflowing with imagination; the public is always awaiting the next "twist." Yet it is important to stress how the machine has increased the imbalance between work and leisure. For if the machine has lightened the worker's tasks on the job, it has done so only too often by reducing his interest in them and his freedom in performing them. On the other hand, the increase in automobile purchases and in the mass media—press, film, radio, television—together with the proliferation of groups large and small to cater to every known taste, hobby, and passion, has piled up the aggregate of leisure activities to proportions incomparably greater than those to which the machine has up to now succeeded in reducing man's sufferings.

Within a period of less than fifty years, leisure has asserted itself as something above and beyond an attractive possibility: It has asserted itself as a value. We know from the Protestant Max Weber what ideals guided the founders of capitalism: "Work justifies gain and all activity that does not serve society is subordinate." This idealistic sociology reflects, in part, Ricardo's thesis on the necessary accumulation of capital. Marx held a similar notion of the fundamental importance of work, but from an opposite perspective: "The essence of man is work." The evolution of leisure in our time threatens the values of Marx and Ricardo both. . . . In 1883, when the militant Paul Lafargue wrote his famous pamphlet, *The Right to Laziness* (8), leisure was still identified with idleness. Today, leisure avows a new morality of happiness. Whoever does not take advantage of free time or know how to is not a whole man, is backward, somewhat alienated. One may fairly well agree with the American sociologist Martha Wolfenstein that we are witnessing the birth, in her words, of a new "fun morality"(9).

Even when the actual pursuit of leisure is restricted for the lack of time or money or something else, the need for it is there, ever more clamorous. In 1955, 15 per cent of France's salaried urban workers had planned to give priority to the purchase of something toward their leisure enjoyment: a reservation for travel or a stay in the country, a television set or a car to run about in. This was as high a percentage as of those who had planned to rent or buy or furnish an apartment or house (10).

Desire for leisure grows with urbanization and industrialization. Studying the changes in economic and family life in three industrialized villages of the high Nourrain valley, Serge Moscovici and his team found that the workers' desire for leisure had been increased by their entering advanced modern industry and undergoing a rise in social and economic standards of living (11). It is not surprising that the zest for leisure activities should most strongly express itself among our modern youth, reaching a peak (according to a nation-wide inquiry) in the age group eighteen to thirty, married and single (12). Want of leisure, indeed, was the reason for most complaints of privation. Forty-two per cent longed for more vacations; 39 per cent desired above everything to have a conveyance all their own for Sundays, holidays, and vacations; 35 per cent simply wanted more amusements. Where the budget won't stretch to such satisfactions, the passion for travel or a television set or a car may lead to a self-imposed deprivation of food, clothing, or shelter; since about 1956, this kind of thing has posed some very new problems for social workers specializing in family aid (13). When wants multiply faster than the means of satisfaction, we have the feeling of pauperization, even though in reality we may be more prosperous than ever (14). The same is true about leisure.

To be sure, the evolution in leisure has not at all advanced at the same pace in all layers of society. There exist in France social milieux where leisure activities are "underdeveloped." Partial or total lack of recreation equipment, paucity of family resources, hardships of the job—all may block or slow the development of leisure—quantitatively or qualitatively. The need in such surroundings, then, for leisure may give rise to particularly acute feelings of dissatisfaction. We cite two instances:

1. Workers living in isolated towns or outlying suburban areas where social segregation and a shortage of community facilities still persist (15). Also, those who have to traverse vast populated areas

to reach their place of work, sometimes so far from home that travel time amounts to two or three hours a day (16). Finally, there are the unskilled manual workers to whom Chombart de Lauwe's observation is applicable: "The pressures of earning a bare subsistence prevent their having any free activities" (7).

While workers of higher economic rank and those in the professions spend an average of 1,556 N.F. a year for vacations, transport, culture, and leisure pursuits, manual laborers expend a total of 174 N.F. (17).

2. The case of the majority of those who labor in the rural setting is comparable. Despite an annual decline in their numbers of about eighty thousand, they still constitute 25 per cent of the employed population of France (as against 11 per cent in the United States). We still have in France five million small landholders and farm laborers: What can the word *leisure* mean to them? The sociologist Henri Mendras, in the course he gives yearly on rural sociology, does not even include the question of leisure; and Marcel Maget devotes one page to it in his 260-page *Guide to Rural Ethnography*. Indeed, in the total rural picture, "Work is never done," as they say in some countries. The daily round of caring for the animals alone makes it difficult for the family to get away. Figures of the Bureau of Tourism, for 1957, show that whereas 65 per cent of urban workers take vacations, only 19 per cent of workers in the country do (18). Nevertheless, new trends are in evidence. Youth on the farm is beginning to value leisure, more and more. A law passed in 1948 limits the hours of the agricultural worker to a yearly maximum of 2,400; it would be interesting to have rural sociology undertake studies of the enforcement of this law. On the other hand, the sociocultural facilities offered by thirty-six thousand rural communities to their nine million scattered inhabitants, of every trade and occupation, can scarcely be deemed adequate.

A movement, first initiated in 1937, to organize leisure activity in the countryside gathered fresh momentum in 1945, but there are still only about a thousand rural centers, two hundred youth hostels, perhaps five or six thousand friendship circles and groups of active young people. Less than one community in four can boast of an organization for sports or youth or instruction and culture of any kind; here we have part of the "French desert." Finally, as we shall later see, in all social milieux, the hours of leisure are considerably fewer for women than for men, and work threatens the relaxation of great numbers of executive and professional staff in every field of work.

What Is Leisure?

First, let us examine the major components of a phenomenon which already in so many ways has affected daily work, family life, our entire culture. Obviously, for Marx or Ricardo there was no leisure to observe in the life of the worker of their day. It took the rise of the huge industrial plant to banish forever the old seasonal rhythms of rural labor relieved by games and religious days. Following the long hours of daily work, as described above, there was left just that little respite Marx referred to as reproduction of the labor force: The ideology mirrored the reality of that period. In our own day, the respite has been replaced by a complexity of pursuits of every kind, not pertaining to required activity or to family and social obligation. We have among us a third order of activity, distinct from the job of production, distinct from social obligation, but raising new problems for both of them, and constituting a revolutionary element within our social culture.

The sociologists of work, and particularly Georges Friedmann, were the first to point out the importance of hobbies, fads, and so on (19). But hobby can mean everything and nothing. It includes useless activities and worthwhile activities, whether positive or negative for society, for culture, for the individual. Collecting cigar bands is a hobby, as is research in mechanics. Playing football, joining a gym, being a comic-strip fan or Shakespearean drama buff—all of these are hobbies. The American sociologist Eric Larrabee (20), taking exception to the confusion surrounding the concept, has noted that some serious writers even include "doing nothing" as a hobby. . . . This notion of hobby, more amusing than helpful, cannot help us discover the secret of this third order of activity.

But if we go further, we may run into a dual pitfall, two opposing temptations that risk imprisoning the young and complex reality before us into an overschematized definition. The great theorizers of the nineteenth century all had more or less of an inkling of the advent of leisure; but none foresaw the ambiguities. All of them fell into the intellectualist error. For Marx, leisure meant "room for human development"; for Pierre Joseph Proudhon, "time for free engagement"; for Auguste Comte, the possibility of developing a "popular astronomy." Finally, Engels claimed the reduction in hours of work as "giving all enough free time to participate in the common interests of society." Such identification of leisure with popular education apparently still prevails in the Soviet Union. Here in France, a certain trend toward "permanent education" reflects a similar conception.

Inversely, the majority of American sociologists have concentrated on analyzing the various forms recreation takes. Many writers have tended to reduce leisure to "an activity freely pursued and without pay, which brings an immediate satisfaction." A critique outlining the various definitions given by American sociology up to the year 1958 has been published by Aline Ripert (21). It was only recently that researchers such as David Riesman (22), R. J. Havighurst (23), M. Kaplan, and H. Wilensky analyzed the complex of leisure as part of the sum total of determinants of our daily lives. In France, we still have only partial ideas, arbitrary and confused, the most deplorable example being the famed "sundries" entry in the household budget.

If you look in *Littré* (1869), you read that leisure is a "time remaining at one's disposal after work," a definition M. Hatzfel and James Darmsteter, fifty-seven years later, were content to copy. Not until 1930, did Augé, in his dictionary, add a new meaning: "amusements, occupations, which one can turn to freely in the time not taken up with regular work." Littré's "time" has become "amusements, occupations," and Michel Augé no longer says that leisure follows after one's "occupations" but after "regular work."

The change in words, however slight, signifies a change in habits; under our very eyes, a profound transformation has taken place with respect to the role of leisure in the life of ordinary people. An exhaustive inquiry conducted in 1953 among workers and salaried employees as to what leisure represented to them made possible refinement of the dictionary definition. Though the majority still referred to leisure as "time," already more than a fourth called it an "activity" and none gave it the passive definition of a "state" (Littré's first definition). Practically all of 819 persons interviewed at random in the cities of the North, of the South and the East, and of the West and Paris, defined leisure *by opposition* to the cares and concerns of daily life called by Augé "regular work." These daily concerns were described mainly by three different expressions: "routine tasks, monotonous and repetitious," "daily chores," "necessities and obligations"—the last used almost as frequently as the other two together.

Under this third category 60 per cent of the respondents stressed the obligations of their job as primordial, although others were mentioned with varying frequency, such as family and social obligations, which, however, we cannot pause here to analyze. For the moment we shall simply give a list of activities indisputably contrasted to the notion of leisure:

1. The job.
2. Supplementary work or occasional odd jobs.
3. Domestic tasks (housework, and the strictly utilitarian aspects of animal care, miscellaneous chores, gardening).
4. Care of the person (meals, bathing and dressing, sleep).

5. Family rituals and ceremonies, social or religious.
Obligations (visits, anniversaries, political meetings, church
duties).
6. Necessary study (for study circles, for school or professional
examinations).

We see now how wrong, how dangerously misleading it would
be, to define leisure by contrast merely to one's gainful occupation,
and if most economists and sociologists so define it, they are
evidently seduced by the overtheoretical formula of the three eights
—eight hours' work, eight hours' sleep, eight hours' leisure.
Briefly, and most emphatically, contemporary leisure is defined by
contrast not just to one's job, but to all of the ordinary necessities
and obligations of existence, and it must be remembered that they
who have and use leisure regard it as part of the dialectic of daily
living, where all elements operate and interoperate. In and of itself,
leisure means little; it might almost be said of it what Henri Wallon
has said of play, which to some extent is part of leisure: "Play is,
probably, a break away from the disciplines and the tasks which
are imposed on every man by the practical necessities of his
existence, the concern for his condition and his person; but far from
being the negation of these, it presupposes them."

The Three Functions of Leisure

However it functions, leisure is first and foremost liberation and
pleasure, and it was so indicated by the respondents to the 1953
inquiry. Their replies fall into three categories, corresponding as
we see it, to the three major functions of leisure: relaxation, entertainment, personal development.

Relaxation provides recovery from fatigue; leisure repairs the
physical and nervous damage wrought by the tensions of daily
pressures, and particularly pressures of the job. True, the need of

physical effort on the job has largely disappeared, but it is still a fact that the production tempo, the complexity of the industrial set-up, the long distances in the large urban centers to and from work—all have increased the worker's need for rest and quiet, for idleness and the aimless small pastimes. Such need is felt even more, according to investigations by Dr. P. R. Bize, among executives and top personnel in industry, 85 per cent of whom reported they were overworked (24). Concern with the recuperative function of leisure ought to lead to broadening the study of fatigue and proneness to fatigue among all classes of workers, heretofore restricted in France to simple observations on the job. A new trend in this direction is discernible. Dr. Stafford A. Metz has instigated medicosocial studies to explore relations between the rhythms of work and the rhythms of leisure. More and more, such studies call for collaboration between the experts in the psychology of work and those in the psychosociology of leisure.

Entertainment is the second function of leisure. If relaxation gives recovery from fatigue, entertainment spells deliverance from boredom. Friedmann has pointed time and time again to the woeful effect of the monotony of fragmented tasks on the personality of the worker. Henri Lefebvre has analyzed modern man's alienations as they result in a sense of loss and lead to an impulse to break away from the daily atmosphere (25). The break away might take the form of an infraction of juridical or moral law in any field—and thus suggest socially pathological elements. Or, going in the opposite direction, it could become a balance, a way of bearing up under the disciplines and constraints demanded by society. From this might follow a search after a life of compensation, or an escape into diversions of a different world, sometimes directly opposed, in fact, to the everyday world. If escape is realistic, it may lead to a change of place or pace or style (trips, games, sports); it may, on the other hand, head toward the fantasy of identification and projection (cinema, theater, the novel)—the resort to the imaginary life, for the satisfaction of what, since E. T. A. Hoffmann and Feodor Dostoevski, has come to be known as one's imaginary self (26).

This was the function of leisure—diversion, in an absolute sense—called up in the minds of the greatest number of respondents to the 1957 inquiry.

Finally, we come to the development of the personality. Here leisure serves to liberate the individual from the daily automatism of thought and action. It permits a broader, readier social participation on the one hand, and on the other, a willing cultivation of the physical and mental self over and above utilitarian considerations of job or practical advancement. It opens fresh possibilities for joining willingly with other people in recreational, cultural, and social group activities. It gives time for the pursuit of voluntary development of skills acquired at school but always in danger of being outdistanced by the continuous and complex growth of society. It encourages a positive attitude toward the use of sources of information, old and new (press, movies, radio, television).

It may even lead to discovering new forms of voluntary learning for the rest of one's life and induce an entirely new kind of creative attitude. And so, released from workaday obligations, the individual has the time to sustain new disciplines freely chosen by him with a view to the unfolding of a new personal and social life-style. This use of leisure for the cultivation of personality, not so common as simple entertainment, is of prime importance to the popular culture generally.

The three functions are interdependent, closely linked even when in opposition. They exist in varying degrees in everyone's life, no matter what his situation. They may co-exist or follow one after the other and in a single leisure-situation, they may be exercised in turn or simultaneously, and often they overlap so closely as to be indistinguishable. In actuality, any one of the three is not so much the more commonly present as the more dominant.

Leisure is activity—apart from the obligations of work, family, and society—to which the individual turns at will, for either relaxation, diversion, or broadening his knowledge and his spontaneous social participation, the free exercise of his creative capacity.

The Culture of Daily Experience

The interrelatedness among the functions of leisure, and of leisure to the obligations of daily life, increasingly determines participation, passive or active, in social and cultural affairs. All this affects the culture of daily experience of our general society. We may safely ignore the theories that explain relations between culture and society in the abstract: One and all, they have come down from a period when the phenomena we are concerned with were not widespread, and we are bound to re-examine all such theories, if we are to move toward a concrete sociology of the leisure both real and possible under our democratic industrial civilization. We say *all*, whether their postulates be democratic or aristocratic, individualist or collectivist, whether they stem from Karl Mannheim or Ortega y Gasset, from Arnold Toynbee or G. V. Plekhanov. For a theory of culture to be cogent, it must correspond not only to a complex of values, but also to the way these values are lived, by all classes and categories of people. Today it is leisure, as an ideal and in practice, that more and more conditions our culture of daily experience.

The creative elite, the educators, and the activists who try to shape thinking and actions know quite well the added difficulty of so persuading the masses of the value of an idea that it becomes a force. . . . But evenings, weekends, and vacations have their own quota of "idea-forces." The serious civic and political indifference that we see among the masses may *not*, after all, be caused solely by lack of enthusiasm or by incompetence on the part of their social and cultural leaders—as we would be led to believe reading the innumerable confessions, and stereotyped self-examinations that line the route of these leaders' failures. Can we be sure that a new leadership could solve these problems? We may venture the hypothesis that, since the entry onto the scene of all those frivolities we call leisure activities, some profound and ambiguous changes have been wrought in people's souls, of every class.

The New Homo Faber

We have seen that time off in a given work period may not be used entirely for leisure. Friedmann is quite right in speaking tentatively and with caution of "nonwork." Twenty-five per cent of the workers at Annecy, for example, had a second occupation or did additional work, outside their regular overtime; this, if not legal, was, at any rate, regarded as obligatory. Out of economic need? Perhaps, but an economic need less likely stemming from any necessity than from a new lifestyle. In countries where the standard of living is higher than in France, time off from one's regular job is used mainly for doing other paid work. In the city of Akron, Ohio, when the rubber industry reduced its work week to thirty-two hours, almost half the salaried workers (40 per cent) took on supplementary jobs, and 17 per cent worked openly at a second occupation. "Less work, less leisure" (27).

Psychological and economic motivations probably are interwoven. Everywhere, apart from the extra time spent in paid work, there is a growing range of manual occupations, half labor of love, half utilitarian, carried on in the family garden or workshop. Leisure—or not leisure? We saw that at Annecy, 60 per cent of the workers regard such activities as part of leisure, against 25 per cent who consider them obligatory tasks, and 15 per cent who think them something of both. According to a national poll conducted in selected areas by the IFOP (French Institute of Public Opinion), executives cultivate their gardens in larger numbers than workers, 44 per cent as against 36 per cent. Here is an activity part practical, part nonpractical, so to speak, in varying proportions; the two parts overlap, but one belongs in the category of obligation, the other, to leisure. We designate these as semileisure activities.[2] In our French city, the nonpractical aspect exceeds the practical; but in such economically less-developed countries as Poland or Yugoslavia, the reverse is probably true. Also, among us these semileisure pursuits consume about half the total leisure time; and everyone knows the "do-it-yourself" vogue in the country even more industrialized than ours. In the very midst of a civilization governed by the division of labor with its attendant social patterns, leisure develops among the gainfully employed, especially in the working class, attitudes typical of the artisan and the peasant, which incline them increasingly toward a kind of work different from their gainful employment. Leisure has indeed fostered the rise of a new *homo faber*, far more independent than the old one vis-à-vis his job in the production process. This, for him, has increasingly narrowed down to making a living, simply a way of earning one's bread, and already for some, of earning one's leisure. Thus a new kind of manual labor, non paid and individual, has asserted its value in the life-culture; it could, by its creative import, redress the monotony of the fragmented tasks of the industrial process, in administration and production. From all this, a new philosophy may come which would put manual labor into its proper place in a civilization based on labor. The handicrafts and modest creations of all sorts we see displayed in shops bespeak a possible use of manual work in the culture of the people—perhaps here is the germ of some kind of renewal for the culture as a whole. However, our new Sunday painters for the most part become totally engrossed in their gardening or puttering. In response to inquiry by Chombart de Lauwe, some Paris workmen reported they spend five or six whole

[2] "This composite whole in which two different elements interpenetrate one another without becoming fused, overlap without mixing, corresponds to the type of relationship brought to lights by modern science under the name of mutual dialectical implication." (G. G.)

hours a day at it! And if such men make good fathers and husbands (though Patachou says in her song that it may not be so lucky for a woman to have a Jack who's a jack of all trades—*"un bonheur d'avoir un mari bricoleur"*), they are unconcerned with what goes on outside their private lives. These are citizens limited by the fact that political, social, and cultural questions do not bother them. All around them are the mass media, from which they derive no benefit. They choose to be isolated, strike attitudes of craftsmen withdrawn within themselves, almost as if they lived in a time without press or movies, and where there is neither division of labor nor class struggle. These highly important facts ought not to be underestimated by sociologists of recreation or of education for leisure.

The New Homo Ludens

Around the midnineteenth century, traditional games and feast days, either civic or religious, were an important part of the worker's life. We know the range of these celebrations, from gay and fanciful to brutal, through the vivid reportage of Agricol Perdiguier. In our own day, amusements have been extracted from their ritual context, and have multiplied, diversified, achieved proportions in our kind of society unforeseeable by the social philosophers of the nineteenth century. Incitement to amusements and contests is uninterrupted, no longer dependent on the ritual occasion or communal celebration, but stimulated daily by radio, newspaper, magazine, and store advertising. This tends to be true even in the Soviet Union, where organs of radio and press are altogether restrained by the doctrinal preaching from higher up.

As for gambling, it is foolish to consider the exigencies of poverty as responsible for it among the masses; it is an upper-class amusement they have seized for themselves as they have seized travel and sports. Betting on the horses is no longer the exclusive privilege of the idle rich at the hippodrome at Longchamps—not since the *Pari Mutuel Urbain* came in, which in 1949 registered more than 280 millions (new francs) in bets, four times the amount spent that year by the General Administration of Youth and Sports for their total activities. Some other amusements, which began around the eighteen eighties as the exclusive province of bourgeois youth, have been democratized, have become active games of "educational value"—sports. Aldous Huxley even goes so far as to see sports as the dominant characteristic of our time. But, alongside the amateurs in action, what about the yelling, banner-waving spectators, the fans who never have played a game in their lives? In a city like Vienne (France), studies have shown, more than a third, closer to half, of the entire population are sports fans, including workers, salaried employees, executives, and professionals. The figures for the year 1947 show that 40 per cent of all Frenchmen regularly follow sports, 35 per cent being "vaguely" interested in the Tour de France bicycle races.

But to go further: This universal bent toward a life of play is something even worse in the larger sense that Caillois gives to it (2). This play life is to one's serious life a kind of "secondary reality," with its own potent influence on everyday attitudes. It is disengaged from all obligation, set into predetermined limits of time and space, regulated, fictitious, "attended by a special awareness of being a secondary reality, or out-and-out unreality in relation to one's ordinary life." But shall we not say the same of vacations, for example, when we play for a time at being rich or primitive—something utterly at variance with our everyday lives? In the same way, we may characterize many of the activities that one by one have appeared among us in the past hundred years.

What are the consequences of all this for our life-culture? Johann Huizinga, in his classic *Homo Ludens,* notes that play has but a feeble role in the serious culture we inherited from the Hebrew-Greco-Latin tradition as watered down by the scholastics (29). In our own cultural development, competitive games, for example, play nowhere near the part they had in Pindar's time.

Nevertheless, games of every kind, serious or frivolous, hold a large place in the life-culture of millions of workers. Play is no longer, as Freud saw it, the badge of the child's world, but has become a necessity, through leisure, in the people's culture. It could indeed work a profound change in academic and avant-garde culture, could inject its own poesy and lightness into the social scene and into efforts toward social involvement.

It could, on the other hand, as Lefebvre fears, engender disaffection for modest daily life, push escape into absolute diversion in the sense of rejection of all cultural efforts and indifference to all social responsibility. Play life opens wide, only to shut out any life of commitment.

The New Man of Imagination

Shortly after the publication of Marx's *Communist Manifesto*, a major inquiry, lasting two years, was instituted into the question of the selection of popular books and the literature offered for sale by wandering peddlers. Directing the inquiry was young Charles Nisard, and while one may take a cautionary view of his testimony, his documentation is impressive. He presents in two large tomes an objective analysis of the contents of the booklets that had the greatest circulation among the ordinary folk of the towns and countryside.

We learn (30) that the comparatively limited number of works of a "moralizing and edifying" nature was nowhere near the number of the occult sciences; humor ("two hundred anecdotes about drunks to give you the hiccups"); parodies of religious discourse; fiction-biographies; dream almanacs "intended especially for our feminine readers" and, above all, the romances of Mme. Cottin *Amelie de Mansfield*, "a romance of delirious love in which the exaltation of the senses mingles with that of the sentiments"; and also "the adventures of a great lady" (1849), a book full of "an ignorance of the human heart which I would call primitive and an abandonment of all moral sense far surpassing the worst smut writers." In addition, there was the *Le Secretaire des Amants* and *Choix de Lettres d'Amour*. The counsels these offer, remarks Nisard, "are base, I do not hesitate to call them infamous. . . . This daring dirty little book has certainly seen more editions than the best book ever issued since books began."

Yet Nisard refused to include a similar analysis of the two-penny romances which were such an essential part of the peddler's crude pack. Who read these? ". . . these serials, this printed stuff, these dramas were available to the most modest purse and in the hands of every young worker. What the last century's depravity produced in beastly ordure and rottenness, our own modern tale-spinners have exceeded"—so wrote the editor of the working-class journal *L'Atelier*. If this would seem dwelling unduly on Nisard, it is because his inquiry showed to what extent half the ordinary people of France who could read at all devoured this type of easy fiction. The popular taste for fiction was not born with the movies; it would be more correct to say that the orientation of the movies toward its fictive character corresponded to profound popular taste. One cannot overstress the point that the working-class culture of 1848, so much admired by Edouard Dolleans and Georges Duveau, could hardly have embraced any but a very small minority of the most advanced and the self-educated.

The growing demand for fiction stimulated by a growing leisure is now satisfied on a scale unprecedented since the discovery of printing, sound, and, of course, moving pictures. In the face of this demand, the influence of Georges Meliès was not long in passing that of Louis Lumière. The movies provide an unequaled means of "visualizing dreams." And television, so perfectly adapted to the direct reporting of vital events, has been swamped with fiction. Fiction, too, is the main ingredient of the fifteen million copies of the weekly magazines catering to women.[3] Novels constitute almost half of all book production, and about 80 per cent of the books

[3] *Echo de la presse et de la publicité,* 1958 edition.

borrowed from public libraries.[4] Still, they are not the same kind
as in the time of Marx and Nisard. Contrary to accepted opinion,
and despite the commonplaceness of most of what passes for works
of art (an informed public opinion judges 90 per cent of such productions in literature and the movies to be "junk"), popular taste is
improving. One must here record an ambiguity in the kind of fiction
that feeds the leisure time of the masses.

In their culture of daily experience, the satisfactions of the
imagination play a much bigger role than in school or university
culture. If the latter is to respond more fully to the needs of our
time, it must undergo a transformation. It has also been pointed
out, by Edgar Morin, for one, that most of our prevalent ideologies
are overrationalistic—fail to take sufficiently into account the
imaginary man. "We must reintegrate the imaginary with the reality
of man" (26). On the other hand, the mechanisms of projection and
identification encouraged by current fiction can drug the critical,
discriminating powers of mind. The imagination may get out of
line and confusion result between the real world and the world of
fantasy in which the personality is lost in the careers of the stars.
Real life gives way to a proxy, where the pleasure of fiction, instead
of simply offering an agreeable dream, deflects the person from
all action or misleads him into maladjusted activity. Fantasy poses
the same danger we have seen in the more real amusements: The
personality may be seduced away from the actual world into a
mythic one, to become no more than a refugee, an exile who has lost
all desire to act along with his fellow men.

The New Homo Sapiens

As much as for recreation, leisure provides time to acquire
knowledge for its own sake. Only a century ago, not even a newspaper found its way into the homes of workers. Around 1846, the

[4] See page 173.

famous journal *L'Atelier*, published by workers for workers, had, at most, a thousand subscribers—and it was a monthly. Workmen bought few newspapers because they were too expensive. Now, of course, a daily paper is part of the domestic scene of the great majority; every day a half-hour or an hour is spent relaxing with it. Almost the whole of the city population (Annecy) reads a weekly, and more than half read at least two. In addition, a good half of this same public views the weekend newsreels at the movies, and 93 per cent state that they listen regularly to the radio news. A poll taken by the INSEE (Institut National de Statistiques Economiques et Sociales) in 1953 showed that 77 per cent of the radio listening public desire "as much or more" news and information programs. Once, working people were isolated in their districts and work was their culture. They lived a life of withdrawal, turned in on themselves. Today, leisure time has stimulated a greater need which is both fulfilled and extended still further by the development of the rotary press, with reduced cost of papers and magazines, and by revolutionary techniques in visual presentation. Digests, of every kind and quality, have had a great success. In all milieux of the population, the taste for nonfiction is growing, especially for biographies and travel books, as shown by publishing figures and library statistics.

For the majority of readers, especially in the provinces, the daily paper is a veritable book, with its editorials, reportage, feature articles, special departments, games and puzzles. Fifty per cent of the readers of such dailies, according to IFOP, follow political events, domestic and foreign, regularly, and about 38 per cent read general reportage and informative articles. A part of the public devotes some leisure time to a more intensive pursuit, self-directed but still systematic, of questions that hold some particular interest for them. In Annecy, about half the heads of families do this, and 40 per cent would gladly accept a paid study-leave of twelve days to improve their knowledge or aptitudes in various fields. In order of preference chosen interests are problems having to do with the job, general culture, scientific and technical matters, economic, social, and political questions, and, finally, preparation for assuming responsibility in their organizations. We may count about 10 per cent of urban workers and salaried employees as self-taught students, who spend a good deal of their leisure hours in their chosen subjects of study. In Paris, alone, they have at their disposal twenty-five schools offering accelerated general courses—this apart from the ordinary grades and technical and trade union training.

Leisure to study is the precondition for this "ongoing culture," which becomes more and more necessary in our complex and swift-moving civilization. It may be that this seeking after knowledge serious in content but attractive in presentation will one day bring about some very notable changes in the mass media of television and periodicals and centers for education beyond ordinary schooling. Leisure to study holds out the possibility for new directions of the mind at each new turn of our civilization. On the other hand, the pursuit of an agreeable knowledge can too readily be limited in kind. If she appears on the front page, Princess Margaret, all by herself, can be the reason for doubling the number of copies in one issue of a magazine like *Point de Vue—Images du Monde*. An IFOP poll on reading the daily paper revealed that local news was most popular, 86 per cent of readers regularly following reports of births, deaths, celebrations, parties. . . . All this abundant local subject matter could be made the basis for an economic, social, political, or esthetic culture. This possibility has gone neglected in the editorial offices of our daily press. After local items, the most popular reading matter is the ads (65 per cent) and miscellaneous news (57 per cent). If not isolated, this kind of reading could be profitable in and of itself. Alone it can scarcely lead to the broadening and deepening of knowledge a modern citizen ought to have if he wishes to keep abreast. To be sure, against a swelling tide of print about national and international, political and economic, social and literary questions, the reader is submerged, unable to absorb and assimilate most of it. He finds himself resorting to what Paul

Lazarsfeld has called opinion guides, those who read and listen for him and give him the gist of the matter.

A reader who strives to do his own reading of serious subjects may soon find that the clutter of general ideas and statistics have left but superficial traces in his mind, and he is tempted to revert to the miscellany of news easier to assimilate. For, despite the advances made by our journals in the presentation of difficult questions, the public's capacity to understand and assimilate has still not developed to meet the needs of any genuine democracy. It has been pointed out by A. Varagnac that if the public now has the time to keep up with what is going on, it still lacks the capacity to develop—to acquire the kind of real knowledge that traditional culture stands for (34). Hence, it is open to question whether the plethora of information and accompanying discussion has not resulted in an ersatz activity in all areas. If discussion in one's free time has pleasurably broadened, it at the same time risks taking the place of, rather than preparing for or supplementing, active participation in community life. The inflation of the information received, given or exchanged, can create an illusion that much social good has been done, when in fact there has been only a good deal said.

The New Homo Socius

Our leisure has also nurtured new forms of sociability, new groupings unknown to the last century. In the course of his inquiries at Reims, and at Lille and Mulhouse, Villermé failed to come across any recreational or cultural association, but only mutualist societies more or less political in character. On the other hand, everywhere he was struck by the great role of the café in the life of the workers. Reading his detailed and moving reports (3), one begins to understand the fierce campaigns waged by the staff at *L'Atelier* and by Perdiguier against working-class drunkenness. Villermé notes: "It is not uncommon to see the workers of the Lille factory working only three days a week and drinking away the remaining four, and," he adds, "this was true even before the rise of the factories." At Reims, "in a working-class quarter that makes up a third of the town, the majority of the best paid laborers work only during the latter half of the week and pass the first half in orgies. Two thirds of the men and a fourth of the women inhabiting certain streets are frequently drunk." And he concludes: "For the worker, everything becomes, so to speak, an excuse for going to the café. He goes there to rejoice when happy, and to forget when beset by domestic worries. The café is where he runs up debts, or pays them if he can, where he transacts business, forms friendships, and even where he gives his daughter in marriage."

Cafés today are still an important place of leisure for everybody and particularly for workers. Yet, contrary to what most Frenchmen imagine, acute drunkenness is probably declining compared with its widespread prevalence in the past century.[5] To be sure, the scourge is still with us, and less to be tolerated than ever. What has increased is the sense of shame it arouses—the country cannot be too zealous in getting rid of this particular affliction. It is fantastic that 40 per cent of all road accidents should be caused by drunken driving (official figure for 1958), that deaths from delirium and cirrhosis of the liver exceed ten thousand a year, and that the national expenditure on alcoholic beverages should far surpass, in France, the sum spent on education and housing combined. True, intoxication is no longer the same status symbol it once was among youth. Within a century, according to Duveau, there has been a substantial decline, relative to the total population, in the number of shops selling cheap liquor for consumption on the premises and in the number of customers.[6] A study by INED (Institut National

[5] Villermé (3). See also G. Duveau, *Villes et campagnes,* A. Colin, 1954.
[6] Georges Duveau, *La vie ouvrière sous le second Empire,* Paris, 1946. See also, Solly Ledermann, *Alcool, Alcoolisme, Alcoolisation,* INED, cahier 29, 1956. In his statistics on liquor outlets, S. Ledermann includes carry-out stores, groceries, and the like. His figures are thus different from Duveau's. From 1954 to 1960, the number of liquor outlets has decreased by 20 per cent (260,000 to 160,000) INSEE, 1960.

d'Etudes Démographiques) in 1960 showed that 16 per cent of the French people visit a café once a week or more. Actually, the great change is qualitative; the atmosphere of the café has been modernized, games of all sorts are played, and the cabarets of ill-repute are kept down to a limited number. The police are fully aware that here criminals or juvenile delinquents prepare their newest exploits. But, of course, all cafés are not hangouts for hoodlums; most are places for a community expression of the many activities permitted by increased leisure.

According to our inquiry at Annecy,[7] reasons for going to a café are, in order of preference: be with friends; social meetings with colleagues or clients; family outings; some conversation after work; talk things over after a get-together; attend a show or match of some kind. These cover about 80 per cent of all reasons given.[8]

But newest of the social forms developed under the new leisure is the group for recreation or education. These organizations, regulated largely by the law of 1901 (which was not made for them), have proliferated right along with industrial and urban expansion. They are not tied to the needs of the job, as are the unions and professional associations, or to the demands of a practical politics or religion, as are the parties or the church groups. They are geared first and foremost to the pursuit of leisure. Most of them are, in principle, open to everybody, regardless of background, class, or education. Around 1930, in the American town he called Yankee City, the sociologist Lloyd Warner counted about four hundred active organizations among the fifteen thousand inhabitants; today a little over 35 per cent of all Americans are estimated to be members of some group. We have no figures for France as a whole, but in 1957, the town of Annecy counted two hundred active organizations, with more than one out of every two heads of family belonging to one or more than one. Thus, while trade unions, political

---

[7] Five per cent random sample among heads of families.

[8] Cf. Joffre Dumazedier and Annette Suffert, *Les fonctions sociales et culturelles des cafés dans la vie urbaine,* report to the Higher Study Committee on Alcoholism, 68 pp., 1961.

parties, and religious action societies could claim hardly 25 per cent of the total membership of all Annecy organizations, 75 per cent belonged to clubs for leisure, most of them for the following purposes, in order of popularity: fishing, sports, outdoor life, bowling, music, and various cultural activities. Those from a working-class background, though on the whole rather less well organized, still have their own fishing, bowling, and music clubs; and about a third of the workers belong to clubs that include members of other classes and social milieux.

Here again, we find a characteristic ambiguity in the culture of daily experience. These leisure organizations provide for the locality the sociocultural ferment studied and advocated by Kurt Lewin (38). Within the framework of the organization, the higher-ups attempt to engage the less well educated in free discussion, while eschewing propaganda. The clubs act as effective intermediaries between remote sources of information and the local public, and help raise the cultural level by democratizing knowledge and practicing mutual education. But not always. Too often, such recreational clubs withdraw into their narrower interests and close themselves to outside influences; they are totally indifferent to the idea of taking part in any general cultural life around them. A sports club of this kind, Georges Magnane has remarked, creates "retarded children playing under careful supervision."

In principle, one may say that the organizations of all kinds, taken as a whole, provide a framework for salutary exchanges between individuals of different social status and education. There is, unquestionably, a general trend of all leisure organizations toward a unified life-style. But, of course, cultural organizations, as such, are dominated by intellectuals, teachers, the élite personnel of all areas—in short, the middle classes. In the minority, workers are never completely at home. Social stratification, if not actively, at least passively resists the organized pressure against it. Finally, we may ask: What influence do all these organizations for leisure (whether sports or travel, whether of musicians or intellectuals) have on participation in the business community or in trade unions, or civic and political organizations. We may say that the leisure organizations furnish a kind of model for these other organizations: the latter are beginning to imitate the activity of the former—holiday celebrations, outdoor excursions, games, reunions. . . . Nevertheless, in the actual operation of our liberal social system, this new *homo socius,* it is to be feared, may come to regard his membership in the leisure groups he has chosen as the only connection he needs with community life. Everything points to a tendency of these leisure clubs to set up marginal, self-contained societies, a kind of new utopianism based not, as in the nineteenth century, on work, but on leisure. And such societies spring into existence despite, not because of, the class structure. They are not concerned with the future, only with the present. They tend to divert a part of the social potential generated in the field of production and the tensions of the clashing relations toward a semireal, semi-imaginary sphere, "where man may escape his humanity and quietly shed his real self."[9]

Will leisure be the new opium of the people? The movement to lead the worker "from alienation to enjoyment" would then be contradicted by a force leading away from enjoyment of leisure back to alienation in work. The worker would be content to sell his labor as a commodity for the sake of simply enjoying the proceeds of his sale in the time away from his job. Is that all he will want? Will he leave it to someone else, to his spokesmen, to win a maximum wage for him? Though a product of the historical process, leisure is being lived, in effect, as if it were a value outside history. The man of leisure tends to be ungrateful for any past, indifferent to any future. To be sure, this is not an attitude which makes a conscientious citizen. It is this aspect of the life-culture of the masses that calls for placing leisure in its historical perspective and in its

[9] Cf., in the same sense, a remark by Jean-Paul Sartre about the ambiguous role of mediator played by associations, according to the first results of our Annecy inquiry, in *Critique de la raison dialectique,* NRF, 1960, p. 50.

present technical, economic, and social context so that we may the better understand what forces operate, or could operate, upon it or because of it.

Chapter 2

What Made
Leisure Possible?
What Will
Leisure Be?

Technical Progress

THERE ARE THOSE WHO BELIEVE THAT THE COMPLEX AND ambiguous state of leisure today is on the threshold of a profound transformation. Thanks to the discovery of new sources of energy and to the spread of automation, the time spent at work should be reduced fairly rapidly for everyone. A new situation would then arise, in which old social problems would disappear. The poets will win out over the sociologists; we shall leave the era of work to enter into the "era of leisure."

Now this prophecy raises a question about the real relations between the growth of leisure and technical progress. First, it is indisputable that leisure is an integral part of technical civilization. Not only will any modification of the latter influence the former, but leisure is itself a creation of our industrial system. Indeed, the "leisurely days" of a time gone by can hardly be compared to the days of leisure we know now. What the forerunner of the sociologists of labor, Sebastien Vauban designated, around 1700, as leisure in the artisan's life never had the liberating character that leisure has taken on with respect to contemporary work (1). Certainly, those old leisurely days brought repose, but of a kind that could offer nothing in answer to the needs felt by the modern worker. At a time when the average income of the workers was below that required for their minimum physiological necessities, what meaning could there be in a desire for shorter working hours— except an increase of poverty? There were only two categories of non-workdays, according to Vauban:

1. Regular holy days set by the Church, often against the will of the peasants and artisans, to foster spiritual exercise. (The poor devil in La Fontaine's *Fables* complains that "monsieur le Curé is always finding a new saint to chalk up a sermon to.") There were eighty-four nonwork days a year.

2. The days when work was impossible because of "illness, bitter cold, or some urgent business" added up to about the same number as the religious days, making the total number of nonwork days each year more than one hundred and sixty.

As for daily repose, it was simply a variation on the theme of the long day's work, that "flow of time" from dawn to dawn that marked the labor of old. The period of rest was indeed a pause in the day's occupation, not a time of leisure.

With the growing mechanization and division of labor within a highly organized production process, a chronological workday came in. It was ever more distinct from, and finally boldly opposed to, the nonwork time which itself was gradually converted into a whole complex of new activity involving relaxation, recreation, and self-development. Thus, while at first an expanding productive capacity served to reduce the worker's free time, little by little it began to increase it, while simultaneously increasing the productive output of the workday. We may, therefore, predict that the discovery of new sources of energy and advances in industrial organization, together with expanding automation, will bring about more leisure time. And we see that leisure is thus a continuous product of technical progress.

Yet the production of leisure is not automatic. The growth of free time, and the shrinking of work time, are among the social advantages that count in the unceasing and continually renewed struggle between opposing interests. It has been pointed out by Pierre Naville (4) that if technical progress in itself meant more leisure for the worker, the sudden spurt in the development of machines at the end of the nineteenth century would automatically have brought in its wake a reduction in hours of work. But the requirements of that society, and the relations among its forces, produced the opposite condition. In 1936, it was indeed a new relation of forces that suddenly, because of a dread of unemployment, brought about the forty-hour week and twelve paid holidays. Yet this same forty-hour week later had to be relinquished, not only because of the war, but also, according to Alfred Sauvy, because the capacity of the country's industrial plant was such that any decrease in the productive forces was bound to block a rise in the general standard of living. From which we see that increase of leisure depends also on the alignment of forces at any given moment.

Social Progress

There was a time when idleness was the mother of all the gentlemanly virtues. This idleness fell into disgrace with the rise of the hard-working bourgeoisie who erected the modern edifice of commerce and industry. Idleness was further discredited in the nineteenth century by the rise of the proletariat. Henri Lefebvre was able to write: "A man of my age has with his own eyes seen, between 1880 and 1940, the final fall of the man who does nothing, does no work, the "rentier-idler." But it must be noted that during approximately the same period, two apparently contradictory movements developed together. As idleness declined, the new notion of leisure began to take shape in the worker's mind. We have no reliable historical records on this development and, hence, can make only an approximation of dates of the principal stages.

The slogan of syndicalist hopes and demands is well-known: "Welfare and Liberty." Leisure is a part of such welfare and liberty, and its history is not unexpectedly interwoven with the history of workers' welfare and liberty. Nevertheless, leisure was a very late demand of the nineteenth-century working class; more immediate needs had to be satisfied first. We know that, in 1833, the printers of Nantes, tired of submitting to individual misery, at last founded a mutual aid society, which issued the modest declaration "Let us say to our master printers: We desire neither your fortunes, nor your pleasures, but only a wage enough to pay for a decent bed, a roof over our heads against the wind and weather, and bread in our old age." The idea of leisure could scarcely occur while the length of the workday weighed so heavily. The initial demand had to deal with a reduction of hours. We have seen that during the July Monarchy there was a thirteen-hour day. The ten-hour day first came in with the Revolution of 1848, but after the June collapse, the Law of September restored the legal workday to twelve hours. Without irony, P. Barrau could write, in a book lavishly honored by the French Academy in 1850: "How many men are there who, weighed down by the burden of their idleness, or dulled by a continuous succession of artificial pleasures, enjoy nothing, are weary of everything, struggle painfully through hours of boredom that seem to stretch out eternally. The worker has no such problem: he is never at a loss to know what to do with his periods of brief and infrequent leisure" (5).

Still, Georges Duveau wrote: "In the midnineteenth century, in France, concentration of industry gives rise to a new problem: What to do with leisure time. But there is only the vaguest awareness of it. When A. Cochin and A. Audiganne raise the demand that there should be a well-ordered use of Sundays, no echo is heard" (6). In 1850 only, after a ten-year struggle, came the reestablishment of a weekly rest.

It was not until 1863 that we find embodied in a text of workers' demands the idea of shorter work hours tied in with the idea of a cultural use of the free time gained. One hundred and eighty-three Parisian delegates returning from a trip to Great Britain where they had studied the trade unions declared: "The length of our workday here makes it impossible for us to take advantage of evening school." A worker named Valin, five years before the Paris Commune, made this statement: "The body needs rest, but a reduction in the hours of work is even more necessary for the mind and the soul. Education is impossible for us since we work all day. We could also enjoy the charm and satisfaction of family life. The kind of leisure a father has, the enjoyments of the hearth, are impossible, unknown to us. The workshop consumes our energies and all our time."

The notion of schooling for everyone appeared at the same time that the right to leisure was put forth as a more and more pressing demand. The French League for Learning was set up in 1864, under the leadership of Jean Macé, "to lay the ground for and assure the republican education of the country." The Third Republic ushered in a new spirit. After the proclamation of the laws of June 16, 1881 and of March 28, 1882, which created free, secular, compulsory schooling for all children, the League vigorously renewed its campaign for adult education, declaring at the Congress of Nantes (March 1894): "The League will not forget its obligations to adults, and in their interest calls for a new kind of activity: the organization of supplementary courses, professional courses, popular lectures. Wherever they do not now exist, the League plans to found associations for popular education." From this time on, there began an intensified drive to establish afterschool societies, adult education courses, and municipal libraries.

During this same period, the aristocracy and upper bourgeoisie, shaken by the crisis of 1870, were looking for means of redress. Writes Pierre de Coubertin: "I had the feeling that the only real remedy lay in a profoundly changed system of education, one capable of producing a collective calm and wisdom, and a reflective force" (8). It was under English influence that the first clubs for athletic sports sprang up among Paris students—the French Stadium and the Racing Club of France and then the gymnastic societies. Coubertin, in 1864, organized the first sports meet in the great amphitheater of the Sorbonne; he also established teaching of sports and proposed the restoration of the Olympic games. Approximately at this time, youth movements were engendered among the bourgeoisie—in France, the Catholic Association of French Youth, headed by Albert de Mun; in England, the Boy Scouts, headed by General Baden-Powell. The Scout movement took hold in France after 1911.

But, returning to 1898, it was to be a serious social crisis that would give rise to a new form of popular education through leisure. Dreyfus had been condemned by the War Council. The Left, under the impetus of the Affair, had found renewed energy, and the socialist movement, led by Jean Jaurès, entered the political arena. The intellectuals "went to the people." Having fought by their side, they then sought to raise their level of culture. In 1898, the first People's universities were established. The future professor André Siegfried was fraternizing with the ex-chef Pierre Hamp. Workers' study circles were formed, amateur theatrical groups, concerts, lectures, lectures galore. Four years later, the People's universities were deserted by the workers; only one, that of Saint Denis, was to survive until the First World War. Later still, there would be a feeble attempt to keep the movement going; but after they disappeared, these universities stood for a long time as a vital example of how the workers' cultural leisure could be organized in the future.

Progressively, the reduction in work hours stimulated among the working classes an ever more widespread and ever more tenacious desire for leisure. Workers' demands finally resulted, in 1891, in the passing of a law to limit the workday of women and children to eleven hours. The General Confederation of Labor was founded in 1895, and May 1 of that year, the young Fernand Pelloutier, founder of the labor exchanges, insisted on "undertaking the moral, administrative, and technical education necessary to make a society of proud free men viable." In 1906, for the first time in a May Day parade, the slogan of the eight-hour day was raised.

After 1907, the first two workers' sports clubs were founded—the Romilly Proletarienne and the Club of Pré Saint Gervais. Jean Jaurès perceived the meaning of this movement: "It is well-known that in all civilized countries the workers have fought for a reduction in their workday; they have won some partial gains. All the while, they have made it clear that it is not only to conserve their strength that they need this shorter day, but in order to be able to live more of a family life, to read, to educate themselves, to become, truly, men."

The law establishing the eight-hour day was passed in 1919. And the Astier law called for work-training for all workers under eighteen. One year later, for the first time, the trade unions included in the text of their absolute minimum demands a budgetary item designated "Vacations and entertainments."

Social teams sprang up, under the initiative of Robert Garric, who desired to see workers and intellectuals together in the same leisure circles as they had been together before in the same trenches. At this time, the workers' movement in Belgium fostered a new branch of Catholic Action—the Christian Workers Youth. The influence of Pelloutier's ideas made itself felt long after his death; from 1933 on, about a hundred workers' colleges flourished.

Then came 1936. The great popular movements succeeded in winning a forty-hour week and collective bargaining, paid vacations, and group travel tickets. The weekend was introduced, the week of "two Sundays." The workers were buoyed up on a wave of optimism. A Ministry of Leisure was created, directed by Léo Lagrange, who would contribute greatly to organizing leisure time sports, travel, and cultural programs. Youth hostels, introduced in France in 1930, rapidly expanded and fostered several movements.

Inexpensive children's camps sprang up, as well as training centers for progressive education. Workers' universities and Houses of Culture were founded, under the impetus of writers together with the vanguard of the trade unionists. The Peasant Foyers made attempts to revitalize the life of the countryside. At Soissons, the first circulating library was launched by M. Vendel. The People's Theater brought together writers and artists around the leadership of Romain Rolland and Arthur Honneger and helped to set up popular leisure programs.

A new style of leisure, not simply a new organization, was born. "We want the worker, the peasant, and the unemployed," said Léo Lagrange, "to find in leisure the joy of living and the sense of their *dignity"* (my italics). The very word *leisure,* up to then claimed by the bourgeoisie, took on a popular resonance and began to replace the more modest *rest.* A host of pursuits, which had been the prerogative of the leisure class, were now taken over and transformed by the urban workers, as well as here and there in rural regions. Nineteen thirty-six marked a high point in the history of the people's leisure.

The "national renewal" of 1940, while taking care to make itself different in all respects from the spirit of 1936, still continued to organize for leisure. Physical education and sports spurted ahead. The Scouts and the Catholic Youth were solidified, and other movements were born. The Youth Residences were founded. But reliance on all this ended, once the Nazi ranks and tanks began to roll in; then it was the Underground and the Liberation.

In 1944, Jean Guehenno was called upon to set up the general program for Popular Education and Sports. And at the instigation of the Minister of Labor, Alexandre Parodi, company committees were set up in factories of more than fifty workers. By a decree of November 2, 1945, these were to take charge of "social programs, aimed at the use of leisure time and the organization of sports [Article 3]; and the professional and educational institutions attached to or connected with the company, such as apprenticeship and work training centers, libraries, study circles, general culture courses, and management training" (Article 4).

Company projects for leisure pursuits spread, and there came an unprecedented nation-wide eruption of groups for leisure and popular culture—the National Federation of Rural Foyers, the French Federation of Cinema Clubs, Work and Travel, Work and Culture, People and Culture, The French Musical Youth, among others.

The general situation later put a brake on the expansion of these groups; but the idea persisted. For the first time, in 1950, the Chief Commission of the Congresses of Collectives included in its minimum budget the item "Leisure activities, culture," and the official report read: "The Workers' organizations have wished to indicate that this item, leisure activities, embodies in principle *an absolute need of the human personality,* and its introduction into an irreducible minimum budget is hereby established."

We see how, in less than one hundred years, leisure had become thoroughly transformed. On the one hand, it had taken on a livelier character among the bourgeoisie, who had become occupied more with physical and social activities alike. On the other hand, once only for the privileged few, leisure had become for the whole body of the employed, first, a possibility, then, a demand, finally, "an absolute necessity." Nor does the story stop there, at the threshold of our own day. The fight still goes on, by trade unions and cultural organizations, to win for the people more and more of this absolute necessity.

The Future

What of the future? A social science, insofar as it looks into the future, does not prophesy, but only analyzes the existing possibilities within the society's evolution. What, as viewed by a sociology of leisure, are the present possibilities?

1. France, since 1950, has entered upon a phase of economic expansion which even the beginnings of a recession in 1959 did not seem to halt. In the six years between 1950 and 1956, taking into account the fluctuations in purchasing power of the franc, average individual consumption increased by 36 per cent. Nonetheless, in 1956, when things were at a peak, to the question "Has your standard of living gone up since last year?" only 8 per cent of the respondents replied that it had; 29 per cent said, "No, it has gone down"; and 63 per cent answered, "neither up nor down." Thus we see that today in France the gap between the wages earned and the wages desired, between the multiplication of wants and enlargement of income, is such that the sense of pauperization remains acute. Probably for the majority of all social categories, the desire to earn more is far more compelling than the desire to have more free time. In 1956, Swedish workers were polled as to whether they wanted a reduction in obligatory hours of work, with a corresponding reduction of wages. The majority opted for the reduction of the then legal forty-eight hours week. How high a standard of living would Frenchmen have to have before accepting anything like this? First and foremost, of course, the total labor output is dictated by the country's national interests; a higher standard of living for all, aid to underdeveloped countries, the policies of defense and of prestige, and so on. Still, the workers' wishes cannot be ignored. A sociology of leisure ought to be able to determine the optimum relation between the leisure desired and the income needed at each stage of the economic development. Such would be the terms of the first possibility.

2. In the event of a reduction in working hours, three phenomena are closely interrelated, and, in fact, advantage for one can only be had at the expense of the others. In effect, a reduction in the country's total number of work hours may mean an increase in leisure time for the body of active workers, an earlier retirement of the older workers, or extended schooling for the workers of the future—the children. Which of these is desirable?

In a study by Jean René Treanton (14) of workers in the Paris region between sixty and seventy years of age already retired for one year, it was found that half among them still felt they could do normal work, but almost half had asked for retirement before age sixty-five; and among the hundred reasons given for quitting work, about 50 per cent indicated fatigue. Should we not follow Jean Daric's proposal and make the retirement age flexible so some may continue to work and others may enter, even before sixty-five, into the leisure of retirement?

Finally, education may be regarded as a social form of leisure of benefit to youth. There is, as we know, a general tendency toward prolonging the school period; in the United States, for example, the majority go to school up to the age of eighteen. France is in this respect backward; but an educational reform anticipates extending the compulsory school years to the age of sixteen. However, Jean Fourastié has pointed out that to prolong by one year the schooling of all French youth would correspond, in loss to the economy, to two additional hours of leisure per week for twenty million employed.

Can the country afford simultaneously to retard the age at which youth enters the labor market and increase the hours of leisure for those already in it? Also, the forty-hour week remains "the ideal working week" for more than half of all workers, salaried employees, and top personnel (54 per cent of the workers, 50 per cent of the salaried employees, 54 per cent of the executives). Unquestionably, advance in the technological organization of industry has intensified fatigue among many workers, and the question of the forty-hour week has reappeared on the agenda of trade union demands. At the end of 1959, Pierre Naville judged the "circumstances were then favorable for the unions to launch an offensive for the seven-hour day, five-day week" (15). But if, despite the apparent advantages of free time in the late afternoons, the shorter workday still meets with resistance in France, the long weekend, on the other hand, wins new adherents every year. "The week of two Sundays" seems to be preferred whenever industry allows it, even if the workday must then be lengthened to nine or ten hours. Also, the French are becoming even more attached to their annual holiday, which since August, 1956, has legally been three weeks with pay. But some recent studies have indicated that 49 per cent of labor, 62 per cent of salaried employees, and 56 per cent of executives would like a month's vacation. The law defining educational leaves of absence, passed in 1957, introduced the new twelve-day unpaid leave of absence for all workers desiring to study some phase of union development.[1] Union and educational forces together with the Ministry Plan for Popular Education have combined to put pressure on the government, Parliament, and public opinion to extend this law to include centers for training organizers of cultural programs.

We see, then, that extension of leisure time depends on both social and technical factors. It may be that in the near future leisure will have to face this clash of interest between the welfare of the country and the social-cultural aspirations of various levels and categories of the employed. Here, too, the chips are not down. The Planning Commission, in its fourth Plan of Modernization, taking the economic view, sees no possible diminution in the work period for the time being.

---

[1] At the time of correcting these proofs, the law has just been extended to include training of organizers in popular education and youth movements.

Chapter 3

Social
Determinisms
And Leisure

To FORESEE WHAT THE LEISURE OF TOMORROW WILL BE LIKE IS
even more difficult than to know how much of it there will be. Too
many philosophers and poets, taking their cue from Aldous
Huxley's *Brave New World,* or Dimitri Maiakovsky's *La Punaise,*
posit for the future "megalopolis" a mechanized leisure, rationalized to the point of killing all natural imaginative impulse. This
kind of forecast recalls Ernest Renan, who prophesied "the day will
come when the artist will be obsolete. The man of science will more
and more take over. Poetry will be killed by scientific progress."
That day appears to be distant as yet. For the sociologist, the reality
is something far less simple. Among the social factors that determine
leisure, three seem to us to be fundamental: technical progress,
traditional holdovers, and the socioeconomic set-up. Without forgetting their mutual interaction, but for the convenience of analysis,
let us consider each factor by itself.

The technical determinants that appeared so abruptly at the end
of the nineteenth century rapidly took on an explosive character
which was bound to cause upheaval in all aspects of leisure.

The first automobile carriage was built by de Dion in 1883; three years later, the invention of the chain transformed the bicycle into "the little queen"; four years later, Clément Ader was making the first flight. A new world was prophesied, and its initial features were already discernible: "Soon," asserted Jules Bois, "everyone will live in the country at a good distance from town." And, at once archeologist and sociologist of progress, he added, "The distances will be traversed by pneumatic tramways or air buses. The automobile will go out; the bicycle will always be in, but it will take the form of a flying machine for the cyclist to gad about with in the air without being run over. . . ."

At the same time that transportation was becoming mechanized, so also were the communication media. In the year 1888, Edouard Branly achieved wireless telegraphy and, in 1894, Louis Lumière, the cinematograph. Radio sets began to appear everywhere about 1921. After 1919, movie techniques were refined and the feature film was invented—and along with it the myth of the star. From 1927 on, the advent of the talkies covered the advanced places of our "shrunken planet" with a network of motion picture palaces.

In 1946, television became widespread, seemingly to usher in a new era. Its import still escapes a great many French intellectuals, but it is television that may cause a greater transformation in modern man's leisure than anything in the preceding period.

These great mechanized agencies of transportation and communication are powerfully seductive. "Magical," some say of this power, by a formal analogy, in any case. And whereas the mechanization of his labor is apt to arouse the worker's distrust and hostility, the mechanization of his leisure has his full consent, not to say downright enthusiasm—his and his children's. There is something marvelous about the world of the mechanical which induces in people from the earliest age a knowledgeable passion for the automobile or an immoderate fondness for the television set. The power of both, however, ought to be studied in detail.

Mechanized Transportation and Leisure

As long ago as 1924, Helen and Robert Lynd, in their study of a typical American city, wrote: "The automobile has perhaps revolutionized leisure more than the movies" (1). In France today, we certainly know the fascination of the automobile for people in every walk of life. The country had 2,250,000 automobiles in 1938; in 1950, 6,700,000. The number of two-seater motorcycles and scooters is even more astonishing; and the yearly rate of increase in motor vehicles of all sorts, among certain social classes is 10 per cent. These immense strides in motorization tend to bring the human body to a halt. The mechanical motor has replaced the human motor, and men no longer walk, run, or leap. The danger is indisputable. But too often we are inclined to stop at this negative side of the balance sheet; let us look at the positive side. Mechanization has fostered activities totally unknown to the premachine age— sports, above all. Lynd, in his Middletown study, has confused the number of those with special qualifications for competition in sports with the number who pursue a sport of some kind; there are in France only two and one half million of the former, but a poll of a typical sample of the population showed that 49 per cent of all Frenchmen engage in at least one activity they call sport.[1] Consider, for example, the growing practice of doing exercises in the morning

[1] Direct or indirect commercialization of certain sport associations has often relegated to second place the original aims of the sport. Hence the appearance of omnisport associations with a purely social and educational purpose. They introduce the sport into workers' circles (Labor Sports and Gymnastic Federation, Labor Sports Union), school and postschool groups (Primary Education Sports Union, French Union of Lay Physical Education Work), religious bodies (French Sports Federation), universities (School and University Office of Sport). They account for about 700,000 members. In 1959, there were in all the associations 2,589,492 members specially qualified for competition, with the number of regular participants amounting to

to the voice of the radio, and in a gym in the evening. In the past twenty years our beaches have become fields of sport (especially volleyball) and the place for all kinds of lessons in physical fitness, some for fun, some for serious corrective purposes. In 1959, there were six thousand teachers and supervisors in charge of this whole effort. Then, too, the growing habit of spending leisure time out-doors evenings, and especially Sundays, is, of course, attributable to the automobile. The meager foliage of Nogent and the dust of the roads leading into Paris have been deserted for the forests of the Ile de France. And the great migration to the suburbs has meant more time spent outdoors in the evenings, puttering in the garden. Thanks to the automobile, there can be suburbs like those of Los Angeles, stretching for miles upon miles of grass and trees. The question is somewhat more complex than the first pessimistic glance would have it.

about 3,000,000. We should add, furthermore, that in 1959 more than 880,000 children had earned their popular sport certificate.

ASSOCIATIONS	NUMBER OF PARTICIPANTS		
	1944	*1953*	*1958*
Football	177,000	439,479	380,352
Bowling	150,700	180,462	177,506
Basketball	53,333	177,137	84,371
Skiing	9,579	78,330	113,960
Tennis	20,445	57,858	76,662
Cycling	10,971	51,940	37,645
Rugby	46,627	34,500	34,328
Track	60,597	33,138	39,187
Swimming	43,679	30,874	27,732
Horseback riding	1,576	28,400	20,418
Volleyball	1,860	23,513	22,710
Ping Pong	2,271	21,599	24,156
Judo	—	20,100	30,070
Target practice	—	16,256	16,211
13-man rugby	—	34,500	—
Physical culture	—	9,912	6,200
Boxing	3,598	13,800	4,541
Golf	1,943	7,118	9,538
Rowing	7,434	7,932	8,955
Fencing	4,162	6,134	7,278
Gymnastics	—	44,218	49,736

Mechanized Mass Media and Leisure

The major dailies and weeklies in France print editions of a million or more. In 1951, some one paper every day was read by 88 per cent of all Frenchmen—an occupation taking a half hour to an hour. It was found by Mme. Gabrielle Letellier that, just as the budget of even an unemployed worker must allow for the daily ration of tobacco, so too does it allow for the daily paper.

However, radio would seem to hold an even greater place in the worker's free time. To Paul Lazarsfeld's query, asked of Americans in 1941, as to which they would choose to forego if they wre forced to, radio or newspapers, the overwhelming vote for keeping the radio once again pointed to the power of this medium (3). Not requiring the use of the eye, like print or movies or television, radio becomes the sound prop of daily life, heard in the home, but also in the car, and at the café and store, in the office, at the factory. Anywhere you happen to be, you may listen to it, hear the orchestra and the songs; 60 per cent of the public wants even more of the songs, a recent poll by the INSEE revealed (4). Radio, as have the movies, has launched stars: Bourvil, Piaf, Robert Lamoureux. It has been pointed out by Roger Veille (5) that there are ten times as many radio listeners as moviegoers in France; a performer in one broadcast can be heard by as many listeners as in ten years at a music hall, where a hundred performances drawing several hundred thousand spectators could well be equivalent to the worst of radio failures. More than 75 per cent of French homes in 1960 boasted a radio.

Movies are not as popular as radio—the elders pass them up, and people living in rural surroundings have very little experience with them. Among city people, movies have their very devoted public, drawn from every social level.

The heroes, themes, and fashions that come out of the movies have brought about some deep-going changes in what people do and want to do with their leisure life, and in what the youth of the world does with its everyday life. A new style, affecting the other arts, has emanated from the greatest of cinema productions.

And now a new phase has begun in cinema development. According to Edgar Morin: "The present period is characterized by a certain stagnation, regression even, of public interest in the so-called Western countries, but of a considerable surge of interest in the public of the 'new' countries, economically and politically new: South America, Asia, the People's Democracies." Between 1950 and 1953 in the United States, 5,038 movie houses closed down, and nearly one third of the remainder, about 5,347, operated at a loss (19). A less pronounced but similar trend is observed in France. This diminution of the importance of the movies for people's leisure results not so much from any widespread decrease in their purchasing power as from usurpation by other forms of leisure activity. Nor is it likely that the American attempts with the three-dimensional large screen—cinemascope, particularly—will succeed in restoring the movies to the role they had in leisure entertainment up to 1945.

The fact is that the cinema now feels the full force of the latest comer in the world of entertainment, a force that promises an unprecedented revolution in leisure habits: the television screen. Again, we have our first statistics from the United States, where watching television quickly became a national pastime. The experts have figured out that a 2 per cent increase in television receivers means a 1 to 10 per cent decrease in movie receipts. Television ownership in the United States has enjoyed an upward curve of a kind rarely seen in matters of household economy: in 1945, ten thousand sets; in 1948, over one and one half million; in 1950, ten million; in 1954, thirty million; in 1959, over fifty-one million.

The United States is not alone in this. England, already before the coronation of Elizabeth, had two million sets; a few months afterward, more than three million. Today, England has ten million sets. The Soviet Union, in 1960, had over four million.

France, in 1954, still had only about one hundred and fifty thousand sets, to the perplexity of the manufacturers who had prepared for a sale of about half a million. Economic hardship, the attitude of the press, and intellectual prejudices were perhaps responsible for the slow growth, about five thousand sets a month. It would be a mistake, however, to think of television as a leisure toy of the rich. A partial poll, taken as far back as 1953, showed that more than half the owners of television were to be found among skilled workers, craftsmen, and salaried employees, and that a percentage of the remaining sets belonged to urban and even rural organizations of various kinds—educational bodies, societies of one kind and another, tele-clubs. Today, the French television network covers half the country; fifty-eight stations (sixteen of them high-powered) assure reception by over 70 per cent of the population. By December, 1959, there were 1,400,000 sets in France, with an average monthly increment of 10,000 to 15,000; since January, 1962, the 3,000,000 mark has been passed.

What influence do these powerful mass media exert on the way leisure time is used? To be sure, there are marked differences between these instruments of communication for use, on the one hand, and for opinion-value on the other. But these powerful mass media, if not of equal importance, tend to coincide in their seductive power over the exercise of leisure. Paul Lazarsfeld has shown the close correlation between attitudes generated by the illustrated newspapers, movies, radio, and television. It would scarcely be incorrect, from now on, to speak of the technological conditioning of leisure time.

Does this technological conditioning spell passivity of viewer and of listener? It is not unwarranted to fear that the peculiarly suggestive power of the mass media, combined with their standardized content, may have some most stultifying effects. Some important observations have been made by Georges Cohen Séat as to what immediate effect "filmic fascination" has on the human nervous system. But the great range of motivations and idea-patterns that a cinema experience, either documentary or fiction, confers on the spectator suggests that the very real physiological effects we speak of can be nuanced, extended, transformed, even contradicted by others, more effectively complex, more intellectually immediate and differentiated. But all such effects vary with the individual and the film being watched. There are films that right then and there work on the imagination, but not to the point of lulling all reflection.

Cinematograph language is capable of expressing the most poetic of fictions as well as the utmost materialities, a theorem or a dance, a song or a lesson. It is polyvalent, can say anything. This language, which seems so simple, can become a thing for new learning. Even the limited experience of the cinema clubs suggests that attitudes toward a film may be conditioned according to the way it is presented or discussed, or, simply, by the fact of its fame. Moreover, the art of cinema must not be judged from particular separate movies, nor even on the basis solely of the predominantly fiction vehicle. "It is a question of film footage," André Bazin has said. ". . . for every three feet of technical film, three hundred of fiction is shot. The film language, so to speak, is used nine out of ten times for writing novels and plays." Finally, the cinema, like all visual techniques of representation and expression, has different effects depending on content and on the spectator's predisposition toward the content.

The final balance sheet of the technological determinants of our leisure is far from being closed. For one thing, this phenomenon is at the height of its evolution, and all the partial observations are bound to make for excessive generalization, too much theorizing. There have been some fairly passionate affirmations, but they ignore the scientific research. Indeed, all aspects of the subject are so fluid that only by experimentally varying the conditions that can produce them will we succeed in understanding them.

Traditional Resistances and Persistences

It would be a mistake, obviously, to regard the change in leisure as having been brought about by a progressively and widely dispersed technological evolution. Actually, as C. Bouglé has pointed out, "Each society has its own structure, traditions, and needs, all of which set limits to innovation." We must, therefore, try to see what are each individual country's determinants of leisure, in both the urban and the rural regions. Even when the forms of a society have disappeared, the old mentality often subsists beneath the new structure—an anachronism that could serve either to redress a dangerous evolution or impede necessary progress. This is a fact of society, and we propose to bring some light to bear on it.

We might take from the work of André Varagnac (8) a suggestion that we study traditional civilizations as we would dig for a buried world. For he speaks of archeo-civilization as a means of describing life-patterns that antedate the industrial revolution. Through him, the sociology of leisure has become aware that "regression of traditional ceremonies, having doubtless appeared much sooner in the cities, would seem to have slowed down in the countryside after the war of 1870–71." It might be of intrinsic interest to resurrect the details of the ancient ceremonials, the torch and the May Day tree, folk legend and dance. And it could be demonstrated how these customs characteristic of an old social order disappeared with the construction of roads, the development of an open economy, the circulation of ideas, and so forth. But this seems to us too static a view of the evolution of leisure activity, and too abstract with respect to all the other forces determining that evolution.

Our own position is closer to that of M. J. Herskovits, who sees tradition as a factor of resistance to change (9). It remains for us to spell out exactly how this works. Tradition may act to reject modern leisure; it may be the cause of inadaptation, or an imperfect adaptation, to it; it may offer a framework of ritual for the integration of the new pursuits, which in turn would give tradition itself a fresh significance; finally, tradition may serve as a force for balance in the development of the new trends. Such are the hypotheses, subject to verification by research.

1. Tradition may put up a roadblock to a modern way of leisure. Thus, attendance at the movies is practically nil in many groups stamped by their rural origins.

Also, as shown by a study of the French radio-television audience, in general, large numbers of aged persons are unacquainted with radio: "In my day, there was no radio; we can still get along without it."

Finally, there are plenty of intellectuals, formed—deformed, perhaps—by poorly assimilated humanities, who oppose a crude "no" to all technical advance. (Oh, television. . . .)

2. Tradition may be the cause, if not of absolute rejection, at least of nonadaptation to the new forms of leisure. Vestiges of the old psychology hamper a new way of doing things, in the same way as models of horse carriages influenced the design of the first motorcars. Country folk are apt to make little use of the modern automobile, which could enhance their pleasure by holiday visits to the city or excursions to nearby or faraway places. Another case: Formerly, conversation was not "directed," but was a spontaneous natural exchange, in front of the hearth or at the table. And we find many people retaining the old habit, listening even now to their radios as if to the inexhaustible voice of a neighbor. In the old days, one went to a fortuneteller to ascertain the future in her deck of cards; now, you may find your future in the horoscope column of your daily newspaper. Formerly, the confessional for everyone—or almost everyone—was a book of responses to questions of conscience; today, people "confess" in the advice columns of the daily papers—there we may follow, if we wish, the correspondence of the heart.

3. How can tradition offer a framework and a method for absorbing the new? Neglected by most folklorists, this is a capital question for a psychosociology of leisure. Cultural innovation makes for a new equilibrium in daily living, varying with the time and the place; old ways of doing things, taking on a new significance as they answer to new uses, may well be a guide to the use of a mechanized leisure.

Here, it seems to us, the traditional festivals provide an interesting case study. Such festivals present a ritualistic context for the new kinds of leisure, which in return give the old rituals a new meaning and role. Thus, anciently, the carnival was the time for donning death masks of the dead who were supposedly going to return to distribute blessings among the living. Today all such festivals still serve as occasions of reunion, but no longer have the old magicoreligious significance; they are not the sacred ceremonies of yore, but only collective pastimes—profane events.

Once upon a time, the ceremonial was sharply divorced from the ordinary life of monotony and misery. "In a more cohesive world than ours," L. Bergé notes, "these ceremonies took on the character of a total collective unchurning of body and soul—an explosive liberation of the human being." The bishops themselves, up to the end of the sixteenth century, allowed the annual orgies of the Feast of Fools, between Christmas and Epiphany, to unfold in the churches. That day, every Tom, Dick, and Harry ate for four; other days of the week villages literally were decimated by famine. On the feast days, the faithful indulged in all sorts of behavior ordinarily regarded as capital sin. In our world, leisure may be indulged in, and even by the underprivileged each and every evening, if one wishes, on the playground, at a movie, seated in front of one's radio. The feast day has been diluted into daily life, and thereby has lost its explosive, perhaps cathartic, character. Certain festivals have vanished—Fool's Day,[2] and the Feast of the

[2] A Middle Age carnival day held in churches on or about December 26.

Innocents; many have more and more become children's holidays, such as mid-Lent or St. Jean's Day.

But the new leisure has by no means abolished all the old holidays; it makes good use of some of them, while often altering their import. Or, in place of the vanished traditional ceremonials, new holidays have arisen, of a secular kind. On the whole, holiday celebration remains in contemporary life the "show of authority and total cohesion" which Marcel Mauss described as the character of archaic ceremonials. The feast day is the occasion for affirming the vitality and unity of the group; at the same time, the distractions offered by it are more and more loosely related to its original rites— it is a day either of ceremony or of leisure. And here, perhaps, the amateur theater in France has taken on its truest significance. From 1947 through 1951, theatrical productions—ballet, concerts, readings—had an audience in France of one hundred million; the cinema dropped sixty million of its audience. Yet the French professional theater counts no more than fifty companies whereas, according to the Authors' Society, more than ten thousand comparatively stable amateur theatrical groups give at least two productions a year. Their success, according to André Villiers, is astounding. In 1946, they gave 28,000 shows, in 1949, 42,400; and the movement continues to grow. Now, this kind of amateur theatrical, whose quality, though generally improving, still remains problematical, is not just an esthetic or psychological phenomenon, but essentially a social one. It is a true chosen, preferred form of celebration—in factory, school, village, district. The group in the midst of such a production is not open to outside influences and pays little attention to such entertainment as radio or the movies. Temporarily, it is a closed society, drawing up the balance sheet of past performances, preparing for future action, enjoying the sense of its drive, its unity, its fraternizing. It is proud of the display of talent by its members, it welcomes parents, friends, and friends' friends to come and applaud and share in the general enthusiasm. We would do well to pursue the examination of this phenomenon, a reaction, perhaps, to the tendency of the modern group toward openness onto a totally open world. It has been pointed out by André Varagnac that it devolves on the youth of the village to organize this new type of celebration: ". . . only a few years back, they [the youth] began to assume the role of instigators of games, competitions, amusements of every kind that are the principal attraction at holiday celebrations. Now, also in their hands are the rural theatricals, and the organization of dances and bicycle races."

But what has happened meanwhile to the religious holidays? Those that persist have been subjected· to a mixture of the ancient and the modern. We shall offer here only a few explanations; elsewhere we shall analyze the many implications of the shifting symbolisms that occur when reluctant participation in a ceremonial succumbs to the newer distractions, that finally make the day one of quasileisure.[3]

Undoubtedly, the one holiday that more than any other in modern times diverts people from the humdrum is Christmas. It claims the greatest number of celebrants (63 per cent). No longer for all a religious festival, it still is, for all, a children's holiday. Basically, it remains a family affair, but, nevertheless, it reveals a tendency to become a collective one; everybody's Christmas tree

[3] Frequency of participation in holidays (10):

HOLIDAYS OF RELIGIOUS ORIGIN	PARTICIPATION			ENJOYMENT WITHOUT PARTICIPATION	NEITHER ENJOYMENT NOR PARTICIPATION	
	ACTIVE %	WEAK %	Total	%	%	Total
Christmas	24	39	63	17	20	100
Easter	9	35	44	52	4	100
August 15	4	20	26	67	7	100
HOLIDAYS OF CIVIC ORIGIN						
July 14	43	—	43	40	17	100
November 11	28	8	36	47	17	100
January 1	11	25	36	30	34	100
May 1	12	0	12	67	21	100

glows in the factory, at the parties, in schools and municipalities. The celebration around the collective tree often has a link with sociopolitics of the group.

In January, the Kings are still "shot at," to the consumption of the pancakes. It is essentially a day of camaraderie, celebrated with the family, with the neighbors, or with one's fellow workers.

Candlemas Day, in February, is no longer the feast of the Purification of the Virgin Mary, but the day when mother fries pancakes because "It brings luck." But in February, despite all organized effort, in Nice, Châlons, Sarreguemines, the pre-Lenten Carnival is on the decline. Virtually all that remains is its tourist-attraction picturesqueness; the masked ball is gone—only the children put on masks.

April Fool's Day seems still to hold its own. Then, practical jokes ordinarily taboo are permitted and even expected, without fear of punishment; the occasion is seized upon to play a trick on some grumpy fellow worker or even on one's superior; a bunch of people ordinarily held in bounds can seize their chance to show hostility toward anyone who annoys them by an excess of originality or authority. Perhaps April Fool's Day is the substitute for the old Carnival Day.

May 1 has become a nonwork holiday, mostly spent in the open. Springtime has arrived, the great trek outdoors begins, the first violets will be picked. The automobile and the motorcycle have vastly increased this movement to the outdoors. Originally a labor holiday, born of the workers' struggles, May 1 now means for some (67 per cent) the gaiety of a spring festival, and for others (12 per cent) anticipation of joyous tomorrows. The songs of social significance underscore the analogy between the coming of spring and the coming of a better world.

Pentecost has been growing in importance, giving workers two or three days of vacation, now made even more enjoyable because of cars and camping. Always longing to get out in the open, young people look forward especially to this holiday; it is often their first night of camping out, the only danger being heavy dew or rain. Two other calendar days remain very much alive: August 15 and All Saints' Day, and their various social meanings need to be analyzed.

But among all secular holidays, new or old, July 14 is still the most vital and boasts of the greatest participation. Parades of trade unions and political parties salute the memory of the taking of the Bastille, but for everybody July 14 is the first summer holiday. In large measure, it has taken on the role of Saint Jean's Day as the great traditional Feast of Midsummer that ushered in the season of fine weather. July 14 is the final holiday of the work year. The children are out of school, and general vacation is in the air.

No other secular holiday is so grandly or so spontaneously celebrated. Victory Day, May 8, suffers from the rupture of the old alliance of 1944; and Armistice Day, November 11, has been effaced by the overwhelming cataclysm of the last war.

Still another holiday should be mentioned, one artificially created, but of great tenacity and growing strength—Mother's Day. Mother's Day makes special sense if we consider that Father's Day, launched as a praiseworthy attempt at balance, tends to be ridiculed or altogether ignored. Do we not in this see the recognition, and the consecration, of the central role of the mother within the contemporary family?

This sketch, while necessarily incomplete, nonetheless does show how the amalgam of the ancient and the modern in the ceremonial holiday conceals new meanings and how numerous holidays are evolving into forms of semileisure in which entertainment is more important than civic or spiritual participation.

4. We have still to examine how tradition may be an element of balance in the mechanized leisure of our time. Friedmann writes: "The Americans, a young people, are lacking in traditions. While we lack the art of living in the new technical environment as much as they do. If we sometimes do better at it, it is evidently thanks to the older traditions of our premachine societies." In fact, certain traditional activities of the peasant and the craftsman tend more and

more to become the leisure occupations of modern society that counterbalance the mechanization and rationalization of work.

Let us take three examples. Gardening is one characteristic of the urban way of life. Rather than dying out, it is increasingly widespread. One of the most important activities of company committees is to develop workers' gardening associations, especially in small towns; gardening is the hobby of 90 per cent of the workers at a big metallurgical firm in Pont à Mousson (pop. 20,000). The reason for this craze does not seem to lie in lack of money or in company policy. This hobby is not dropped when there is a sudden rise in the standard of living. Industrial managers are as fond of gardening as are the workers (1).

Could it be because the old peasant base has not yet been undermined and many city dwellers are still peasants of recent date? The popularity of hunting in towns and villages, and of fishing in the cities, makes the case even more plain. In 1958, about 1,640,000 fishing licenses were issued and the number of anglers was estimated by the Higher Council on Fishing at 3,500,000 (11). When good weather comes, neither radio nor movies can hold back the lovers of the chase or the line. The opening day of the fishing season is more and more treated like a new rite.

On opening day, invite any fisherman to a party or a wedding, even one who never catches anything, and he replies without hesitation: "Impossible, it's opening day," writes Montmousseau in *La Musette du Père Brecot.*

The growth of camping is another example. The high cost of hotels is certainly one cause of this development, but an ever larger number of campers, especially those having a car, "are going back to nature" for their own pleasure. In 1959, about 450,000 camping licenses were issued and the number of campers was estimated at two million. Pierre Daninos, the humorist, draws his own conclusions: "I have," he says, "the most profound admiration for those who, for the sheer fun of it, go back to the age of the mammoths in the era of television and, in the midst of the forest, set about making fire by rubbing two stones together."

But we must agree with Arnold Van Gennepp on the total change in meaning to be derived from these activities, which are transported from the realm of work to the realm of leisure (12).

To put a stop to all the talk about "the good old days" when life was better, listen to the ethnographers who have seriously studied rural life in the old days.

"Not only are we very far from folklore itself," writes Van Gennepp, "but also from the actual conditions of shepherd life, a harsh life of rain, fog, and wind for hours on end, and, up to the middle of the nineteenth century, a life tormented by fear of wolves. City dwellers may amuse themselves lunching on the grass from time to time and call this passing moment a picnic; nowadays, we have made a sport called 'camping' out of this life in the open fields—and it delights us because we know it won't last" (12).

So it is that the opposition between the technical and the natural environments takes place according to an evolutionary and dialectical rhythm in which the mixture of tradition and progress in daily behavior is highly complex. The subject merits a more dynamic study by ethnographers and folklorists, from the viewpoint of adaptation to modern life. Sociology needs this work if it is to make progress.

Socioeconomic Influences

We have stressed the ambiguity between the technological conditioning of leisure in its relations with traditional conditioning. One may ask if some writers sometimes don't attribute to the technical environment reactions that are economic and social in origin. This question frequently arises when one reads essays inspired with the idea of progress. The ambiguity created by this confusion reappears in innumerable generalized indictments of the "machine" in the name of "man," where the real culprit, the socioeconomic organization of the machine, is seldom mentioned. An objective study of the conditioning of leisure should seek to emphasize the effect of these socioeconomic determinants.

In an analysis of consumer spending, found in the French financial balance sheet of 1950, Jean Bernard lists as an entry "Luxury goods and leisure." This association of words is not entirely satisfactory, but it does have the merit of making it appear (1) that leisure activities cost money; (2) that money spent on leisure is bracketed among "luxury goods" after the expenditures on prime necessities, such as food, medical care, clothing and housing. It follows from this that leisure activities are also determined by customers' potentialities and habits; here is the foremost socio-economic determinant.

Too many educators concerned with cultural leisure, too many sociologists heedful of the main currents of technical progress or of traditional civilization forget the financial aspect of leisure.

The drop in prices resulting from mass production has expanded the consuming public. For example, until the middle of the nineteenth century, when a newspaper cost five sous, a day's work brought the worker about thirty sous. In 1882, there must have been among the twelve thousand subscribers to the *Constitutionnel* few workers who could afford it. Today, in France almost everyone can afford to read the newspapers, go to the movies, or buy a radio set. Technical progress has, therefore, destroyed some of the inequalities deriving from unequal incomes. Preceding chapters illustrate how leisure habits are standardized by mechanization. But we have encountered only one aspect of the problem. The other is quite different but just as real and important.

Because it is often neglected, we will insist on it even more. In his critique of daily life, Lefebvre observes that "the dividing line between the classes, while not rigid, nonetheless exists; it exists in all the areas of daily everyday life: housing, food, clothing and leisure," and, above all, "class does not imply solely a quantitative difference in the amount of wages, salaries, or incomes but also a qualitative difference in the way incomes are distributed and expended" (13).

The low purchasing power of part of the working class determines standards of consumption which in turn can influence expenditures in general. So it is that leisure activities which exceed working-class standards of consumption will rarely be indulged in by workers, even though they may be less expensive than others that do conform to these standards. For example, in a provincial town a wrestling match at which the cheapest seat costs six new francs will be popular while a theater ticket costing two new francs will be considered "too expensive."

A free leisure activity which does not fall within the standards of consumption will hardly be acceptable. Low incomes bring about a common way of life among people of the same income level, so much so that even free spare-time activities that do not take account of this miscarry, especially among the working class.

For example, some large Parisian factories made several tennis courts available without charge to their employees. The office employees came, while the workers who did show up promptly departed. They felt ill at ease.

After all, the space and the services needed for modern spare-time activities are obviously offered for sale in accordance with the laws of the system. There is a strong temptation for the seller to succumb blindly to the passion for maximum profits, so much the more since competition forces him to.

We don't share the indifference or the scorn that certain idealistic educators express for leisure-time business. To say "this is commercial and therefore doesn't interest us" is to give up the ship at the very point where every educator ought to carry the fight against the bad product in order to make the good one prevail. Editors and booksellers, theater managers and film producers, have not all hatched a black conspiracy against culture and education. . . . There are those who make strenuous efforts to raise the cultural

level of popular leisure activities. We shall give some examples of
them later on. Not to help them, because they are in business, would
exhibit an idealism worthy of a simpleton, for one would be depriving himself of the most efficacious means of attaining the desired
result.

But we must recognize that, in our present system, the first aim
of most of the wine merchants or movie theaters or evening newspapers or women's magazines is not to satisfy, still less to develop
to the maximum, the cultural needs of the masses during their
leisure time. Lynd was saying as early as 1924, about private
commercial radio stations in Middletown, that while the community
tried to preserve its schools from private commercial schemes, this
new and powerful instrument of education, which was taking over
Middletown unexpectedly, was in the hands of a former peanut
vendor, a former motorcycle racer, and a former racetrack operator,
whose principal concern was to make money.

What is the matter is not the occupations[4] mentioned but the
cultural incompetence of certain producers or impresarios. Certainly, there exist other types, even some highly cultivated ones;
however, most of them seem to be seeking only the greatest profit.
"Art and money," writes Réné Clair, "creative intelligence and
financial rules are here locked in combat."

Advertising can perform services; that of the toothpaste and
shampoo industries has undeniably developed hygiene. It can contribute to the spread of art. Cassandra, Paul Colin, and Savignac have
exhibited *chefs-d'oeuvre* on the walls of our cities. A large international company producing photographic equipment has put on
art expositions. Since 1949, public relations firms that set out to
win the customer's sympathy for some enterprise or group, and not
just to sell products, are tending to develop education of the public
through advertising. Finally, let's not forget that we owe the birth

Cf. for example seminars on photo-journalism and the responsibilities
of the magazine reporter organized by picture people in Boulouris, 1960.

of one of Robert Flaherty's great films, *Nanook of the North,* to an order for advertising by a fur store.

But advertising can cause ravages as well. It works in the most intensive way even where the product is emptiest of any real value, where its virtues are the most illusory: prefabricated stars of radio and song, monotonous stereotyped films accounting for 90 per cent of the production, "best sellers" concocted according to elementary recipes. This is so obvious that the most varied commentators join in denouncing the misdeeds of these enterprises.

"Most people," writes Caillois, "easily become accustomed to their daily ration of mechanical stories and crude pictures, cooked-up legends that are prepared for them at the lowest selling price, in immense kitchens, where, for sure, there can be no question of encouraging gastronomic research nor of educating the customers' palate." A certain system of capitalist production, instead of satisfying the most noble needs, on the contrary starts with the easiest object to produce and tries, chiefly by advertising, to create a need for it.

In France, scientific study has hardly even begun of this social conditioning of leisure through advertising of every sort (employing more than six thousand experts) (1). Yet it is possible to formulate several hypotheses based on observation:

1. The education factor in leisure is constantly impeded in favor of the entertainment factor. A whole atmosphere, a whole web of suggestions, incitements, and pressures, encourages attitudes of escapism, at the expense of attitudes of reflection; the most healthy reactions to the constraints of daily life are exaggerated, distorted, denatured. Certainly, the advantage of the system is that it erects a powerful barrage against annoying pedagogues and hostile propaganda. But its most serious drawback is that it standardizes the choices of the majority at a primitive level.

Through sports, Pierre de Coubertin wanted to bring "calm, philosophy, health and beauty" to the nation (8). Sports news and sports columnists stir up stadium and velodrome fans, concentrate attention on the professionals alone, transform them into demigods; and their devotees become the countless customers who finance the whole business. In fifty years almost all of Coubertin's ideas have been betrayed: mass participation in sport is not the essential, but the accessory; champions are not models, but stars. Nobody gives them a social purpose. Outside pedagogical circles, there is no serious stimulus to make sports a style of life, a form of esthetic, dramatic, social, or human culture.

How could the mass of sports fans find a means of improvement in sports? Even the Olympic Games, once foreseen as "an educational manifestation which, as in olden times, should concentrate the collective thinking of people on the cult of youth," are for most sports association directors and sports writers nothing but world championships, without any great educative impact. Only a few obstinate ones in this unfavorable atmosphere strive to demonstrate the original meaning of these games.

Another example. Television has within itself the means to make us discover all the countries we cannot visit and explore museums, to transmit the great works of cinema and theater to us and initiate us in the great discoveries of technology and science; it can communicate with us directly from festivals and distant events. It is instantaneously universal. Television in France frequently succeeds in realizing these possibilities, but the commercial TV stations almost completely ruin these good opportunities.

American stations, state Dallas Smythe and Robert Merton, devote almost 75 per cent of their program hours to entertainment paid for by advertising. And the best is eclipsed by the worst, they report. R. Rubicam, one of the founders of the advertising firm Young & Rubicam, writes after retirement: "There is one thing to which I am obstinately opposed, and that is the present widespread monopolization of radio and television by the advertisers; freedom of choice in programs is more theoretical than real, and these two communications media are paying much less attention to the public interest than they should."

In France, the women's magazines, with their photographs, games, and stories, could be an attractive tool of education as well as of entertainment. Some of them are heading in that direction. But in the fifteen million copies that go into homes every week to be read by an average of two or three persons, scarcely 10 per cent of their pages show evidence of any concern with developing the general culture of the public (16).

2. In this system, it all seems as if leisure activity is simply a way to lead man back to his childhood. It is not a matter of a refreshing dip into childhood memories, nor of nurturing in the adult heart the freshness of feeling that is the source of poetry. All too often, there is a conscious or unconscious effort to put thinking to sleep and to replace reality with a simplistic mythology. In the United States, 90 per cent of American parents state that the over-use of low-level "comics" prevents their children from practicing sports, doing their homework, or studying music. Only 50 per cent, however, are opposed to this kind of reading, which also is tending to become the sole reading matter of certain adults themselves (17).

Similar findings could be made about magazines in all countries devoted to the wonderworld of princes, princesses, and film and radio stars, a world maintained and developed during hours and hours of broadcasting, newsreels, and printed matter, throughout the whole year "because the magazine must sell."

3. Yet the evil is perhaps still worse. To be more certain of selling merchandise, the content of the mass media need not be convincing, but only striking, not informative, but overwhelming. It all seems as if man must be reduced to instinct and pocketbook. In this way the system is simplified: It's enough to excite one to empty the other.

This is why some radio and television commercials and some movie advertisements prefer to stress people's desire for money, violence, or eroticism.

Luck is not only the raison d'être for the older games of chance, *Pari Mutuel Urbain*, lotteries at fairs, the National Lottery or the newer slot machines, advertising contests, elections of the Miss of the Year or of the Queen of the Day, but is also the leitmotif of innumerable stories, serials, and novels in which the Prince Charming offers his riches, the count donates his chateau, or the good boss sets up his secretary for life. And all is arranged for by magic in a world where there is nothing to change and where one can expect all to depend on fate, one's lucky star, or the turn of a card (16).

Aggressive tendencies arise not only among those who are dissatisfied or frustrated in their daily lives; they are stimulated day after day among a growing number of people reading their newspaper or seeing a movie. The big newspapers are often "buckets of blood." A film, to make money, has to show at least one scene of violence. It's not a question of condemning cops-and-robber movies; they are the new form of a very old genre; they provide a pleasant pastime; some have been masterpieces. Indeed, according to the theory of catharsis, they make us experience fictional dramas that may let us be good little boys in real life. But what may be the effect of these programs on certain children?[5]

Finally, on the screen or in the magazine, it is woman who is everywhere. This is not a matter of crying "scandal," the favorite occupation of blue noses of all latitudes and beliefs. Entertainment is often comparable with daydreaming. What do young men dream of, if not of girls, and vice versa. No doubt, it is a serious matter that censorship feels obliged to forbid many films to be shown to "under sixteen." What is still more serious is that so limited or even deformed a picture of the eternal feminine is shown throughout the length of most films. For the few great films that portray woman as she is, the whole woman, her instincts and ideals, her adventures and her work at home, at the office, in the factory, in the neighborhood, in civic activities—how many exalt her as an idol while at the same time reducing her merely to the role of

[5] Seven TV chains in New York were studied for a week by a team of sociologists. In 1952, they found 2,970 acts or threats of violence in one week, and in 1953, 3,539, of which 742 were telecasts specially aimed at a children's audience, that is, six acts of violence an hour.

female (18)? In these films, she is neither comrade nor friend, nor wife nor mother nor citizen; she is exclusively in love and made solely for love. If one looks carefully at the list of films today distributed in France, the most common are those with titles beginning with "Woman," "Girls," or "Love." Of course, not all these films reduce the relationship between the sexes to their most instinctual or idyllic aspects. But the most common titles are *The Naked Woman, La Femme Fatale, The Ideal Woman, Anybody's Wife, Woman at the Crossroads, The Lost Woman, The Rebellious Woman, Women Like That,* and so on.

In conclusion, it is impossible to gauge either the benefits or the ill effects of leisure or to predict its evolution without taking the traditional and socioeconomic technical determinants into account. Most of the time, commercial exploitation of the great entertainment and communications media looks at man merely as a ready customer. In offering him enjoyment in a world limited, deformed, and false, it not only can put the brake on human growth, but even worse can cause man's stagnation and regression.

But beware of the prejudices and stereotypes that influence most of those responsible for censorship or for education when they decide about this "effect" on the total number of possible cases; they point only to those few examples that favor their thesis. One of the most urgent tasks for the social sciences is to promote exact knowledge of all the social conditionings of leisure and the effect leisure has on the various parts of the mass public.

Chapter 4

Relationships
Between Work
and Leisure

Effect of Work on Leisure[1]

I N THE ABOVE GENERAL CONTEXT, THE RELATIONSHIPS BETWEEN
work and leisure have developed and continue to develop at a rapid
pace, though in what direction and at what rate is not clear. There
are those who describe our society's style of life in terms of a
work civilization, while others are already evoking a civilization of
leisure. Some consider leisure as simply a phenomenon that comple-
ments or compensates for dehumanized work.

For others, leisure is a determinant affecting work itself. How
do things stand today in France?

First, we have made some basic distinctions that writers often
forget. Friedmann was the first French sociologist to underline the
capital importance of leisure in the humanization of our technical
civilization. In the industrial enterprise conceived of as a *technical*

[1] This chapter utilizes part of an article, "Travail et Loisir," which
appeared in the *Traité de Sociologie du Travail* under the direction of
Georges Friedmann and Pierre Naville, A. Colin, 1964.

system, Georges Friedmann stressed the evil effects of the division of labor and the mechanization of work. The splitting up of skilled trades and the fragmentation of tasks often leave the worker with a sense of unfulfilment and dissatisfaction. From this comes the need for compensation through accomplishment of a completed task or of a work freely created; hence the importance of hobbies and do-it-yourself activities. Friedmann contrasts this need of compensation with the simple need for amusement which comes from doing interesting work involving one's person.

This idea has become a familiar one not only to researchers but also to social workers, industrial managers, and educators. But popularization of the idea has also oversimplified it. It is certainly desirable to compensate for demeaning work by work that enriches But is it always desired? On this subject, Georges Friedmann has drafted some subtle comments that little by little empirical research has defined more precisely.[2]

Thus, monotony is far from being the predominant quality of fragmented tasks, such as those performed by many specialized workers, especially women working in small businesses. "Thirty-four per cent of employees work in enterprises with fewer than ten employees, and, in spite of appearances," observes Jacqueline Frisch-Gautier (2), "there is such a variety of specialized tasks that no general characteristic obtains except that of variety itself. And variety also describes the abilities of the women who work at these jobs."

J. Gautier remarks that some of these skilled workers are aware they are performing difficult tasks. Probably, these women do not feel that their work is demeaning and do not feel the need for compensatory leisure. Our own systematic observations in enterprises at Annecy, Valence, and Lens of attitudes toward leisure in relation to degree of skill lead us to believe that leisure is far from

---

[2] Pierre Louchet and Jacqueline Frisch-Gautier, "Pigeon-fancying among Miners in the North." Preface by Georges Friedmann, CNRS, 1961.

being a factor compensating for fragmentized and repetitive work.[3] Let us not deceive ourselves into thinking that spontaneous activities compensate for the dullness of daily work. Awareness of a style of life and a general education are required; otherwise, dull work is most often accompanied by dull leisure.

Not only is the enterprise a technical system; it also is a social organization. Friedmann, analyzing the technical environment, has shown that the worker's job does not amount to a mass of fragmented tasks. It is subordinated to an organized and rationalized set-up of which workers are perhaps more aware than they are of the fragmented nature of their tasks; resistance to the time-clock system is a major constant in worker attitudes.

We may ask if the campaign against wasted time and spontaneous rhythms in today's industrial production has not led to reaffirming in leisure time the value of those natural rhythms that involve wasting time in the traditional way.

Would not a possible explanation for the extraordinary rise in such activities as gardening and fishing lie in the above? We know that there are about three and one half million fishermen in France, particularly among the working class. It is possible that these minor leisure activities play a major stabilizing role in the workers' lives. They are as widespread as they are inexpensive. They can play a stabilizing role within modern industrial organization by allowing some aspects of traditional work to survive or be reborn, at the same time giving them new meaning.

Varagnac's thesis on survival of an "archeo-civilization" would, in this case, uncover a veritable treasury of evidence. "Many a

[3] According to the observations of Nicole Leplatre on the activities of three hundred working-class adolescents in the Paris areas (3), the most skilled workers have the most "active" leisure. In the Annecy study, while 20 per cent of the skilled workers who belong to some association and take responsibility in it, only 10 per cent of the less-skilled workers do likewise. Michel Crozier (4) has established that those responsible for difficult and interesting work have only an "average activity" in their free time, but the effect of fragmentized and subordinate tasks is uncertain—some relate to a higher amount of activity during leisure time, some to a lower amount.

misunderstanding of the concept of leisure would be avoided if we were willing to recognize it, not as an escape into activities foreign to work, but as a return to activities precedent to our modern forms of work" (5).

A modern enterprise involves an organization not only of work time but also of social relationships. In spite of efforts at reform, the old hierarchical structure often weighs down on the employees with immense heaviness. In the midst of a society that is becoming ever more democratic, business has retained an autocratic system of organization which lies heavily on everyone from the bottom to the top of the social scale. From this, no doubt, derives the need for more human relationships, more fraternal associations, where the supreme value is not the measured material output but the spontaneous interchange. Wouldn't this explain the attraction of café acquaintances? The most common reason for going to cafés is connected, as we know, with the need for sociability. In Annecy (6), 11 per cent of the skilled workers never go to a café, as contrasted with 16 per cent of the average population.

After all, an enterprise is an economic system. In our country, this system is based, in general, on the division between wages and profits. The employee works for someone else, his boss, even in a large corporation. He often has the feeling that he's not paid what he's worth. He dreams of setting himself up in his own business. He wants to be his own boss. This tendency is general (even in the United States), but France has the largest percentage of small businessmen in all Europe. In 1954, counting both city and country, there were about nine million small businesses in a labor force of nineteen million.

Another way for the employee to escape his situation is to try to change it by joining a trade union. But in France today, according to figures provided by union headquarters themselves, probably fewer than 20 per cent of the employees belong to unions, and they number probably about three million (7).

Under these conditions, one can speculate about the possible significance of the employees' passion for do-it-yourself work at home for their own benefit. In this semiutilitarian, semidisinterested activity, they are masters of the work they do; whatever profits there may be are theirs alone; they have the feeling they are the "boss." Isn't this, at least in part, a reaction to the subordinate position they suffer in the big company?

So, in relation to the employee's economic status, would it not seem reasonable to assume that puttering around at home is not a minor pastime, but a reaction comparable in its significance to the desire to establish one's own business or to take part in the collective defense of employees through the union?

Yet it must be repeated that in the present state of research, all these ideas about the relationships between work and leisure are only hypothetical. We could come up with still others, but we simply wanted to stress that the study of these relationships is not limited to studying leisure as a compensatory phenomenon of one aspect of modern work, namely its division and fragmentation.

The Effect of Leisure on Work

We plan to analyze at greater length the effect of leisure on work. This has been studied to a lesser extent by industrial sociology than the preceding analysis. This gap both theoretically and practically creates a false picture of the general problem raised by the entry of leisure into industrial civilization. It prevents scientific inquiry into the present and future state of the worker's social consciousness as shaped by the growth and need of leisure. It can imprison labor sociology within all sorts of worker ideologies that were born when work was almost the sole activity of the worker. This is why, at present, a study of the effects of leisure on work is important for the future of industrial sociology.

We have seen that leisure, backed by a growing prestige, provides models for behavior and can even stamp a style on everyday life. Its effect is felt even at the moment of choosing a job. Naville stresses that the main problem in this choice is how to transform an illusion about the nature of the occupation into an objective awareness of the job and its actual conditions (8). Of course, hope for more interesting and better paying conditions of work is a basic consideration in this choice. But is it not the fact that many young people are looking for the leisure possibilities in any job they are choosing, and that this is the source of their occupational illusion? We have already seen the preponderant place occupied by leisure activities among young people. Research would seem useful in this area; it could help us understand in detail the exact reasons for the overrapid growth in France of occupations in the tertiary sector (services) in comparison with those in the secondary sector (industry).

In Annecy, about 350 sales outlets of 650 directly involved leisure goods or services—that is, about 50 per cent: cafés, fishing supplies, sports and outdoor equipment, music, movies, newspapers, photographs, books, toys, and so forth. Interviews with a large number of the managers of these stores revealed to us a direct connection between youthful tastes for leisure activities and the choice of their work.

Another example. France is carrying out a systematic effort at industrial decentralization. One would think that the choice in industry's implementation of this plan would be, above all, governed by economic reasons related to outlets and energy sources. Twenty years ago, these were the only controlling factors. Today, they are frequently less important than the psychosociological factors involving greater or lesser means of material comfort, and recreational or cultural activities provided by the local community to the executives and technicians and their families. This is an aspect ignored by purely economic studies. Now, this is the determining factor in more and more management decisions about manpower decentralization.

Likewise, the main reason for failure of this decentralization,

according to the same sources, lies in the refusal of executives and
their wives to accept a local situation where afterwork life is underdeveloped. The need for recreational and cultural leisure demands
minimum equipment. It determines a sort of sociocultural vital
minimum which constitutes, for every local environment, the limit
below which a work force accustomed to big city life will consider
it unacceptable. It is reasonable to suggest that industrial decentralization will fully succeed only if it is accompanied by cultural
decentralization.

The very atmosphere of the company tends to change under
pressure from these leisure requirements—whence comes the search
for a new plastic and musical décor in newly constructed or rebuilt
factories. "Functional," or work, music is controversial. It would
be a mistake to look at it only from the viewpoint of output or of
strengthening interest in work. It is also an answer to nonwork
needs that today are felt in work itself; it turns out, in a study of
two hundred workers in a local factory (Valence), that music is
appreciated by the majority as a prolongation of radio-listening
hours. Today, the demand for music, light or serious, modern or
classical, has everywhere become inescapable.

In the same way, little by little, the example of sports has forced
itself in the activities of modern life. For example, company
organization often is based upon methods of emulation, cooperation, and competition borrowed from sports. We know of the
growing success of intershop or intercompany sports matches,
especially football: of two thousand people employed in the biggest
metallurgical company in Annecy, more than six hundred take part
in such events with an incredible enthusiasm. This kind of event and
the way it is set up often provide a style for production or training.
Numerous methods of job improvement find their inspiration in
techniques well known to sports instructors—for example, "Training Within Industry" (TWI), mental training and fifteen-odd deriva-
tive techniques. These methods are already being taught by a
hundred engineers of the Office of the Scientific Organization of

Work, in Paris, and by a much greater number of founders of new enterprises.

Let's go further. Research into the efficiency of sports activities came before research into the productivity of work activities. It prompted several studies and meetings in the United States well before Robert Taylor had begun his work on time and motion studies in industry. Indeed, the rise of the sports movement in the United States, according to Coubertin, began around 1860.

Taylor himself took an active part in it. He won the American tennis championship in 1881, two years before obtaining his engineer's diploma at Stevens Institute. He was greatly interested in improving sports performances. After considerable experimental research, he invented a new tennis racket and a new surface for tennis courts.

Henri Dubreuil, one of his most recent biographers, describes the work and influence of Taylor, the engineer, in *Robots or Men* (1958).

So it isn't surprising that in his famous book devoted to the scientific organization of work in 1911, Taylor should have made a precise comparison between the organization of work and of sports, nor that in 1912, before a committee of the House of Representatives he should have been led to develop this same comparison.

In stressing this example, we have not sought to give one-sided credit to the influence of sport on the scientific organization of work. Many other more important factors played a role. But what we wanted to suggest was the possible existence, even in Taylor's mind, of a relationship between leisure and work activities. This has rarely been emphasized by sociologists or psychologists.

In fact, the work group, whether in an enterprise or a company committee is more and more taking the form of leisure organization. From now on, the social function of the enterprise will be expanding into a sociocultural function. Under French law, since 1945, the organization of these recreational cultural activities at the place of work is to be independent of the management of the enterprise and of the leadership of the unions.

Very few company committees, in fact, have this independent character. Some are under union domination; others, greater in number, under management control. But whatever may be the ideology of these committees, the organization of leisure activities is a new preoccupation for modern business. This fact is evident in the United States and the Soviet Union as well as in France.

Despite the opposition in principle that this trend may bring forth or differences in situations that it may encounter, it is widespread. In France, organization of leisure activity by company committees has already attained considerable importance (9). In a decreasing order of expenditures, it involves (1) vacation camps for children, (2) company parties (Christmas, Mother's Day), (3) sports and outdoor activities, (4) libraries. Work-study shops and entertainment performances are growing less rapidly, but have been increasing over the past ten years.

Out of twenty thousand enterprises with more than fifty employees, which are subject to the law, about ten thousand had established a company committee by 1954. About three thousand of these committees (under management, worker or mixed direction) were organizing leisure activities. Thus, around 25 per cent of the active nonfarm population were benefiting from activities paid for by 2 per cent of the employees. These sociocultural expenditures amounted to ninety million new francs in 1954.

This sum plainly is insufficient in comparison with the needs of all the employees who should have benefited from the law. But this sum was already equal to the entire national budget of the Ministry of Education's Office for Youth and Sports allocated for subsidies to all national, regional, and local recreational and cultural leisures associations, for financing the training of managers, and for related administrative costs. . . . These few facts make one stop and think.

Thus the expansion of recreation into the very place of work, the penetration of models of leisure activity into occupational activities, raises new questions. In a country like ours, leisure is no longer content to co-exist with work. From here on, it will be conditioning the practice of work itself. If leisure becomes one of the factors of the adaptation of work to man, one may once again ask: Where is human labor heading?

David Riesman (10) notes among American workers an "offensive against the preponderant place held by work" (1956). Eric Fromm in *The Sane Society* foresees "radical changes in the work process so that it may become bearable for future generations" (11). Finally, according to an investigation recently carried out by the *Harvard Business Review* (1959) among five thousand industrial managers, the share of time given over to leisure tends to increase as compared with that accorded it in the preceding generation observed by Burnham.[4]

The age of the organizers is certainly not dying, and American businessmen are not about to become Oriental pashas, but ideas do change. Even for the "executives," leisure is no longer a futile, unmentionable activity; quite the contrary, it is asserting itself as a value. This fact is general; could we not make similar observations in France, among all categories of employees? What will be the consequence for work? What will be the consequence on workers' attitudes toward labor problems?

Wolfenstein has correctly noted the progress being made toward a "fun morality," a moral obligation to have fun. But what kind of fun is involved? For what kind of workers? In relation to what social or cultural context? When the contexts vary, what becomes of the content of the fun? We must define these things. We believe it essential to distinguish once again among the differing functions of

---

[4] The average work week at the company is a little less than forty-three, to which must be added about seven hours of business work at home, hence *fifty hours*. Semileisure activities connected with work (entertainment, social activities, and so forth) take up about four and one half hours a week. Leisure time ("hobbie, Ingres violin playing," sports, reading, study for pleasure, voluntary civic activities, television) takes up about thirty hours a week, and most managers find this free time insufficient.

leisure and to throw light on the several attitudes that they bring about (or may bring about) toward work in accordance with differing social and cultural contexts.

We have seen that semileisure, particularly "puttering around" occupies a major place in the activities of a French worker. As Havighurst noted, American workers' interests tend more and more to be based not only on their company but also on their home, where the family workshop has an important place (13).

This do-it-yourself work can play a role of equilibrium in relation to the job. Contrariwise, it can cause or continue maladjustments within the labor movement or in the scientific organization of work. There may be an opportunity to balance relations on the job and family relations, or, on the contrary, the worker may turn away from having social relationships in the company or in the union. It imprisons work within itself, far from any economic, political or cultural concern outside the little daily trifling in the family workshop. For what do the values of productivity or of solidarity matter to the man concerned only with his "do it yourself" activities?

It would be interesting to know if the meaning of this semileisure changes in its relationship with work proper, when big companies such as Charbonnages de France, the SNCF, or Kodak make "puttering" workshops available to their employees at the very place of work.

How does the influence of leisure on work make itself felt when it is a matter of the recuperation of muscular and nervous energies? We have stressed the importance of fatigue in today's urban and industrial civilizations. In France, medicosocial research has thrown light especially on the unfortunate effect on the organism of certain work schedules (night work, three shifts), certain cycles of work gestures, certain rhythms. Dr. Louis Le Guillant's research on the neuroses of telephone operators is still one of the most striking examples of this kind of study (14). Still, the effects of work fatigue on participation in cultural and social life so far have given rise merely to stereotyped or impassioned assertions. It would be useful if research could separate what is true and false in every systematic effort to impute the cultural indifference of the masses to work fatigue.

Dr. Claude Veil asserts that the equilibrium between leisure and work activities ought to be the subject not only of a study but also of a "controlled education" (15), so difficult is it to fight against the numerous and fatiguing distractions of industrial and urban civilization.

What would be the effect on work of various types of repose? The need for physical or nervous relaxation plays an ambiguous role itself. It can, on the one hand, result in a healthy "recuperation of the work force," as Marx says, or, on the contrary, in the growth of a taste for laziness and idleness. Repose is indispensable if the spirit of initiative and invention is to recapture all its strength. It is also, in situations as yet little studied by sociologists, an alibi for apathy or social and cultural withdrawal. Certainly, repose can give value to time itself. It can stimulate a taste for contemplation as a counterbalance to the dominant values of a century of action.

This theory of repose is upheld by Josef Pieper (16). On the other hand, repose can strengthen opposition to work, go against the dominant values of both capitalist and socialist systems that lay stress on the production of consumer goods. Strengthening idleness weakens work, as we see in certain Oriental societies. In France, we are far from that, so great are the material needs to be satisfied; even so, the "right to laziness" was claimed as early as 1883. We cannot be sure that with the rise in living standards the increase in material needs will be without limit.

In 1958, in the *Age of Automation*, G. Soulé made some interesting comments on the growth of needs on certain social levels in the United States (17). The search for repose, therefore, can be a balancing factor in a civilization dominated by the spirit of enterprise and production. In these complex conditions, where does laziness begin or end, especially willful laziness (18)?

As we already know, the need for entertainment is closely related to the nature of industrial work. "Dissatisfaction in work," says Friedmann, "whether conscious or not, has a permanent and many-sided reaction on life outside the job, since it leads through various escape mechanisms to sideline activities." We couldn't be more in agreement. The results of the study made by C. Benassy-Chauffard and J. Pelnard of adolescent workers in the Paris area (19) have shown that more or less conformist leisure activities are more common among young people dissatisfied with their work. Still, leisure activities attract all workers, whether satisfied or not. Riesman is perhaps correct in emphasizing that boredom tends to become a widespread phenomenon in industrial civilization (20). It would be interesting to collect scientific observations on this question, not only from the United States but from Poland, the Soviet Union, and Yugoslavia in varying economic and cultural contexts. We already know that the need for entertainment is growing in France, especially among the younger generation. What may be the effect of this on work attitudes?

Work activities can be balanced by play or by membership activities tied into a partly imaginary, marginal way of life governed by rules and values other than those of real life. These side activities can prompt positive changes in work activities and improve working conditions. They can bring poetry into life. Business and union relationships are strengthened by ties born of sharing in recreational activities and associations. Lipset takes note of this in his study of a typesetters' union, *Union Democracy* (21).

To sum up: These pleasure activities can add a sense of play and sport to the values of productivity and solidarity. On the other hand, pleasure-seeking often leads to an unfair downgrading of everyday life. From this follows a failure to adapt to the inevitable monotony of work. Friendships born out of leisure activities can cause one to forget friends on the job. Enjoyment of recreational activities often results in denial of any commitment to either company or union. The adult henceforth takes delight in an infantile world where any sense of professional or social responsibility is wiped out.

This is perhaps what already faces some of the Americans; according to Dwight MacDonald, Peter Pan would be a better symbol of the United States than Uncle Sam (22). But this is not simply an American problem. All sociologists of political life raise the same question, whether they study a capitalist or a socialist environment (Poland, Yugoslavia).[5]

Employers and union leaders both are running into ever greater difficulties in their efforts to interest the mass of workers in matters affecting either their company or their union, and the parallel rise in escapist activities seems in varying degrees to raise problems common to our industrial society.

So we know that leisure offers to people in industrial society three possibilities: information, self-education, and benevolent social participation. What are and what can be the effects of this on activities and values in the world of work? First, this function of leisure is much less common than the former one. Traditional conversation is limited to small talk about the home, the shop, or the neighborhood. More than half the workers in Annecy have never tried to learn the facts about any subject whatever. They see no point even in a paid annual educational leave for the purpose of improving themselves. They take no part in the life of any association. A still greater proportion (80 per cent) state that they are wholly indifferent to any company or union problems. For them the only things that count are their salary and their nonwork life.[6]

If leisure can contribute to the worker's real individual or social

[5] Cf. the theme of the International Seminar on Political Sociology held at Bergen, Norway, June, 1961 (Rokkan, UNESCO).

[6] This is one aspect of what Alain Touraine calls "cultural withdrawal" (23). In the same sense, Janine Larrue concludes her investigation of workers' leisure in the city of Toulouse by stressing as one of their constant traits "a sort of passivity as to how they spend their free time and a basic indifference as to the ways of spending it. . . ."

development, it is also a cause of adjustment or failure of adjustment to life in the company or the union.[7]

Obviously, it would be simple-minded to imagine that workers concentrate their thinking essentially on their work. The ideas of socialist realism, social literature, and the populist novel clearly play but a feeble role in the hopes of a working man. We are, at the moment, in the process of studying how workers educate themselves, and, in this regard, Solange Hervé recently made a study in the city of Mantes, near the Renault factory at Flins (24). What is interesting is the great variety of their intellectual interests, some in the job itself, some in social action, some in recreational or cultural pursuits.

Problems of Improvement in Relations Between Work and Leisure

One question that has not been studied as much as it should have been either by sociologists of leisure or of work is this: What role do these new leisure activities play in the growth of social relationships and of a social consciousness? It was not until the eighteen seventies that activist workers could read in the first French edition of *Das Kapital* Marx's ideas about the social relationships brought about by the system of production. What could they see around themselves? The working class was crushed by the length of the workday and the sordid conditions of their life; the normal social relationships of the working class were still determined almost entirely by their work and their neighborhood. At that time, workers had their own organizations, their own folklore, their own amusements. Newspapers were expensive. Radio, movies, television and rapid transit didn't yet exist.

[7] In the answers to a poll of 141 workers in Annecy, 37 stated that their trade was the basis of their general education, but 38 indicated general mechanics, 32 mathematics, 34 geography, thirty puttering around, and only five answers mentioned economic or social questions.

Since then, the work week has been shortened and group and individual activities of a new kind have become possible. In a broader sense, relationships on the job, in the neighborhood, and in the family are supplemented by other types. Mass transit and individual means of transport have shrunk both geographical and social distances. Since 1936, and especially since 1945, thousands of organizations have begun to take pride in being democratic and have opened their doors to everyone without regard to their social background, in the same way as did the public school in 1881. Don't these new types of groups and activities have a different, almost an opposite, effect on social consciousness and class consciousness to those of work activities?

Meanwhile, recent studies by Lucien Brams and Paul Henri Chombart de Lauwe[8] of French working class families also remind us in what a state of material and cultural underdevelopment certain industrial neighborhoods and communities remain in France. From the standpoint of leisure, social distances still are very great.[9]

Doesn't awareness of all these new possibilities of leisure alongside the persistent feeling of economic and social inequality stir up rather than diminish class antagonisms? It is probable that a certain kind of proletarian consciousness is on the way to disappearing along with the conditions that brought it about; but in that event, how are both this standardization and this differentiation in life style reflected in the new social consciousness of workers?[10]

[8] See "Condition, Attitude et Aspirations des Ouvriers" in *Sondages,* Institut Français d'Opinion Publique, Paris, 1956, No. 2.

[9] We have given the results of inquiries by the French Institute of Public Opinion which have calculated the well-known social differences in the use of leisure. We have been able to determine for the last twenty years that worker participation in so-called "popular education" groups rarely amounts to 5 per cent, even though manual workers made up a majority of the active population of the locality.

[10] In our opinion, one important approach would be empirical research bearing particularly on the study of the effects of the use of and the need for leisure on workers' attitudes toward work. This is the present approach of Wilensky and his collaborators in Detroit. It is also interesting that the second number of the latest sociological industrial review (*Industrial*

Leisure is a major social fact that is obviously conditioned by one's type of work, but that in its turn influences the latter. Both form a whole. Work is human only if it leaves the possibility or promotes the desire for human leisure. But if leisure is merely escape outside of work, or a fundamental refusal to take any interest in the technical and social problems of work, it is only a false solution to the problems of industrial civilization.

It is, similarly, impossible to deal with the problems of leisure and work separately. Indeed, the humanization of work through the values of leisure is inseparable from the humanization of leisure through the values of work. Certain conceptions of work no longer correspond to the reality of this work-leisure relationship. In our view, we must liberate the social sciences of work from models borrowed from the last century. Ignace Meyerson has perhaps achieved the most systematic French analysis of the "psychological function" of work (26). He properly stresses the compulsory character of work today. We deem it useful to verify if work is really experienced "as a need, even a psychological need" by the majority of industrial workers. From our inquiries, it is the activity, but not the work, that is felt as a fundamental need. For some, the principal interest is found in work on the job; for others, in union activity; for still others, in fishing, traveling, vacations, and sports.

Unskilled workers at Annecy answered a question as to which activities gave them the "maximum of satisfaction" as follows: 25 per cent, leisure activities; 47 per cent, family activities; and 24 per cent, work. Apparently, skilled workers had a different attitude: 25 per cent also selected leisure; 53 per cent, family activities; only 15 per cent, work. It is hard to analyze the meaning of such answers.[11] Nevertheless, before affirming that work is a psychological need, it is well to ask about which categories or types of

---

Relations, published at Berkeley in 1961) was entirely devoted to relationships between work and leisure (February, 1962).

[11] ". . . We are driven toward a civilization of creation far more than toward a civilization of work. . . ." François Perroux, *Arguments* 3, 1959.

workers. In any case, one can only agree with the general comment of Alain Touraine in his conclusions about the Renault factories: "The social aspects of work tend to assert themselves over and above the purely negative and perfectly inhuman reality of the job. In this perspective, the problem of leisure is seen in a new way, not as a search for compensation but, exactly like work, as part of the social system" (27). The existence of quantitative or qualitative underdevelopment of leisure in many strata of society perpetuates inequalities and tensions.

It is important to appreciate and to measure its effects objectively. Whatever may be the basis on which we define social classes (level of income, types of culture, general attitude, economic status in the productive process), it is impossible to make a sociology of class consciousness without comparing the social relations created outside of work, especially in leisure activities. Without minimizing the importance of occupational status and economic condition, one can still ask if class consciousness, its content, the attitudes of cooperation or of opposition that follow from it, have not been profoundly overwhelmed by the growth of the leisure practices and needs.

In each situation, the social struggles and tensions, as well as the real potential of the workers' strength, must be calculated.[12]

"Active leisure" activities reveal the same ambiguity. They help humanize work only to the extent that they aid the growth of a social culture and provide balance to the worker's life. Improvement in human relations depends on the search for a balance in active attitudes during work and leisure.

This balance cannot be spontaneously achieved. Every society must become aware of the equilibrium that it is attaining and that it is hoping for. It must bring about the economic, social, political,

---

[12] No "objective" sociology can seriously provide an *a priori* definition whether it be Marxist or non-Marxist. Only investigation can, in each case, clarify the effects of work-leisure relationships upon social consciousness and the real attitudes that result from it with respect to social change.

and cultural changes necessary for its realization. A sociology that is both critical and constructive regarding the manifest or latent relationships between work and leisure should study these problems against the background of a social and cultural dynamic in industrial civilization.

In each step of this process, the democratization of knowledge and power demands a common culture which, beyond leisure, conditions the active participation of workers in the life of the company, the union, and the community. Routine, prejudice, frustration, or alienation can create an imbalance between the theoretical needs of society and the real-life aspirations of the various social groups living within it. As we have seen, Engels wanted the reduction in work hours to lead to greater participation of the citizens in public affairs. Marx stated that "individual education corresponds to the reduction in required work, thanks to the leisure and the means provided for all." In fact, schemes for political or social participation are often opposed by purely recreational activities or by new kinds of semiutilitarian, semidisinterested manual work at home. So democracy becomes impossible for lack of democrats.

People find easy answers for these time lags and imbalances. It's the fault of the public mind, national education, management attitudes, social organization, worker conditioning, structures of society, and so forth. On their side, the social sciences of leisure are not yet in a position to give answers to these questions. There is not, however, any objective more important for them. We must try to establish a sociology of experimentation, concerned with the conditions suitable for developing active attitudes toward both leisure and work. The dynamic study of the relationships between work and leisure demands research into the active or passive attitudes promoted by leisure, taking into account the spontaneous and artificial variation of the social situation.

In this way, the social sciences of leisure can hope to close the gap with the social sciences of work, and furnish some verified answers to the problem of the real and the possible relationships between work and leisure. These answers are essential if we try to learn what man can become in the various social structures of industrial civilization.

Chapter 5

Family

and

Leisure

Some Effects of Leisure on the Content of Family Life

SINCE VEBLEN (1899), MANY SOCIOLOGISTS HAVE STUDIED THE
relationship between leisure and work obligations[1] and labor in
general. Studies of how leisure relates to family responsibilities and
family life in general have yet to be made. The role of housework
and family responsibilities vis-à-vis leisure during time off the job is
still poorly understood.

In the schema of the "three eights," household chores are
treated as if they didn't exist. This is astonishing, since recent studies
of housework show that it takes up an impressive amount of time
of a given country's labor. On the basis of an inquiry into the time-
budget of married women, conducted in 1947, by the National
Institute of Population Studies (2), Jean Daric calculated that of
five hundred billion hours worked by the French people in 1946,
housekeeping accounted for forty-five billion hours, the largest part,

[1] Introduction to a section of the European Study of Social Policy in the
face of the evolution in French needs (European Office of the UN), Arnheim,
The Netherlands, 16, April 26, 1961.

91

exceeding even the time devoted to working on the job (forty-three billion hours) (3). These findings were confirmed by a second investigation carried out by the same Institute after a ten-year interval.

In 1958, in the city, the housekeeping workweek amounted to forty-one hours in homes without a child, and sixty-five, seventy-seven and eighty-two hours, respectively, in homes having one, two, or three children, if the hours devoted to this work by the housewife and other persons helping her are added together (2):

	No Children	*One Child*	*Two Children*	*Three Children*
Housewife	34 hrs., 7 min.	52 hrs., 5 min.	64 hrs., 6 min.	70 hrs., 3 min.
Other Persons	7 hrs., 8 min.	13 hrs., 1 min.	13 hrs., 1 min.	12 hrs., 9 min.
TOTAL	41hrs., 15min.	65 hrs., 6 min.	77 hrs., 7 min.	82hrs., 12min.

Under such conditions, what is family leisure? It is a reality. Its significance raises new questions that are but poorly perceived and analyzed by a sociology imprisoned by traditional attitudes. As William Goode remarked recently in *Sociology Today,* many a hypothesis is needed to grasp the reality contained in the old word "family" (4).

Jean Stoetzel, however, returning to the classic analyses of W. F. Ogburn (5) of the functions of the family, properly emphasizes that despite appearances, "the recreational function" of the family is expanding. Little by little, it is tending to change the whole system of family activities, roles, and values (6). This point has already been made in the recent study by the CREDOC.[2] of twenty thousand household budgets: the "leisure item" (vacations included) is the only budget item that is increasing more rapidly than total expenditures, thereby causing retrenchment in other items in the budget (7).

[2] Centre de Recherches et de Documentation sur la Consommation (Consumer Research and Documentation Center).

Work, Leisure, and Semileisure in the Time-Budget of a Mother

Besides doing domestic and family chores, the various members of the family enjoy a certain time for their leisure. How much is it? Given the division of labor which presently governs family organization, we should differentiate between and compare the free time of a man and of a married woman.

We have calculated the time a city worker devotes to leisure each week. There remain to him from twenty to thirty free hours after his work on the job, whether regular or supplementary, and after completing household chores. In 1958, the INED estimated that the average daily free time of a married woman without children and without a job amounts to four hours (2). For other types of women (those who hold a job and those who have children, even if they stay at home), daily leisure time is not more than two hours and ten minutes, on the average. It is even less for women who hold a job and also have one, two, or three children. Taking the workweek as a unit of time and taking into account these variations, the free time of a married woman would vary between fourteen and twenty-one hours a week.

These studies call for some comment. Estimates of free time, especially for women at home, run into certain difficulties deriving from the very nature of household duties. Domestic work splits up into a multitude of activities varying greatly in their obligatory character—such as, for example, certain kinds of sewing, knitting, puttering around, and gardening.

In the studies cited, these activities were systematically classified as housework. Now, they are not always done in response to necessity. Often, they are done willingly and considered by the individuals themselves as a form of relaxation. These semiobligatory, semipleasurable activities we call semileisure. They are particularly widespread in the daily life of married women remaining at home. They do not fall into the same class of strict obligations such as cooking, dish-washing, and the like. They count, in varying degrees, both as obligations and as leisure; they overlap. In mathematical language, one could say they are situated at the intersection of two sets.

In studies of time-budgets, then, there is reason to distinguish between the degree of compulsion of the different obligations and the degree to which they overlap with leisure. In this way, an intermediary zone of semileisure may be marked off. According to the study we made at Annecy, its extent may be as great as, and even greater than, the zone of leisure properly so-called. Absence of this distinction leads to overestimating the time devoted to "work."

A second difficulty one runs into in studying the free time of married women has to do with the very quality of time. As Jean Fourastié emphasizes, this field of scientific research has remained practically virgin territory (8). Such a gap limits our understanding of the problem of leisure in the family. In fact, it is difficult, without the frame of reference that is built by family responsibilities, to know how leisure fits concretely into the warp and woof of domestic and family activities.

Incomparable differences exist between time on the job and time spent in household work. In no case should they be considered together. The first is practically incompressible. The duration of each task has been measured without regard to the rhythm of each individual. There is a direct connection between the task accomplished and the time it took to be done. The same cannot be said for domestic chores. Delays in completing each of these chores are subject practically to no control, other than that imposed by the housewife herself.

Time devoted to housework is extremely elastic. It can be expanded or compressed according to the aptitude, the mood, or the caprice of the person doing it.

It is characterized by great fluidity where "lost"time spent either in solitude or with the neighbors has highly variable meanings; it makes one think of the "waste" time of the traditional artisan. The workday of a housewife is of the same type as that Naville calls "the porous day" (9). It is made up of tiny distractions. It is practically unmeasurable. Into this formless and inconstant time-framework, the activities of leisure fit themselves. Can we still call leisure time a period composed by adding together these lost moments pieced out and spread over the day?

It must be emphasized that the amount of free time a housewife enjoys depends upon the *value* she places on having it. For some, it is a sort of unconditional victory; there is a transformation in domestic work. The woman who wants more "time for herself" organizes her work, invents a rational program so as to waste less time. In this way, she gains time for fulfilling her responsibilities. Then, as her personal needs increase, leisure in its turn takes on greater value; certain kinds of housework are eliminated or abbreviated to make way for leisure activities. How she makes use of her time is then determined by the choices she makes among these newly valued leisure opportunities—another concept of the relations between leisure and work. We see, therefore, that the enjoyment of leisure is conditioned by the actual use made of time. Any understanding of it is difficult if we employ purely time-measuring methods.

Modernization in Living and Reduction in Housework

According to Jean Fourastié, an American housewife on the average devotes an hour and a half a day to her housework (10). A French housewife would spend five hours of her day on similar tasks. Why such a difference? It is not likely that this is due entirely to differences in the amount of mechanization or the number of household appliances. The reduction in housework and the increase in leisure result from the modernization of a whole set of factors affecting all aspects of daily life, both materially and morally, in all industrialized and urbanized countries.

Despite material and moral obstacles, the movement toward modernization is expanding everywhere, in all groups in all countries. For the past fifteen years, France has been engaged in a considerable effort to transform its urban environment. The technical revolution is beginning to transform housework, at least among the more privileged classes. In three years (from 1954 to 1957), more apartment houses were built in Paris and in all France than in the preceding thirty years.

The figure set some years ago (three hundred thousand new dwellings per year) was almost reached this year. Housing problems occupy a large part of current social policy of the government. Architects and city planners are engaged more or less successfully in finding optimal conditions of living and environment. For the first time, French sociologists are studying the hopes and needs of individuals and families in terms of their housing (11). Social services are providing consumers with personnel to help them adapt to their new kind of life. Functional rearrangements of apartments are reducing the number of tiring steps and movements. Hot water, bathrooms, and trash-shutes are eliminating the worst chores. New surfaces for floors and furniture require only hasty upkeep.

Household equipment has been mechanized. Of course, depending on the kind of appliance, only a fifth or a tenth of our city dwellings enjoy them; whereas in the United States, the figure is about 80 per cent. But for some years, new expenditures on appliances have been shooting upward like arrows. In 1957, they amounted to 25 per cent more than in 1956, while prices rose 8 per cent.[3] The most favored social groups obviously were the higher-paid executives, but workers are beginning to put forth great efforts to purchase appliances (7).

[3] In 1954, only 19 per cent of housewives owned a vacuum cleaner, 11 per cent a refrigerator, and 10 per cent a washing machine. In 1960, 29 per cent owned a vacuum cleaner, 26 per cent a refrigerator and 24 per cent a washing machine (12).

As a matter of fact, moving into a new dwelling stimulates the purchase of modern equipment. Applicants for middle-income dwellings, regardless of their social category, put the purchase of electric appliances at the top of their shopping lists. For long the privilege of the well-to-do who had servants, technical progress in the home was at first linked with the idea of improving comfort in the home. Today, it is more concerned with liberating woman from household chores in all social groups.

In addition, equipping the great housing developments has created a new need for a community approach to household chores. In the traditional home, the housekeeper did all the work alone, like an artisan. From now on, certain jobs are being taken over by the community. Automatic laundries arc often installed in the new housing developments. Common maintenance services for windows and floors are provided the tenants. Ready-to-eat dinners are often easier to find. Consumer cooperatives with home delivery are being organized. People in cities eat at least their noon meal in a canteen (in Annecy a thousand children, or one in five, eat their noon meal in a canteen).

In spite of great difficulties, collective organization is nevertheless progressing. Chombart de Lauwe shows in a recent study that if the great majority of people (two thirds) reject any increase in close relations with their neighbors, 60 per cent of them, on the other hand, demand community services and would be ready to hand them over to collective management. These practices could bring about some changes in housework (11): better distribution of chores among the various members of the family, a firmer organization of housework to help shorten the time spent on household chores. Of course, sharing these tasks is more widespread in the United States than in France, where the husband's contribution is often limited to doing the dishes or the big jobs. The most numerous tasks (and often the heaviest) are left to the wife: housekeeping, washing, shopping, cooking, and so on. Yet it cannot be denied that in young households the tendency for the husband to cooperate in housework is stronger than in older ones.

Furthermore, family responsibilities are not limited to housework. Being a mother involves a number of absorbing material tasks that often are painful. Indeed, they are the most serious obstacle to a woman's enjoyment of leisure. Still, they are diminishing. First, during the last one hundred years, the size of the family has been dwindling. In spite of a spactacular population growth since 1945, family size is in the process of stabilizing at two or three children, without the number of multichildren families increasing appreciatively (13). There is a feeling that raising children is not the sole purpose of the family group. The couple asserts its right to happiness. On the other hand, taking care of children is often simpler than it used to be because of modern advantages. Diapers are mass produced and simplified. Child care is more standardized. Mothers are taught these things in maternity wards and clinics. It would seem that the time a mother must necessarily devote to her children is in the process of diminishing.

No longer is it exceptional for a woman with young children to have a job. In Paris there are one hundred and fifty thousand who do. In the three-to-five age group, 60 per cent of the children are already at a nursery school, thus freeing their mothers during six hours of the day. Likewise, many women go to work once their children are of school age.

The curve of work rates of women according to age makes a sharp upswing around the age of thirty-five. Today, despite an utterly inadequate network of nurseries and nursery schools, the job of being a mother generally takes up only one fourth of an adult woman's time. The time-budgets of married women and of households ought to be studied in terms of cycles of existence, as B. Seebohm Rowntree has down for household budgets.

While the presence of younger children produces a real limit on free time, once they are grown, the woman's free time in certain cases can exceed that of the man, notably among women staying home. Thus, under the influence of technical progress, collectivation of chores, and progress in domestic organization, housework is losing in absolute value, and the possibilities for leisure tend to increase.

Integrating Leisure into Family Life

We can't, however, determine the importance of leisure in family life simply on the basis of how many fewer chores must be done. Leisure activities take up a large part of an individual's time, often despite daily demands. In reality, the present-day phenomenon of family leisure is chiefly the result of an evolution in values and family structures linked with technical civilization and its social effects, the dying-out of traditional ceremonies, the growth in means of transportation and communication, among other factors. The need for leisure is born and grows out of the enormous expansion in entertainment devices designed to satisfy it. The day these devices (radio, television, hi-fi) become part of the home furnishings, this need is implanted in the family. From this comes a new function of the family, which now should be analyzed in accordance with the appropriate categories of leisure sociology.

In France, some city architects have foreseen what the revolution brought about by the need for leisure implies for the very concept of a habitation and a habitat. In 1945, Le Corbusier put among the first rank of needs to be satisfied what he called the need for "recuperation" and the need for "self-improvement" (14). This is an important point, but to our way of thinking Le Corbusier set aside a little too hastily the need for amusements, outings, shows, and the like. The variety and intensity of the desire to escape have a meaning he seems to miss. Was he not guided by the proposition that a well-conceived home ought at least to diminish, if not eliminate, these needs? This is still a debatable proposition. Studies have shown that the leisure needs of modern civilization do not arise essentially from dissatisfaction with one's habitation. Riesman has strongly emphasized that boredom develops in a modern family, even one well housed, still faster than the extraordinary variety of ways to escape from it (15).

In addition, the need for "self-improvement" above all was conceived by Le Corbusier in terms of the collective means of obtaining an education outside the home: schools, organizations, groups. This is a good idea, but inadequate. Under what conditions do such institutions develop or decline? What role do telecommunications play? The development function of leisure also tends to be carried on inside the home in more or less suitable ways adapted to each person.

The sociologists of housing have themselves encountered this problem of leisure. We can mention here the work of the social ethnography group in Paris. In his study of worker families, Chombart de Lauwe attacked the question of relaxation. Thanks to him, the need for relaxation has been well identified. Even so, the significance of the need for leisure in the modern family is understated in this type of study. Other problems have been much better studied—for example, the economic and social limitations that stand in the way of certain low-income families in satisfying such needs. Chombart de Lauwe has demonstrated very well that in these families free-time interests are thwarted by the daily preoccupation always present in these individuals' consciousness. Even when these "preoccupations" prevent full enjoyment of "free-time interests," the need for leisure is still there, in all its forms, ever more pressing. Above all, in young households, it creates new consumption and behavior habits, thus threatening to break up the traditional equilibrium of the family economy and culture.

First, the recuperation function of leisure has taken on a larger importance in the modern home. Repose is the highest aspiration of most mothers. A man coming back from work is above all else seeking quiet. The most frequent complaint in apartment houses is against noise (11). That is why the need for rest, insisted upon by every member of the family, results in a search for optimum conditions of fresh air, sunshine, open space, and privacy.

Today, these conditions tend to be part of the vital minimum that everyone is within his rights in demanding for his relaxation. Likewise, in our day, people satisfy their need for relaxation through entertainment. Up to our grandparents' day, family merrymaking took place on holidays, on fixed dates: Christmas, Easter, August 15 (The Virgin's Day). They were organized according to almost invariable rules. This family merrymaking on calendar holidays still persists and is very much alive.

Yet their family character tends to displace their social or religious character. In Annecy, these are the preferred family holi-days, but they are gradually losing their ceremonial character.[4]

For example, in Annecy, in a ratio of 6 to 1, people consider that since 1900 the ceremonial aspect has been diminishing rather than increasing or remaining static (16). Holidays are becoming like another Sunday; their activities are of the semileisure type in which civic or spiritual participation is less important than pleasures enjoyed for themselves as a form of leisure. Still, for the modern family, there are other ways of enjoying leisure.

As we have already said, possibilities for amusement have become everyday occurrences. Of course, Saturday evening is an evening consecrated to amusement, but every evening of the week may be an occasion for going out. In our city, half the heads of families go out at least once a week. For 52 per cent the movies are a conjugal or family outing.[5]

It is the same for country driving, which has been multiplied by the increase in scooters, motorcycles, and automobiles. Last, in most cases, vacations are leisure enjoyed by the whole family. In

[4] Twenty-three per cent choose family parties, 12 per cent religious, and 10 per cent public festivals. We should add that the carnival sort of festival which most often takes on a family character received 19 per cent of the votes (Annecy 1954).

[5] Thirty-five per cent responded that they went to the movies with friends (inquiry by the Centre National du Cinema, 1954).

1957, of one hundred persons who took vacations, fifty-one took them with the family; this is the preferred style of vacation (17). Young households often decide to make their first expenditures on the car rather than on the house. An investigation of youth (18) has shown their first need is for increased vacation, the second for acquiring means of personal transportation, and the third for more entertainment. The need for amusement overwhelms the aspirations of young families.

Recent inventions are fanning the flames of this need. Activities that used to take place at the café or the dancehall are penetrating the house; at home, the radio both stimulates and satisfies what is often a permanent need for musical surroundings. The sudden spread of transistors and record-players is accentuating this still more. We found record collections in 20 per cent of the homes in Annecy. Young workers and students are increasingly bringing these sound-machines into the home. Once allowed in the house, there follows, depending on the social circle, informal dancing, balls, and "blasts." But the greatest revolution in family life and intrafamilial relations has unquestionably been brought about by television.

In French families, on the average two or three persons watch the set. Movies, variety shows, theater, exhibitions, debates, and news all flow into the home. We have observed in all circles that television sets are being installed in the home with rising frequency. Today, the average spectator watches television, more or less intermittently, over a sixteen-hour period. This results in housework being organized in terms of programs. Chores are shortened; time spent puttering around diminishes. Family entertainment may take on new values.

Leisure is not limited to amusement. In earlier times, members of the family kept themselves informed almost entirely through conversation with parents, neighbors, and friends. This, of course, continues. In Annecy, we were struck by the extent of the persistence of this kind of exchange, above all among workers of rural origin (one fourth of the population). Almost half the households in

Annecy hold family reunions or make visits, whether for pleasure or by routine, more than once a month.

But in the modern home, a growing portion of one's free time is taken up listening to information coming from outside by way of telecommunications. Besides music, the radio provides information. The daily newspaper is of such importance that it takes up from one half to a full hour of the time of the head of the family every day. Women and children read it too. Stories, knitting or sewing patterns, and recipes are provided in abundance by almost all women's magazines.

Not only is the home tending to become a small news agency covering the whole world, but it also creates more and more an atmosphere for mutual education. At first, it was believed that the great media had a *direct* influence upon the masses. In reality, they act through leaders who transmit and interpret their content for the benefit of the public.

Often, the family provides its own leaders. For politics, the father generally plays this role; for the movies, it is the oldest daughter (19). In this way, a home may become a discussion circle, more or less organized and impassioned.

Yet the children's games and studies probably create the prime area for mutual education. The child's improved status in the modern family brings the parents more closely in association with their children while playing ball or Monopoly or with electric trains and toy racing-cars. How much does this parental participation derive from a sense of educational duty and how much from a desire for amusement?[6]

Perhaps sharing in the children's schoolwork gives parents a

[6] In Annecy, parents who said they joined in the games of their children out of pleasure were fourteen times more numerous than those who felt this sharing was an educational duty. We find about the same proportion in the parents' participation in their children's homework. A study of two thousand parents of schoolchildren in Chambery (2) showed that the parents spend an average of one and one half hours every evening helping their children learn their lessons and do their homework.

chance to learn something forgotten or something new, in a world where knowledge for its own sake is increasingly becoming a way to advance one's social prestige.

We were likewise struck by the relative importance of family libraries in all sections of the city. The modern home, especially under the pressure of studies on the child, could thus become, given certain conditions, a veritable group study center. Family leisure, therefore, offers possibilities of permanent growth in self-improvement, knowledge, and aptitudes.

For those lacking intellectual or musical culture, manual work is something like Ingres playing the violin. The do-it-yourself movement increasingly takes on more varied forms: in the family, for the individual, utilitarian, for its own sake, conformist, or creative. The effect of this semileisure on the growth of the individual within the family is ambiguous. While the effect of it often is limited, it indisputably has an effect.

A First Step in the Study of the Influences of Leisure on the Functions and Structures of the Modern Family

"To the extent that the workday is shortened," Riesman writes, "We can predict that the family with many children willing to live in the city will be increasingly rare" (21). The minute it has the means, the American family looks for a residential set-up permitting a pleasant life on weekends and even during vacations; the family residence tends to be established near the preferred place of leisure and no longer near the place of work. Since the last war, many fewer families in the United States are leaving the country for the city than are deserting the city for the suburbs. In France today, the current problem is the construction of great urban centers. This type of habitation represents an immense improvement over the slums. It provides the best financial solution. But when people are asked their tastes, the majority prefer a house with a garden.

Sociologists insist on the inconveniences of great distances. Should people be asked to restrict themselves or on the contrary to spread out, to the degree that possibilities develop for renting or building in the green suburbs and the home becomes motorized?

Our hypothesis is that we will have to pay much more attention to the public's aspirations for leisure if we are to solve the housing problem, proportionately as the standard of living rises and the value of free time increases. If the cities and their metropolitan areas are not radically transformed, we can foresee that in ten years apartment houses without space, without silence, without pure air, without trees, without walks, without meeting rooms, without play or garden areas, will be deserted, and we will see an urban exodus as massive as that of the Americans toward houses in the new and distant suburbs.

Is not such a movement a silent but irresistible revolt against urban civilization which, born of work, has been unable to satisfy man's need for repose? Will our great French cities be any more protected from such a reaction than were the cities of America?

One is struck by the lack of long-term imagination in this respect among city planners and architects. At present, they are building houses that should still be in use in the year 2000, and they hardly even inquire into public taste as of now, let alone of how it will evolve. The boldest thinking in architecture dates from the Bauhaus movement of the twenties. Housing sociology on the whole is too static or lacks the means to make the great studies of the future that are needed. In any case, it hasn't made much of a penetration into this area.

Leisure brings perhaps the greatest and the most ambiguous confusion into patterns of family life. As Stoetzel remarks, the system of values worked out in the family circle is based on a utilitarian morality, traditionally oriented toward housework and the prosperity of the clan. Now "the right to laziness" proclaimed against the sovereignty of the job is being reasserted seventy-five years later against the tyranny of housework. The system of family relations dominated by the community's ideology is threatened. The right to leisure is accompanied by the right to individual happiness for each member of the family, whether within it or outside.

These new trends have appeared more swiftly among the middle classes than in the working class, where persisting difficult living conditions have favored the survival of the traditional modes of life (economy, work, domestic virtues, mutual assistance). But these new tendencies are already felt in the young households of all milieux. They will grow. Probably, they will be one of the dominant traits of the "civilization" of 1975.

What is and what will be the effect of all this on the internal cohesion and external relations of the family group and on its participation in cultural and social life?

For many French families that are still poorly housed and badly furnished, as we have seen, leisure does not bring much change in habits of life. Family responsibilities lie heavy, especially on mothers. Yet some of these today seem to be more or less useless to the proper functioning of the modern home. There are true obligations, semiobligations, and pseudo-obligations that depend on a traditional system of values and frequently amount to no more than an outmoded conformism. These are related to fear of what people will say (it's bad to be separated from one's children, to take a sunbath during the day, to spend hours reading novels, to go out in the evening without one's husband). They also represent a lack of hope and are a cause of maladjustment of the home to modern life and of the family way of life to the new needs of leisure. On the contrary, the need to escape may become tyrannical, especially in younger households. Dreaming, going out, dancing, reading, prolonging the evening, the weekend, or the vacation—these are activities and preoccupations that encroach upon the essential tasks at the very heart of a home and upon the harmony of the marriage or the raising of the children. What today is the favorable setting for the family to function, for a new family morality, or for the blossoming of the personality?

To give solid psychosociological bases to these new cultural patterns, it is essential to consider the entirety of family activities *as a dynamic system of obligations and leisure, of semiobligations and semileisure, in balance or imbalance, from the viewpoint of both individual and institution.*

During the last thirty years, family sociology has mainly been stressing the cohesive factors of the family group. What becomes of them with the growth of leisure? The family adapts itself poorly to its new situation. Some sociologists, like Edward A. Burgess (22), have noted the decline in discipline in the typically contemporary family such as the American family.

The development of family games, automobile trips, and family watching of TV programs brings together all the members of the family, young and old. These improve interpersonal relations. Some, like Rolf Meyersohn (23) and Leo Bogart, on the contrary, think that sharing activities does not necessarily result in interpersonal exchanges. Anyone in a family group can remain quite isolated. On the other hand, leisure has increased interest in organized or spontaneous groups outside the family that attract people around the same pastime, the same conception or the same passion. How can the family rediscover its unity among all these antagonistic tendencies? For the couple, leisure has multiplied occasions for sharing recreation. E. L. Scheuch has studied the importance for the couple's harmony of conversation and common activities during free time (24). The right to free choice of leisure activities and relationships being greater for each member of the couple, there can result a more complete personal and social realization of each one's personality. Equality, however, is still distant. In worker families in Malakoff, Pierre Fougeyrollas noted that while 30 per cent of the husbands go out alone in the evening, only 5 per cent of the wives do so (25).

Here again, traditional patterns are tenacious obstacles to satisfying new aspirations. Should we not see in this situation one of the reasons behind those tensions among married couples that seem so much more numerous than in an earlier day?

Relations between parents and children have altered. There has been an increase in the number of amusements enjoyed in common —ball games, tennis, bowling, parlor games, radio and TV games and variety shows—in the evening, on vacations, or on Sunday. The time for this kind of leisure shared by young and old is much lengthier than in the last century. Also, the educational function takes on new forms.

This change makes for a much easier dialogue between parents and children. The father is less isolated. He has lost his false dignity. Thanks in part to these common activities during free time, parental authority is changing.

Yet, in some families, has this camaraderie in play between parents and children not also wiped out respect for certain adult roles, certain family values necessary in training the personality of the young? Excesses of a certain kind of liberal pedagogy have been blamed partly for the inadaptibility and delinquency of a growing fraction of American youth.

Thus it is in leisure, in spite of it and also through it, that the modern family is seeking the basis for a new cohesion, one so difficult to attain. This family cohesion, however necessary it may be, is not an absolute. Talcott Parsons and most American sociologists have analyzed the ways the family group adapts internally. But it seems to us at least as important to study the forms of its participation in social and cultural life outside the family. Such outside participation does risk dispersing the various members of the family among different groups, which, because of their significance, may take the place of the family itself. Yet, without this social participation, the family group turns in upon itself, and its members remain strangers to the onward movement of culture and society.

What is the effect of leisure on the balance between family and social activity? This is perhaps one of the major problems for family cohesion in a leisure civilization.

We have seen to what extent leisure can transform the way in which the household participates in social and cultural life. Radio listening, newspaper reading, television shows, sharing in children's games, and joining recreational groups can enlarge one's curiosity and develop the social sense. But do the majority of families have the desire and the power to organize their time so as to reduce material tasks to the minimum, diminishing useless puttering and gossiping, so as to find a balance between the entertainment and the cultural aspects of leisure at the day's end, on the weekend, during the annual vacation—for the group and for each person?

Here again traditional patterns persist, not adapted to family needs nor to preparing for a leisure civilization. Some housekeeping improvements may actually be a sign of lack of social and cultural life. For the American housewife whose home is well equipped and well mechanized, "Taking excessive care of the children and the house often are for her a self-justification and at the same time an escape" (21).

Above a certain standard of living, do not people cling to some old-fashioned family constraints because of a dread of or an inability to attempt new forms of leisure that would stimulate personal or social life? The gap between new needs and old-fashioned norms of family life results in a growing imbalance. New norms are not clear yet. A growing number of families oscillate between conformist patterns in which they hardly believe any longer and anarchistic patterns that lead to break-ups. A new balance must be sought between dull servitude and duty, between obligation and leisure, between recreational activities and enrichment, between individual and family leisure.

Theories of the family, whether Christian or socialist, conservative or progressive, communal or individualist, often seem inappropriate or inadequate to deal with these imbalances or to create a new equilibrium. These theories must be thought through again on the basis of a concrete study of the new needs of the family and its members as they stand on the threshold of leisure civilization. What is the new type of life that is really taking over, leaving aside any ideology? Which culture experienced freely by people corresponds both to individual aspirations and to the family's and society's needs today?

To reach this *new culture*, the family generally needs help from outside. Are social workers who counsel families prepared to answer these questions? Alfred Sauvy speaks of the need for new cultural assistants for families. Will the priest, the teacher, the doctor, or the social worker be able to take on this job? It is possible, provided they have been so trained. The directors of family associations and social centers in the new housing developments have a heavy responsibility in helping the growth of a popular culture associated with the new types of habitation.[7]

[7] From the start, there are two deformations awaiting them: first, the "social" deformation. The cultural institution is conceived of as a social service (an organization of social cooperation or assistance). This is the first mistake. Of course, the cultural center has a social function, but people do not come to it as they come for a consultation. It would be dangerous to base a policy of cultural improvement on a sociology of social service.

If we want to base a sociocultural policy on a scientific study of needs, we must realize that these needs are not identical with those that drive people to the social services. These are leisure needs with all their ambiguity: the need to be amused or to initiate other social relations.

The second deformation—and it is quite frequent in the teaching world despite fifty years of adult education—is the "school" deformation. Integrating sociocultural equipment with equipment that is an extension of the school seems equally dangerous. The problem of school equipment and its full use by adults as well as by children is very important—even of prime importance. But it is related to school responsibilities and their extension, whereas sociocultural equipment is related to a voluntary involvement. Voluntary activities in the fields of entertainment, learning, and self-improvement take place in free time. Here cultural behavior is in permanent competition with recreational behavior. It is, therefore, important that sociocultural training be related above all else with the functions of leisure.

In addition, sociocultural training does not wait for the student who has been obliged to come under threat of a visit by the truant officer. There must be action taken in the group in order to convince the family. What are the needs of the family? The word is ambiguous. In the first place, we must not confuse a cultural need with a material need. The latter is not created or developed; generally the demand is greater than the supply. But cultural needs must often be created and developed. These are the demands the society makes up for the individual. Here the supply is greater than the demand, even when the public proclaims its desire for community services in the cultural domain.

Leisure sociology can forearm us against the illusion that it is merely necessary to provide the equipment to bring the demand for culture into being. Institutions stand open and are never fully utilized. Therefore, it is important for sociology to emphasize the permanent ambiguity of leisure and of its corresponding needs. For leisure to be able to increase the participation of a growing number of families in cultural and social life, social and cultural stimulation of residential neighborhoods is at least as important as their material arrangements.

Part 2

Leisure

and

Culture

EXAMINATION OF THE RELATIONSHIPS BETWEEN PROFESSIONAL AND family life and leisure has led us to the question of popular culture. It is time to define the effects of leisure on this problem. In a society based on democratic principles and equipped with powerful communications media, mass participation in cultural works and the development of works suited to this vast new public are essential. This participation and this development may be more or less widespread, the quality of the works presented or created may be more or less high, but all modern societies, whatever their dominant ideology and the level of their technical growth, must face this problem after their own fashion.[1]

At every stage in its development, an industrial and democratic society is seeking out the form and content of its popular culture. In underdeveloped countries, in the process of industrializing themselves, when the struggle against misery, disease, and traditional fatalism comes ahead of everything else, the development of a

[1] In a capitalist society like the United States, mass culture (even under the vulgar name of *Kitsch*) seems to many sociologists to be the sign of a vast esthetic awakening among the classes who formerly just accepted what-

modern mass culture is basic if the masses are to take an active part in the economic and social transformation of their own lives (3).

In advanced countries that have attained the level of production and education of most of the nations of Europe, development of popular culture helps to narrow the gap between the creator and the public, between the specialist and the layman, between the educated classes and the others. It alone can prolong and adapt the effects of schooling, stimulate active resistance to simplistic propaganda or short-cut advertising, and prompt individuals to take an active part in social and cultural life. Without it, there is risk that technocracies and oligarchies will redouble their powers.

In postindustrial society (4), popular culture is even more essential. Not only do all the previously mentioned social problems remain, but others are added. When the need for food, clothing, housing, comfort, and recreation is satisfied for three quarters of the population (5), a rise in the cultural aspirations of consumers is probably the basic requisite in order to prevent the "society of abundance" from dragging man down into a world where material values alone reign supreme. "Abundance for what?" sociologists like Riesman are asking. A growing number of economists are echoing them (6).

There is, perhaps, reason to restrict and reorient advertising aimed primarily at increasing the sponsor's profits, through a powerful, permanent effort at cultural emancipation of the mass of the people. This would give popular education a central place in our society of consumption. In every democratic industrial society, popular education is more than a possibility; it is a necessity, something worth having. Yet those who are trying to improve the daily life of the working population rarely see the connection between the spread of education and leisure for the mass of the people. But,

ever was given them and who had practically no access to esthetic expression or understanding (1). According to the rulers of the Soviet Union, culture has a solid base capable of unlimited and smooth development only when the whole mass of the population has been integrated into the cultural structure (2).

in reality, what one does with one's leisure time does influence and increasingly will influence what kind of a cultural life one lives in a mass society. It won't be a waste of time to analyze this all-too-often ignored relationship.

For more than a century, we have known that allowing the masses to enjoy the fruits of culture would require shorter working hours. Modern culture, whether technical, scientific, artistic, or philosophical, cannot be acquired or developed through the sheer performance of daily obligations. Acquiring or creating it requires time. As the time spent in school becomes less and less adequate for acquiring the knowledge and the aptitudes needed in an ever more complex and changing world, time free from the job and from other obligations is all the more necessary. Even this essential condition is not enough. We have seen that leisure is not merely free time, a temporal framework, or a "space for human development"; it is an ensemble of ambiguous activities conditioned by values and patterns that to a certain degree determine the very content of popular culture.

For the working man, any active participation in cultural life— that is, any creative activity or act of learning, whatever it is—is a leisure activity. It is, therefore, in *permanent and direct competition* with all other leisure activities, particularly with all forms of relaxation and recreation. For the masses, going to the theater, reading a literary work, or studying a work on popular science are leisure activities, just as taking a walk, puttering around, playing a game, dancing, or going on a trip. All these activities have the same character. None of them is basically obligatory, as are work or raising children. In the first place, they are not considered as ways of making money, but rather as pleasurable. They can be substituted for one another at will, according to the situation or to one's fancy. Even in a society that encourages efforts at personal improvement to the maximum, the gap between the aims of the propagandists or the educators and the real attitudes of the people is probably very large. The Soviet state, for example, has put forth an enormous effort to spread literary works among its people. While some authors are excluded, a large number of the works of Hugo, Balzac, and Shakespeare are available (7). But how many read them? According to the satirical magazine *Crokodil*, books are used in various ways; many use them for learning, others for different purposes—to hold up a table leg, to light a fire, and so forth. This is a joke in *Crokodil*, but statistics on the distribution of cultural goods give only a vague idea of how the masses of consumers actually use them.

One of the first sociological studies ever made of leisure among the Soviets shows that 25 per cent of their leisure time is devoted to action, pure and simple, that a sizable portion is taken up with receiving guests, and that, despite educational policy, leisure is far from being for everyone a way to develop himself culturally (8).

In the United States, the effects of leisure are even more complicated. Every sociologist confirms that in a context where freedom of choice is greater but where the pressure of mediocre commercial amusements is so very powerful, only a minority of citizens take part in any cultural life. That is why the most important inquiry into adult education currently under way has selected leisure as its central research focus (9).

The influence of leisure upon mass culture is not limited to this. The *life*-culture is in a sense the way society or an individual behaves; studying this process we find the patterns, the representations, the values that make up different stages in the cultural range. These stages are tied in with types of practical, technical, artistic, or philosophical patterns. Their level of quality varies a great deal. These types are developed to a greater or lesser extent depending on the individual, the class, and the society. The sum total of all the activities of daily life may be the basis for this life-culture. They can form the support for cultural growth. But the increasing, attractive, and even prestigious activities of leisure exert a special influence. We have seen that almost one fourth of the workers in the city of Annecy concentrate on them.

According to Riesman and Wilensky (10), at a more highly

industrialized stage the number of workers concentrating on leisure would be even greater. Indeed, if the Soviet rulers make such a great effort to organize free-time activities and to connect interest in entertainment with interest in work, is this not because they recognize the special power of leisure in the personal life of the people, in the most spontaneous expressions of their culture (11)?

Two recent anthologies of American sociology make a distinction between mass leisure and mass culture in terms of activities (12). This distinction, which is explicable because of the present confusion between leisure and amusement, is unjustified. In these two books, it results in whimsies. An educational study group is classified as mass leisure, while a card game is part of mass culture. Why? Because at the level of activities themselves it is impossible to find simple criteria for making distinctions. In reality, all the activities listed in these two anthologies are leisure activities—card playing, belonging to a club, reading a book, or going to the movies. Each of these leisure activities has cultural content; popular culture is largely blending with popular leisure. "Tell me what your leisure is, and I'll tell you your culture."

There is probably no problem more difficult and at the same time more important in popular culture than that of *levels of quality*. We reject the currently dominant a priori split between humanist and popular culture. In fact, as Shils says, we are facing the entire problem of "culture in a mass society."[2]

The life-culture of a given mass society is a continuum of differing levels that interpenetrate each other in every class and milieu. Sociologists with a Marxist or a liberal tendency properly consider popular culture as a concept "both humanistic and sociological" (13). This leads us to ask the crucial question: To what degree do old and the new works of art penetrate into the cultural patterns of the masses? In broadening its public, isn't culture threatened by oversimplified art, oversimple science, conformist morality, and

[2] Edward A. Shils, "Mass Society and its Culture," *Daedalus*, Spring, 1959, Vol. 89, No. 2, pp. 288–315.

superficial philosophy that can be sold or distributed to the greatest number with the greatest of ease? These fears are shared by most American sociologists who study "mass culture" (14).

In the socialist countries, despite systematic efforts to educate the people, who fill the museums (one out of three inhabitants of a Polish city goes to a museum), and guarantees of enormous sales of major works, is not art for the people usually accompanied by a lowering of artistic and literary standards (15)? Since 1956, this abasement has often been denounced by writers' congresses in the socialist countries.

In France, the struggle against "cut-rate popular culture" is one of the permanent themes common among all popular education groups. So, in spite of diverse social and ideological contents, this problem of the standards of mass culture is everywhere present. If a concrete solution to the problem is to be found, it will probably be in the standards of leisure in which culture is really experienced.

This is why in a given society, if we are to find out not only the ideal but also the real and *possible* levels of popular culture, it is important to examine the real and possible leisure activities of the masses.

We have, therefore, decided to analyze the contents of several kinds of leisure.[3] The following are the activities we have selected and the reasons therefor:

1. *Tourist travel*. This occupies a privileged place; it is a recent, still incomplete social conquest. Its influence is growing, expanding among all urban groups. It expresses with force the need for escape.

2. *Movies and television*. They are the vehicle for particularly prestigious models (movie stars, and so on). TV, along with the automobile, is probably going to be the most powerful leisure tool.

3. *Self-improvement*. We have tried to find out the extent of reading and the aims of free intellectual curiosity in the various social groups of the city. To us it seems that spontaneous self-

---

[3] Of course, they do not include the major leisure activities we have previously found to be seven in number.

improvement efforts during the leisure time of the masses are of great significance for the future of cultural democracy.

We offer these findings to the thoughtful reader. Investigations are still going on; the most important ones have hardly begun. It is by exploring the content of leisure activities in the various social groups that the most important part of the complex content of popular culture will stand out in its true form, unified and diversified. From this there may possibly arise a true science of mass culture in a given society. Little by little, it will be possible to identify the patterns of cultural growth that are common to the whole population or that differ according to the milieu, the class, and the specific groups that compose it.

Chapter 6

Vacation Leisure

and

Tourist Leisure

The Birth of Mass Tourism

Vacations are perhaps the most important leisure activities, both because of their length and their attractiveness. Of course, vacations don't eliminate semileisure or housekeeping tasks, especially for the woman. Nevertheless, on vacation, chores are simplified. In a general way, relaxation, getting away from it all, and free individual or social development can be enjoyed more fully during vacation than in other periods of leisure. The possibility of traveling plays a very special role. At the time when Stendhal invented the very word "tourist," only a few rich bourgeois enjoyed vacation trips—often Englishmen (Hotel des Anglais, Promenade des Anglais). Today, such trips have become a rapidly growing reality.[1]

[1] In 1957, according to a survey by the INSEE (National Institute of Statistics and Economic Studies) ten million Frenchmen took a trip during their vacation (1). Today this figure must well exceed twelve million. Resulting expenditures have risen to about sixty million new francs, a figure equal to what French employees pay each year in income taxes or what all Frenchmen pay for their rent or apartment maintenance.

123

Having become a social fact of the first magnitude, this mass tourism raises questions of growing importance. It is hardly surprising that vacation organizers and travel experts should have looked to scientific research. Individual experiments are ineffective in finding an efficient and harmonious solution to the problems of adapting the tourist industry to the new needs of vacationers.

From now on, vacation leisure is part and parcel of the great economic and human problems raised by the interrelationships among city, country, land management, public health, popular culture, and so forth. No longer is it possible to tackle this general question seriously without taking into account the special problems of mass tourism. What are the first fruits of research, and, above all, what are the main problems facing us today in France in this new sector of leisure sociology?

Travel for pleasure originally developed in France along with the growth of cities and the spread of love for the outdoors popularized by romanticism. The real spurt in mass tourism is more recent. As noted, 1936 is its legal birthday: Twelve days of paid vacation a year mandatory in all enterprises and a cut-price railway ticket gave birth to popular tourism.[2]

It can be estimated that in the last twenty years the number of tourists has increased about six times. Should we expect expansion of tourism to continue at the same rate? Answering this question demands a study of the relevant factors. First, vacation travel is linked with the degree of urbanization of a country. This is shown by the INSEE study made in 1957;[3] among people who take a vacation trip, there is a majority of big-city dwellers.

[2] In one year (1937) the number of tourists increased from a few hundred thousand to nearly two million according to the estimates of the SCNF (French Railways). After years of stagnation, a sudden growth in travel took place around 1950, along with an improvement in living standards. In 1951, 49 per cent of our citizens took vacations, about the same number as in 1946. In 1957, the figure had risen to 62 per cent. Between the two surveys, the legal duration of paid vacations had been lengthened to three weeks (1958).

[3] The National Tourist Center has asked the INSEE to undertake three

Those living in metropolitan Paris, 18 per cent of the population, accounted for 51 per cent of the expenditures on vacations (1); 72 per cent of the inhabitants of Paris or the Paris area took vacations, as against 62 per cent in Angers, 56 per cent in Nantes, 55 per cent in Lyon, 48 per cent in Toulouse, and 37 per cent in Lille. Despite the size of Marseille, only 31 per cent of its inhabitants went on vacation. Yet, even though the reasons for this have never been studied, we may at least surmise that the sun and the sea play some part. Crowded cities obviously have a powerful influence on the desire to get away on vacation, especially cities lacking much sunlight.[4]

nation-wide surveys on the subject since the Liberation: 1949, 1950, and 1957. In 1958, in the principal professional journal (*Le Repertoire des Voyages*), M. Sandro Sorbeli, director of the International Tourist Center, wrote that for him, an international director and organizer, the tourist market is an unknown quantity. But research in this area is outstripping market studies (4). At the same time, we were asked to prepare, with Roger Girod, a project on tourism for the Institute of Sociological Research (5). Besides, the International Association of Tourist Experts, under the direction of W. Hunziker has produced several serious works on the subject (6).

At its 1959 convention, this association for the first time placed at the head of its agenda the problem of interdisciplinary research methods common to experts in the social sciences: geographers, economists, psychologists, and sociologists (7). Under the impetus of Georges Deffert, a French association of tourist experts was founded in 1959. At long last, French psychologists have taken up the matter of tourism. H. Raymond, starting with the sociology of air transport, has begun studying leisure travel and its "concrete utopia" (8). Nicole Faivre-Haumont is completing a series of interviews on the motivations of vacationers at the Mediterranean Club. Psychological and sociological studies of vacations and tourism have, therefore, become a major current concern in France.

[4] Leisure travel (day's end, weekend, or annual) increases with the move to the cities and the use of motor transport. Any study of these ought to be as dynamic as the subject itself. The sociology of tourism needs to be far-seeing. Polls on the current state of tourists' habits provide only limited results. What is most important is research into what conditions, according to what processes, and at what rates vacation travel develops, so as to facilitate knowledge of its probable growth in the future, whether short or long term. René Duchet, in his essay on tourism, takes the history of this phenomenon back to the pilgrimages and the crusades of the ninth century (9). In spite of certain secondary analogies, it doesn't seem to us that such travel belongs in the history of leisure travel. We prefer to lean on the hypothesis of a historian of tourism in the southeast, Marc Boyer, who takes the "prehistory" of tourism back to 1815 and its history to around 1850 (10).

It would also be interesting to know if vacation travel helps one adapt to city life, or, on the contrary, makes such adaptation so difficult as to lead to chronic dissatisfaction or outright departure— this is particularly important for the future of decentralization. One other fact worth mentioning. Marc Boyer noted that in a growing number of cases tourists from provincial towns generally travel about two hundred kilometers (125 miles) away from home. Perhaps this fact should be measured and an appropriate program of lodging, transportation, and amusement be organized. Little is usually done about this aspect of the development of a given region. Are tourist information bureaus doing any research in this regard? They give, rather, the opposite impression, that they are concerned almost exclusively with travelers coming from afar, especially foreigners.

On the other hand, those who do travel far from their own region almost all head for the same places, substituting for the crowded city crowded sea coasts and camp sites. One third of vacations in France are spent in nine departments, and half the overnight stops are made in ten departments: Alpes-Maritimes, Haute-Savoie, Morbihan, Puy-de-Dôme, Var, Basses-Pyrénées, Savoie, Allier, Ille-et-Vilaine, and Côtes-du-Nord. There is a growing vogue for the sea. In 1951, 45 per cent of our tourists chose the countryside for their main vacation, 25 per cent the sea. In 1957, the trend was the opposite—32 per cent chose the country, 35 per cent the sea. The mountains attracted at that time about the same number of fans as in 1951, a mere 15 per cent.[5]

We all know the success of the Riviera (Côte d'Azur). St. Tropez stands out as a curious example. There are 360 hotel rooms and some 500 furnished rooms available; still, according to official figures, nearly 20,000 people spend their vacations in St. Tropez (11).

The vacation exodus from the cities everywhere creates human

[5] Watering places, other cities, and touring maintained their percentages : 10 per cent against 12 per cent; 9 per cent against 8 per cent; 7 per cent against 8 per cent.

problems closely related to economic questions. There has been much new building in tourist areas, but they are still poorly equipped to handle the influx. The local populace is not adjusted to meet it. No serious effort to inform or train them has been made (12). These vacationing crowds, on the other hand, often cause problems of safety, hygiene, and unfamiliar social relationships. Some under-developed areas could be improved if projects for expanding tourism took account of the leisure needs of various kinds of city dwellers, instead of being oriented mainly toward foreigners.

Urban sociology should henceforth be studying the conditions of the annual leisure migration between home and vacation spot, just as it has studied daily migrations between company and home.

The *means of transportation* has determined and will continue to determine the way in which people solve the problem of traveling between home and vacation resort. We are aware of the spectacular railway traffic figures on holidays such as Christmas, Easter, and the August vacation period. Between August 1 and 2, 1959, 412,100 passengers departed from the six main railroad stations in Paris (13). Yet these statistics are misleading. In reality, although we are not able to isolate the proportion involved in vacation travel, there has not been a net increase in railway traffic. Quite the contrary. In 1931, 773 million passengers traveled on French railways; in 1958, 553 million. In fact, the number who take "Sunday special" railway trips out of Paris (reduced fare) has varied very little since 1938.[6]

Of course, the total number of traveler-miles since 1956 has exceeded that of the prewar record level, but the chief means of transportation is the automobile. This, obviously, has had the greatest effect on tourism.[7]

In six years, the proportion using cars had almost doubled, and the number of people using cars for vacationing is becoming bigger

[6] 2,373,038 in 1938; 2,408,234 in 1958 (13).
[7] The auto boom is extraordinary. In 1951, 60 per cent of vacationers used the train to reach their vacation spot, 24 per cent the automobile. At the end of 1957, 47 per cent were still using the train, but already 40 per cent were using automobiles.

than the number going by train. Will this rate of growth continue? If one looks at the United States, the answer is yes. There, 85 per cent of vacation trips are made by automobile, against 13 per cent by train (14). In the cities, a growing number of people are buying autos, not to go to work but for making trips on Sundays, holidays, and vacations.

Leisure traveling is often the motivation for buying a car. The general trend toward family car-ownership obviously can only increase the amount of traveling. Remaining in one spot during one's vacation has been replaced by keeping on the move. The average stay in a given hotel grows shorter every year.

Tourist accommodations are trying to adapt themselves to these new consumer tastes, but the placement, equipment, and personnel training of hotels create new problems that cannot be effectively solved except after studies have been made into the growth of tourists' needs and into what results have been achieved by new-type accommodations. For example, couldn't there be experiments with stopover hotels reserved for overnight travelers?

Because of the spectacular number of accidents, we are all aware of the problems arising from the sudden expansion of traffic during weekend and holiday travel. Up to now, strict enforcement of traffic regulations and police surveillance have had little effect.[8]

There are twice as many accidents in July and August as in January and February (about 20 per cent as against 10 per cent of the annual total). One accident in three occurs on weekends. Leisure-time travel is more dangerous. Man is not prepared for this new facet of city life, which has arisen suddenly in less than ten years.

Experts in highway control estimate that 95 per cent of body accidents are the individual's own fault, out of 250 possible

---

[8] In 1956, more than 200,000 were injured in auto accidents, and 8,783 killed, of whom 1,400 were children. Twenty per cent of the child deaths that year were caused by accidents, mainly on the road. In the United States, it was 37 per cent (15).

causes (15). Modern governments seem paralyzed before this problem. They have perfected their system of statistical highway control and taken measures against drunken drivers, bad tires, and so forth, but their policy of repression and prevention is not enough. There has never been a true policy of experimentation, short term and long term, to introduce broad innovations subject to scientific control. Up to now, the attempts made (such as in "Operation Annecy") have little in common with true research by dynamic sociologists.

Of course, there are other, more general, factors in the growth of mass tourism: first and foremost the *general improvement in standards of living.*[9]

A sizable minority of people cannot go on vacation because they lack the means. We should not ignore the effects of social measures aimed at expanding tourism among the lower-income groups: vacation savings, vacation bonus, group travel, or double-salary as a legal requirement, as in Belgium. Which of these is really effective? If advances in popular tourism are subject to economic restrictions, there are also psychological obstacles. The small number of country people who go on vacation (19 per cent in 1957) can't be explained away solely on financial grounds. Most reasons currently given by those who fail to go away on vacations are not of an economic but of a personal nature: health, taste, various reasons (51 per cent).

In the United States, where living standards are higher than in France, a nation-wide sampling in 1955 showed that on the average

[9] In 1951, 52 per cent of those who did not take vacations blamed the high cost of travel. In 1957 it was 47 per cent. The influence of income, while diminishing, is still significant. Figures on those leaving for vacation, by socioprofessional categories, correspond approximately to differences in income. Eighty-two per cent of the industrialists and big businessmen go away for their vacations, as against 59 per cent of the handicraft workers. In the working class, 70 per cent of the foremen, 61 per cent of the skilled workers, 57 per cent of the less-skilled workers, and 23 per cent of the laborers go away on vacation.

only 65.5 per cent of people earning more than $5,000 a year and only 54 per cent of the entire nation took vacation trips (14).

It would be interesting to have psychosociological research shed light on the evolution in motivations concerning vacation in accordance with class, group, and individual preferences. Economic factors will have to be placed alongside cultural and psychological factors if we are not to make errors.

Work season, Vacation season

Another series of problems affecting the future of tourism is raised by the time of the year that people take vacations. For more than half the people of France, August is the month for going. The inconveniences caused by this are many: underemployment of tourist facilities during the work year and their inadequacy during the vacation season; abnormal price rises, overbidding, speculation, which profit the rich and increase social inequalities in the matter of vacations; growth of new patterns of segregation at vacation resorts comparable with those in housing developments in worker suburbs. Those on "paid vacations" are ignored or treated as minor customers. Gangs of a new type appear, suited to operating among concentrations of tourists. Here again, economic problems are inseparable from human problems. . . .

How did this trend toward concentration, causing so many difficulties, arise?[10]

Contrary to what one might expect, this trend is diminishing, not increasing. From 1951 to 1957, the proportion of those who took their main vacation out of season rose from 6 to 10 per cent, and in 1957, 16 per cent of the French tourists went on a short vacation beside their main one. This change results in great part from the increase in the number of people who do not take their vacations

[10] Principal vacation periods away from home: July, 8 per cent; August, 51 per cent; September, 8 per cent; school holidays, 8 per cent; out of season, 10 per cent.

all at once but generally in two parts. In 1951, one adult in twenty-five enjoyed this privilege. By 1957, it was one in ten. This change reflects mostly the rapid growth in winter vacations. During the 1957–58 season, their growth, compared with the preceding year, was estimated by experts to have been between 13 and 15 per cent (16). Before 1914, there were only a few thousand ski amateurs; today the number of skiers is considerably more than a million (16).

In 1956–57, 225,000 adult French tourists stayed at hotels attached to winter resorts. And, according to professional estimates, the total staying in all types of accomodations at these resorts was about 400,000. It is likely that the rise in living standards and the growth in public awareness will further increase in this kind of vacation. In the United States 30 per cent of the tourists take their vacations in two parts, especially in the winter (14). Organizations such as the Mediterranean Club, Travel and Work, and the National Union of Mountain Camps have succeeded in substantially reducing the cost of such vacations (often by half). The National Union of Mountain Camps provides young people with lodging, ski monitors, and atmosphere. The number using these camps increased sixfold from 1945 to 1958. In 1958, in spite of 13,960 members, there were three times more applications than places (17). The same remarks would apply to the growth in snow-sport classes. They currently number 151; the demand is immeasurable compared with present supply. Here the problem is primarily economic. The equivalent of camping in tents has not yet been found for winter vacations. The capital needed obviously is of quite another dimension than that for summer camps. There is a question whether the hotel construction and facilities are not imprisoned in a conception of winter tourism that places them beyond the reach of the potential new clientele. It is time for sociologists and economists to examine these latent needs and to propose bold experimental formulas both for the commercial sector and for the noncommercial, so as to take care of this new wave of tourists.

The trend toward split vacations, while substantial, is quite small. It is not certain whether this trend will lead automatically to a solution of the difficulties caused by the huge concentration of arrivals and departures during the month of August. Propaganda in behalf of spacing out vacations over the year has not up to now met with any great success. This spacing out raises a number of economic difficulties beyond the control of the individual. In 48 per cent of the cases, the vacation period is regulated by the employer (1). Attempts at adjusting vacations from work to vacations from school have never been seriously carried out. Spacing out vacation periods raises the whole problem of weaving this annual leisure travel into the rhythm of the work year for adults and for children. The economic and human problems of vacation leisure are inseparable from the general problems caused by the expansion of production, the humanization of industrial work, and the rational arrangement of school work. It is at this level that basic research ought to be undertaken in order to learn the optimum rhythm for alternating between periods of work and periods of vacation, in the interests both of society and of individuals.[11]

The growth of tourism, especially in the lower classes, runs into the problem of shelter. According to W. Hunziker, this is "the crucial point for mass tourism" (6). Every year more than four million foreign travelers visit France, "good customers," tourists for the most part (18). But the sharp rise in the number of French tourists has raised the problem of shelter in new dimensions. Henceforth, is the hotel going to remain the most important form of accomodation? It has often been said that most French hotels are not adapted to satisfying a deluxe clientele, especially foreigners accustomed to the English style of hotel, but that they are even less well equipped to answer to the new needs of mass tourism. So, many hotels are closing down. Seasonal labor employed by the hotel

[11] It should be noted, however, that during the summer of 1960, on the initiative of the Planning Commission, several big automobile producers gave their personnel one week's uninterrupted vacation.

industry is estimated at five hundred thousand. In 1957, however, only 23 per cent of French tourists used a hotel. Account must be taken of the growth in travel abroad, where hotels are used in 59 per cent of the cases. But of the tourists who traveled only in France, a mere 17 per cent utilized hotels or boarding houses. One grave problem in adapting hotels to the taste of vacationing customers is the growing demand for individual accomodations: villas, houses, and rooms. The State favors providing rooms in peasant homes, as a source of supplementary income. For the tourist, this is an assurance of tranquility in a "natural surrounding." In 1951, 19 per cent of French vacationers, and 16 per cent in 1957, used this kind of accomodation. But there are still only 2,750 rural tourist lodgings in all France, and only 400 rural family houses providing services for the mother of a family.

As we have seen above, one shelter formula has been expanding enormously since 1945: camping in tents. Nine per cent of the French tourists who spend their vacations in France use this formula (against 6 per cent in 1951). There are about two thousand camp sites and a hundred tent villages. Among the most important are those of the Touring Club, the Mediterranean Club, and the great undertakings of such as the EDF (French National Power Company) (19). Why does camping enjoy such success? The economic reason plays an important part, but it is not the only one.

According to the 1957 survey, there are as many executives from industry and commerce as there are workers who like camping. It would be interesting to know what their motivations are (informal relationships, open air, nature, pleasure in camp life, breaking with daily comforts?). And it would also be useful to study the conditions necessary to prevent overcrowding and to assure a minimum space for each tent. Organizing the safety of individual campers creates difficult problems. The return to nature exacts a high price.

By far the most popular place to stay is still the home of one's relatives or friends (41 per cent for all tourists, 43 per cent for those who spend their vacations in France). Of course, economy plays a major part in this. From 1951 to 1957, the rise in living standards was accompanied by a drop in the number in this category. Still, in every social group, rich or poor, this way of spending one's vacation was chosen by one third to two thirds of the total.[12]

It seems likely that vacations provide an occasion for tightening family ties. A sizable number of tourists pass their vacations within the family. A still large number, almost all, go on vacation with their family. This raises the question of children's vacations. Since 1936, we have seen in France a growing effort to create inexpensive vacation camps. About 1,100,000 children attend them. These camps are the biggest noncommercial group-tourist business. Should we encourage children's vacations outside the family, or, on the contrary should we encourage family vacations, as rural family houses providing services for the mother of a family do? Should we alternate? What do people want? There are few such family-type houses supported by family associations (four hundred) and they are overwhelmed with applications. And they are expanding to the maximum. It would help if we made an inquiry, from the viewpoint both of family cohesion and of the development of children and parents, to find out what would be the best balance between vacations on one's own and vacations in common, according to the type of family and the various social groups.

In a more general way, the problem of accommodations and family-group living on vacation ought to be compared with those of accomodations and family life during the rest of the year. We have seen that all the functions of the family, except recreation, have been declining for a century. Vacations are part of the recreational function and can be the occasion for tightening family bonds. Foreign sociologists like Yrjö Littunen (2), however, have undertaken some interesting studies of fatigue within the family group and the need for separating the family during vacation time in order to restore it with new vigor. A whole series of human prob-

[12] In the United States, this category still accounts for 45 per cent of all vacationers who earn more than $5,000 a year (15).

lems arises, beginning with accomodations on vacation. They could be clarified by family sociology.

A New Culture?

Vacation activities raise problems still more complex than the question of where to stay when vacationing. These activities involve hygiene, an ethic, a culture that may have profound and long-lasting happy or unhappy effects on the individual or the society in every-day life. These activities may be responses to quite different needs. In 1947, the French Institute of Public Opinion asked a nationwide sample: "What do you count on doing during your vacation?" The most frequent reply indicated people most wanted repose: "Take it easy," "Breathe fresh air," "Eat and sleep well," "Take naps," "Enjoy the view." This type of response, given by 55 per cent of those questioned, was far more common than all the others. These are not the tourists who travel very much. They are voluntarily sedentary. They are fleeing the pressure of the world, the tumult and the noise of the vast built-up areas, heading for "an inexpensive little spot." For these the rustic retreat is the best answer.[13]

But how many vacationers will, for any length of time, put up with mere repose without suffering boredom? How many know how to enjoy the relaxation they need after a tiring year of urban life and work? The repose afforded by vacation will, henceforth, be an important factor in the public health, the physical and mental hygiene of modern societies. What kinds of countryside, plant, equipment, and activities are conducive to repose without boredom? Vacations should be considered first of all as a broad means of prevention and treatment of the "aggressions" committed against man by the noise, tumult, and tension and cares of modern society.

[13] The two thousand rural refuges provide about ten thousand beds. mostly on farms.

A policy of systematic public education could be worked out after cooperative research by sociologists, psychologists, and medical experts.

Other vacationers, chiefly the young, are looking not for repose but for escape. They dream of suntans in Capri, hunting in the snows of Kilimanjaro, dancing at the Rio carnival, or living with love in Tahiti. Some are looking for "life at the château," to be served like a king. Others are seeking the Bohemian life where all restraints are gone. Still others dream of wonderlands where everyone can be Alice or the blonde Iseult, Alladin or Tristan, Don Juan or the Prince Charming.

Travel advertising abundantly stimulates this desire for escape, often in quite primitive ways. But it doesn't create the desire, a need as old as the world. In this advertising can be found, in attenuated and degraded form, all the great rhythms that have always excited the imagination of peoples and poets. Vacation occupies a special place, a "concrete utopia" as Raymond calls it (8).

Then everyone acts in a real world but at the same time can project himself into or identify himself with a situation which, during the rest of the year, remains in the realm of dreams. A study of the film content in *Last Vacation* or *August Sunday* would furnish a pertinent analysis of this process.

We should ask ourselves whether vacations are creating an authentic poetry of forms, lines, colors, feelings, and sentiments unknown in the daily routine or, on the contrary, are they an occasion for faking, degrading, or perverting tastes, attitudes, and ideas? To what extent are vacation activities regarded as games without a morrow rather than as serious activities that change the personality in a lasting way? There ought to be research into the influence of various ways of life on vacations and the influence of different types of vacation on daily life.

For some, vacations afford time for the free cultivation of the body or the mind which the work year makes impossible for lack of long periods of freedom. The immense variety of hobbies and amateur pursuits so widespread in our "standardized" era can better be enjoyed on vacation than during the rest of the year. Theatre enthusiasts attend festivals that now number thirty a year. Art lovers haunt museums and exhibitions. Sound and light spectacles improve monuments for the benefit of tourists. Vacation camps for volleyball and mountain-climbing fans are the rage.

There are not enough summer courses for lovers of art, music, and theater to satisfy the demand. From this standpoint, a special study of the growth in England and the United States of vacation camps with cultural purposes would be worth making. In this area, France could well make use of vacations to bring together amateurs of all sorts who are looking for companionship with those sharing the same interest. This kind of vacation lodge or camp so far occupies only a small place in our country's tourism.

We should stress that, in any case, vacation travel stimulates every kind of curiosity. How are they satisfied? The traveler goes away from home because he wants to discover new countries. Varagnac has shown that vacations are a fine time for city dwellers to get to know country people (21). There can develop either an interpenetration of education and information or a reinforcement of mutual misunderstanding and hostility. Vacation trips let Frenchman from one area become acquainted with those from another.

Some successful efforts at developing knowledge about France, especially among the young, have been undertaken: visits, interviews, sharing people's lives, and the like. Other efforts on the contrary (and the most numerous) involve only the most conventional tableau of each region with its folkloristic specialties, customs, costumes, and dances "cooked up" solely for the benefit of tourists.[14]

The vacation trips can promote mutual understanding between people of different nations; such contacts, however, are often

[14] Cf. Raymond's research on tourism as a system of images.

inadequate to produce a real exchange. Some preparation is needed. Ignorance of foreign ways may cause these meetings to produce negative results,[15] as Otto Klineberg's research into the role of exchanges in international understanding has shown (22).

It is said that vacations permit different social classes to rub elbows with one another in the same hotel or camp. Some think that the fact people find one another dressed in the most casual fashion helps lower the social barriers. Is such a rapprochement real, and lasting? Some studies we have made seem to give a negative answer. A new kind of social segregation results, often more accentuated than in everyday life, because of prestige spending and fancy activities that emphasize to an even greater extent the differences and the antagonisms among social groups. Tourism can probably help the masses acquire a new culture, but what will it be like? What lasting effect on the standards and the ideas of daily life will it have? These questions will provoke only uncertain and contradictory answers so long as there have not been greater advances in research into the relationship between leisure and popular culture.

[15] More than four million foreign tourists come to France each year, and about 1,300,000 French citizens of all sorts traveled abroad in 1957. Twenty-one per cent were professional people; 19 per cent, employers; 11 per cent, midrange executives; 9 per cent, white-collar employees; and 9 per cent, workers (1).

Chapter 7

Leisure
and the
Movies

Ambiguity in Public Choice

Examination of public attitudes toward the movies will lead us to the same conclusions. In France, the film public has already been the subject of numerous statistical studies, the latest of which have been collected in a book by Jacques Durand (1). They tell us that the movie industry, contrary to what the newspapers sometimes say, is not as important as the automobile or the petroleum industries. In France, it is seventy-sixth on the list of industries (in the United States, forty-fifth). We also learn that in spite of René Clair, Jean Renoir, Louis Malle, Alain Resnais, and others, French people go to the movies on the average of eight times a year, which puts France twentieth on the world list.[1]

Investigation tells us that the quarrels over public taste between

[1] Far behind Israel (38), Costa Rica (30), England (29), and the United States (22), on the same rung as Norway, Czechoslovakia, and Cyprus. In 1954, 65 per cent of the French people went to the movies (30 per cent of them once or more a month). After age twenty-five attendance drops off progressively until old age. If one omits the impoverished, it is a fact the lower-income people go to the movies more frequently than the middle classes; women, contrary to what some would think, go less often than men.

pessimists and optimists are quite in vain. Public taste is basically ambiguous. It has been improving, however, since before the war. Today, the biggest receipts generally are earned by the best-known films—by that 10 per cent of the production that the critics praise. But the votes don't go automatically either to the best or the worse of the 10 per cent; sometimes they go elsewhere. In 1954, the highest box-office receipts were earned by *Salaire de la Peur,* followed by *Porte des Lilas, Si Versailles m'était conté, Gervaise,* and *Napoléon.* Among foreign films, *Sissi* broke all records. But *La Strada* and *On the Beach* were not far behind. Mere mention of these titles shows how ambiguous the public's choices are.

All this economic and sociological information gathered through investigation lays an objective foundation for thinking about the movies. It would also be interesting to find out by experiment what attitudes go with such differing or contradictory choices. What is their structure? How do attitudes vary according to societies, classes, groups, or in the same individual? Under what conditions and by what process do types of attitudes and levels of expectation change?

Probably thinking of the partial, formal and static character of current empirical sociology and of the overmetaphysical character of the current theoretical sociology of the film, a UNESCO expert, W. D. Wall, wrote to the International Film Congress of 1955: "A recent bibliography lists a few more than 600 titles of works, lectures, and articles dealing with the influence of the cinema. We are, nevertheless, still as far from an exhaustive understanding of the spectator's psychology and of film production as we are from a sociology of the cinema" (3).

While awaiting the happy results of a marriage between the most subtle theory and the most rigorous experimental analysis, we shall limit ourselves to offering some empirical data about movie leisure as actually experienced.

It is important for the creator and the educator to know about the different cultural levels of the consumers of movie leisure. This is the way to measure the gap between the levels observed and the levels hoped for by those who are striving to develop the cinematographic culture of the public. We are going to study the cinema, starting with a study of motivation (Why do you go to the movies?) and a study of ideal models (What do you expect from a good film?), carried out among the heads of family in Annecy.

We should emphasize the limits of this type of inquiry. We know, in fact, that the answers reflect only the conscious motivations, those approved by the prevailing moral standards, and that all these answers can and must be interpreted in the light of theories of alienation and frustration. In addition, the results are incomplete. Having no other French sources for dealing with this problem of the movies, we have, nevertheless, decided this first glimpse may not be altogether useless.

Release, Escape, Education

In Annecy, movie attendance is about the same as the average in French cities; about 75 per cent of the inhabitants go to the movies at least once; a third of these 75 per cent once or more each month.[2]

A. The reasons given by movie-goers for their attendance are primarily negative; they are seeking a release. The movies are merely a way to break the monotony, to shed the daily routine, "to put one's mind to other things." The movie spectator does not even feel he has to be on time; one engineer admits preferring the movies to the theater, "less because of taste than because the movies open up more possibilities. You can go even after the show has started." About 13 per cent of the answers give this kind of reason.

Movie-going is not experienced as if it were a dream foreign to daily life. On the contrary, it is in permanent competition with

[2] Those who attend the least are the workers, heads of companies, and the craftsmen (56 per cent of the latter never or very rarely go). Those who go the most often are executives and professionals.

one's responsibilities. The responsibilities most often mentioned are those to the family. "I rarely go to the movies. I can't go out because of the children, and I won't go alone," says one worker. Others go to the movies not to see a film but to accompany their wives. "I go to the movies because my wife takes me, otherwise they don't interest me much." The pressure of family responsibility often may lead to a rejection of all movie-going. "The movies? I'm thinking of my new apartment and the furniture I'm making," one citizen who doesn't go to the movies told us. Some even consider the movies as a wholly unacceptable antithesis to their family responsibilities: "Since the death of my wife, I never go to the movies any more."

The movies are in competition not only with family responsibilities but also with other forms of leisure. We found some individuals who exclude all but one type of leisure activity. "I don't go to the movies. I just go bowling. It's quieter there," says a twenty-nine-year-old worker. "Since he's gone wild over fishing, he doesn't go to the movies any more," explains the wife of a thirty-year-old employee. "I'd rather engage in sports than be a spectator at the movies," declares an active small businessman of twenty-eight. Conversely, the movies may be preferred over all other activities, such as the theater, for example, with which comparisons abound in all social groups, often more in favor of the first than of the second. "The movies are easier to figure out. The action is more realistic. In the theater you have to pay closer attention." Or "I like the movies better. They aren't as lifelike, but they move faster," says a forty-year-old worker, in about the same words as a forty-eight-year-old woman baker.

B. Our city folk are expecting not only a release but a pastime when they go to the movies. Their expectations are as numerous and varied as are the functions of leisure activities themselves. Not everyone goes to a movie theater as they go to a cathedral. For 23 per cent, the movies are simply a way to pass the time, having about the same significance as other pastimes. "I go when I haven't anything to do on Sunday," says a technician aged thirty. This simple relaxation brings satisfaction without requiring any effort at understanding or thinking. "For me it's simple amusement; I don't like films that are too complicated," says a worker of twenty-seven. And a clerk adds: "I don't remember a thing about the films I like. I just watch them for the fun of it."

Sometimes this satisfaction would resemble sleeping, if it weren't for the action in the films. We ran across this particular reaction to *War and Peace* when a thirty-five-year-old worker said: "I liked *War and Peace* a lot. I like movies where there is plenty of action. If the film isn't full of action, I fall asleep."

C. The largest number of persons interrogated (40 per cent) are looking for an *imaginary life* in the movies. Such people have a richer and sharper sense of why they go to the show. They are looking in the film for the pleasures of imaginary situations. They hope to feel emotions and experience feelings. The movies make it possible for everyone to project and identify himself—each one has the power to "visualize dreams." Each one can be who he believes he is, who he doesn't dare to be, who he desires to be. The movies let everyone satisfy this "double" which is part of his semi-imaginary reality.

In our inquiry, we found the themes of love, eroticism, luxury, battle, adventure, and laughter were most appreciated. Yet we were struck by the fact that the most numerous votes, one out of five, went to movies that are gay. *Mr. Hulot's Holiday* is often mentioned. The star best remembered is neither Brigitte Bardot nor Jean Gabin, but Fernandel. "I don't like seeing sad movies. Life is sad enough as it is." Or "At a movie I expect to laugh, because you don't have much chance to laugh," says a mechanic. "I have strong preferences for funny, very funny films," reports a businessman. Executives and intellectuals especially appreciate Charlie Chaplin. What Lefebvre calls the inverse image of daily life is what seems most sought after by this public.

D. The function of the movies is not merely to amuse. About

24 per cent of the replies indicate that for these persons the movies are primarily a source of information—"to become better informed," "to educate myself," "to think about problems," "I like what is lived, what is true." A twenty-five-year-old worker says: "All I remember are the documentaries and the newsreels." A fifty-year-old clerk says "Fiction leaves me cold." "I like documentaries like the *World of Silence,*" says a young worker. For these people, thanks to the movies, reality surpasses fiction.

What Do You Expect from a Good Film?

We already have better measurements of the wide variations in motivation of people attending the movies. To complete and deepen our analysis, by approaching it from a quite different viewpoint, we have tried to understand the ideal models that guide the spectator in his appreciation of a good film.

The question we asked, although directed to works of fiction in general, in fact brought us information primarily about the movies. These responses follow.[3]

A small number of movie-goiers (12 per cent) want the film to be "beautiful" and well played. What spoils their film enjoyment beyond all else is vulgarity. "The hardest thing to find," says a thirty-five-year-old clerk, "is an amusing film that makes you laugh and is not vulgar." He likes Chaplin and Fernandel in *Angèle.* "I want feeling, art, and beauty. I loathe vulgarity," says a thirty-year-old woman employee, who very much liked *The Ransom of Fear.* Fakery is as much disliked as vulgarity. "I don't like feelings or situations that are too conventional and artificial" (a twenty-nine-year-old worker). Also, for the public, the actor often is more important than the hero or the heroine of the scenario. "The only thing I remember about *Gervaise* was that Maria Schell played to perfection."

[3] The total percentage is 95. Five per cent did not concern our subject.

Another 18 per cent primarily demand that a film present a "true" picture of life; they insist on reality, objectivity, and realism in the production. In support of this thesis are these quite diverse examples. Concerning documentary films: "I remember only the documentaries and the newsreels. Fiction doesn't interest me. I like studies of reality" (a fifty-year-old clerk). As to biographical films: "I like what is lived, what is true," says a forty-five-year-old worker who admired *Moulin Rouge* because it evoked the life of Toulouse-Lautrec. In films on social activities, a sixty-year-old businessman likes things that are experienced in reality, such as in *The Blue Veil*. As for sport films, a twenty-nine-year-old worker says: "I don't like the movies much, except the documentaries on sports." Last, concerning film-reporting: "What we are looking for is what increases our knowledge, especially reporting from abroad . . . a film that can show us the complex life on different social levels and that shows there are honest, decent people everywhere," states a worker.

The majority of replies (65 per cent), however, stress not the quality of the film nor its faithfulness to reality, but interest in the content (theme or subject) dealt with by the film. On this point, the results of inquiry into the qualities the ideal film should have cross-checked almost precisely with the results of the preceding study. Comedies come out ahead. Those favoring them are equal to the total number favoring combat, action, and adventure (15 per cent altogether). The themes of love and sentiment come next. It is worth stressing that about one fourth expect the film to evoke an ennobling picture of life. If it is realistic, it should not be "too black." If it is true, it should be "moral." It should have a social and human sense. Most examples reveal a need of identifying oneself with a strong and generous hero. A clerk says: "I liked *Spotlights.* There was magnificent courage in that film." If a twenty-nine-year-old worker liked *The Battle of the Rails,* above all others, it was because in it "you saw people sacrificing themselves." The memories that remain longest are those of generous exploits and lofty deeds. "I remember a scene from *The Heroes Are Tired* where the two aviators come face to face. . . ." The most-mentioned scenes are the bits of gallantry in *Les Misérables* and *Notre Dame de Paris.*

This need for greatness can take many a form. *"Napoléon* thrilled me because he had ambition," says a twenty-six-year-old clerk. "I take great satisfaction in the triumph of a man's will in conflicts that set him against other men," says a thirty-seven-year-old employee. Pierre Fresnay is admired in his roles. "He's a man who stands up and fights back." The same for the life of Dr. Schweitzer, who is admired "for the work he has done in Black Africa." "He has a strong, generous personality," says a twenty-five-year-old clerk. These are but few of many examples. They all converge on exaltation of the "hero double" who lies dormant within a great number of moviegoers.

What tentative conclusions can be drawn from this investigation of motivations and models? It reveals that the meanings of a movie experienced by the public are as diverse as the functions of leisure and as ambiguous as its content. It is not enough to assert that the movies are part of the daily life of our times. Movie attendance must be studied in the light of the problematics of leisure and responsibility.

The influence of the cinema should be analyzed in terms of its relationships with both family and social leisure and responsibility. Edgar Morin correctly insists on the difference between reality and the image of reality (4). The cinema always stresses the charm of the image. Image of what? The films produced by Meliès and by Lumière are perhaps similar in formal outline, but they differ fundamentally from the viewpoint of *content.* Morin also properly stresses the importance of the imaginary man and of the "double"; yet there are fundamental differences in an identification with Scarface and one with Pasteur, with Don Juan or with Dr. Schweitzer, even when the same individual identifies himself with different or opposite heroes one after the other. Still, from our point of view, there is no possible confusion between those who attach the highest importance to the cinematographic art and those who are indifferent to vulgarity and fakery. This is not a matter of defending a morality or an esthetic—but of insisting on the variety of concrete functions of movie leisure and on the necessity of making distinctions among the different cultural levels of public participation.

Film research has given rise to elaborate philosophical, moral, esthetic, psychological, and sociological theories. In the manner of Balzac, Morin proposes a brilliant synthesis in an essay both anthropological and sociological in nature (4). He demonstrates that it is the film, more than the airplane, "that has been sent ever higher toward a dream heaven, toward an infinity of 'stars' bathed in music, peopled with adorable and demoniac personages, escaping from daily life instead of being its servant and its mirror as originally intended." He emphasizes the charm of the image and its magic power; he makes the cinematographic attitude analogous to an "awakened dream." In a penetrating way, he analyzes the mechanisms of projection and identification connected with the spectator type of participation. He boldly reconciles this modern form of participation with the system of participation in archaic societies. In brief, he insists on all aspects of the "imaginary man" discovered by the movies. Yet he points also to the works of those who have emphasized the rationality of the film.

"In the languages of the film appear the laws and rhythms of ideation (René and Bianca Zazzo), the eloquence of speech (Georges Cohen Séat), a logical system (Pierre Francastel), the movement of conceptual thought (Henri Bergson)." Edgar Morin is trying to develop a synthesis of ideas about rationality and magic. Unquestionably, all these theories have enriched knowledge of both cinema and man. Anthropology gives a doctrinal basis for the intuitive awareness in movie criticism started thirty years ago by L. Moussinac and developed with finesse by critics such as André

Bazin (5). Anthropology already plays a role in movie criticism that it has scarcely yet assumed in literary criticism.[4]

If one wants to achieve a better understanding of the various functions of the cinema and the different levels of culture as experienced by the masses, however, one may ask if present-day analyses, including the sociology of the cinema, are really adapted to the subjects.

In spite of the exhortations of film makers, critics, and educators, the sociology of the cinema, at least in France, has not succeeded in identifying the criteria for classifying the contents and the forms of the cinema art. What are the criteria of quality at various social levels? This question has both a theoretical and a practical interest of the highest importance. Analysis of the film spectacle, however interesting it may be, provides only hypotheses that are too general to provide an empirical study of the relationship between a film production and a public. How are the different levels of cinema culture to be identified? How does this cinema culture become integrated within the general culture? How is this integration differentiated according to age levels, sex, class, and so forth? Is it increasing or decreasing according to differences in content and in conditions of reception? The answers to these questions would first require that the sociology of the cinema, without abandoning its remarkable efforts in theoretical thinking, begin worrying more about the exact nature of this thinking at the precise level of the attitudes of the spectators themselves. In order better to know the conditions for advancing cinema culture among the masses, a dynamic and experimental sociology, of active behaviors, must replace the static and analytical sociology of average behaviors. In the complex bundle of reactions produced by the sociocultural situation, how is the problem of increasing these active attitudes faced by each society, social group, and individual?

In connection with these attitudes, how do we measure the

[4] R. Bastide, "Sociology and Literature Compared," in *Cahiers Internationaux de Sociologie*, PUF 1954.

differences, the time lags, the imbalances between levels of cultures that are typical of the average attitudes in the various groups. Finally, how may we observe experimentally the way in which the reactive attitudes of the public can be improved by the action of social organizations, groups and leaders? From our point of view, these would be the most important questions to ask.

Chapter 8

Leisure
and
Television

M ANY INTELLECTUALS CONSIDER TELEVISION IN THE SAME WAY they consider the cinema, and fail to apply to it the leisure standards to which it is entitled. They analyze the content of the programs from the point of view of an absolute concept of culture with a capital C. When one looks for the basis of this more or less explicit concept, it is found in the system of values and ideas bestowed upon them during their university studies. By comparison with this "high culture," the content of television programs seems inferior (6). From this perspective, any entertainment culture is labeled more or less "decadent."

Huizinga has long criticized this approach. As early as 1930, he accused university culture, with its Greco-Hebraic-Latin origins, of being a stranger to the values of play (7). More recently, Leo Lowenthal, speaking out against the distinction between "high culture" and popular culture, remarked that the first problem is how to integrate entertainment with culture (8).

Long before the advent of "mass culture," entertainment had been seized upon by the authentic spokesmen for culture. On the morrow of the Renaissance, Montaigne was defending escapism against the champions of the culture of the Middle Ages. Voltaire praised entertainment that Pascal condemned as an obstacle to spiritual life. In the midnineteenth century writers were opposing the excesses of man-centered art with a doctrine of art for art's sake. All these criticisms take on new strength in a civilization where the masses have access to a new form of culture, through leisure. So we should be on guard against this doubtful point of view of "high culture" regarding television. It is useless insofar as it is exacting, but it is debatable because of its implied value judgments, and it is utterly foreign to the conditions under which popular culture works.

We are going to study television as a leisure phenomenon that is becoming common to all classes and social categories.[1] For all viewers, watching television is a free-time occupation. In large measure, this fact determines what the public expects from the content of the telecasts. But it is a complex expectation, representing both a desire for escape and for participation, for entertainment and for conformity, for information and for self-education. It is dominated by values and patterns that permit understanding and appreciation of the content of televised culture as well as study of its variations and contradictions and ways of avoiding them. We shall look at the television audience, at the reactions of the public to TV content, and at the effects of TV on other forms of leisure. The French data we are using are very limited. In closing, we shall raise the most important questions that we do not yet have the means to deal with.

The information we can provide comes from several sources and the results are incomplete. The sources presently available for this research in France (May, 1960) are debatable from several standpoints. We drew our information from the survey conducted by Radio Television Française (RTF) during the first half of 1959. This survey was made in three different ways: by written question-

[1] Since writing this book, there have appeared two very good research works by Hilde T. Himmelweit and Wilbur Schramm (1959 and 1960) on television and children. These studies have a very broad import and are devoted to the phenomena we are analyzing.

naire, by interviews in the home, and by telephone calls. During this period, 700 interviews took place, 13,700 telephone calls were made, and 9,000 questionnaires were sent through the mails. Three thousand questionnaires were filled out and returned. We have made use of the results of a scrutiny of these questionnaires.[2]

As a precaution, we have retained only those that were cross checked with results from two other sources. We will compare this data with those from nationwide RTF surveys made in 1957 and 1955, as well as those we were able to collect in 1954 in fifteen villages in the Aisne Department (9). This was a slightly different experiment, since the people of these townships had created tele-clubs; watching TV was a collective, not a family affair. The majority of the TV audience were small farmers. We had no way to make a serious differential study of these results. In general we limited ourselves to throwing light on the *most widespread reactions of the whole public*.

The approximate socio-occupational composition of our sample follows. According to the public relations department of the RTF, it corresponds almost exactly with the current owners of TV sets.

Higher executives	2%
Professionals and industrialists	16%
Middle-range executives	11%
Craftsmen and small businessmen	24%
Workers	9%
Farmers and farm workers	4%
Retired employees	9%
Women without occupation	9%
Unidentified	16%
	100%

The questions asked by the RTF in 1959 dealt with the different programs that make up a week of French television. The following

[2] We are greatly obliged to Jean Oulif, director of public relations of the RTF for having furnished us the documents which allowed making the analysis.

table indicates the hourly volume devoted to these programs and gives an indication of the distribution of programs during this period. Weekly program time amounts to about fifty-three hours, much less than in the United States.[3]

Content of a Week's Programs on French Television

1.	Programs for children		6 hours	11.5%
	Education	2 hours		
	Entertainment	4 hours		
2.	Practical programs		1 hour	2
	(cooking, women's			
	magazine)			
3.	Games		2 hours	4
4.	Entertainment		15.5 hours	29
	(variety shows, circuses,			
	songs, minor comedies)	10 hours		
	Serial stories	2 hours		
	Sports	3.5 hours		
5.	Productions		7.45 hours	15
	Films	2 hours		
	Theater	3 hours		
	Classical and			
	modern music	1 hour		
	Arts and letters	1.45 hours		
6.	News		15.5 hours	29
	Paris Club Journal	13.5 hours		
	News Magazine	2 hours		
7.	Documentaries and		3 hours	6
	reportages	2.5 hours		
	Interviews and			
	debates	0.5 hour		
8.	Religious programs		2 hours	4
			about 53 hours	100%

As shown in the table, France spends fifteen and one half hours on entertainment programs—29 per cent—while similar programs

[3] Cf. Evelyne Sullerot, "Television in the USA and Great Britain," *Bulletin of CEGMAS*, No. 1, 1960.

in the United States, depending on the station, amount to from 60 to 75 per cent of the total (10). The reactions of the public to these programs are measured by two criteria: on the one hand, by the size of the audience, on the other by the rating or index of satisfaction. The rating is calculated on the basis of statements about the program given by the viewers themselves. A rating below 35 is considered bad, between 35 and 50 mediocre, from 50 to 65 good, 65 to 80 very good, and above 80 greatly appreciated and deemed excellent.

Time Spent Watching TV

It is widely assumed that TV is a form of tyranny and that programming in most cases is too long. Is this well founded or not? Inquiries made in the United States do not all give the same results. According to Rolf Meyersohn, the American citizen watches his set on the average of eighteen hours a week (12). This is obviously a very high figure, yet others insist that individuals may sit before their sets four or five hours a day (12). In France, most people watch TV on the average of sixteen hours a week, or a little over two hours a day.

In this connection, we should point out that the time per week not devoted to work or sleep is about sixty hours, and for the majority of city people leisure time amounts to nearly twenty-five hours. If we hold to these figures, the amount of time spent watching TV does seem relatively high, even in France.

If, however, the situation in America is compared with that in France, one may ask if the French televiewer doesn't feel himself at a disadvantage. To the question "Would you like more hours of television?" 80 per cent of the public indicated they were satisfied, while only 18 per cent wanted more.

Furthermore, the time spent watching TV seems to decrease after one has owned a set for a long time. One third of the Frenchmen who have owned a set since 1955 stated in 1957 that they were watching the programs less frequently. Half the public were watching TV about the same amount of time. In the United States, Leo Bogart notes the same tendency, stating that some of the viewers were spending less time watching TV. Yet this general assertion has but a limited interest. Survey results emphasize great differences in length of time spent watching TV, according to different groups in the public. Bogart stresses that in the United States the length of time varies according to educational level, between one hour and twenty minutes to eight hours a day.

One of the arguments echoed and re-echoed to prove the tyranny of television is the trouble it causes with sleeping and eating habits. It is true that many people in France, as in the United States, acknowledge that they go to bed later once they own a television set. French inquiries in 1959 indicated, however, that from 60 to 80 per cent of the people are abed at 10: 30 P.M.

What happens at meal time? Between noon and 1: 30 P.M. the percentage of viewers does not exceed 30 per cent of the public. In the evening, it appears that the majority of people eat before looking at TV and at eight o'clock the percentage of viewers suddenly jumps from 40 to 75 per cent and after 10: 30 to 85 per cent.

Along the same lines, it is sometimes said that TV has restrictive effects on family outings. Sunday mornings, it is true, the programs are essentially religious. The audience amounts to barely one third of the public. But Sunday afternoon, when the programs are aimed at everybody, the number of viewers, varying by seasons, is from 30 per cent in winter to 20 per cent in summer (not counting vacation periods). None of these figures take account of a most important factor: the continuity and discontinuity of viewing. TV watching can be continuous or intermittent, and its variations depend on both the audience and the programs. In other words, the amount of time spent viewing does not indicate the type of viewing. The different attitudes that can be counted among persons watching the same program give an idea of the complexity of the problem.

Thus, TV can be considered a conversational prop, an accompaniment, or simply background noise. For example, some investigations in Great Britain found out that many women knit or sew while watching TV (13). The hours of attentive viewing probably do not coincide with the number of hours the set is turned on. In estimating the hours spent viewing TV, we must undertake a study of the kinds of viewing that correspond to the different attitudes.

Reactions to Program Content

It is widely accepted that the content of TV programs is basically aimed at entertaining the public. The RTF slogan "To entertain, to inform, to teach" gives expression to more ambitious goals. Taking this into account, what are the public reactions to the various programs fitting into this over-all purpose?

ENTERTAINMENT

About one third of the program time consists of variety shows, and they are the most preferred programs. This preference is as obvious in the answers to the nation-wide RTF survey as in the sample taken from rural tele-clubs. Theatrical plays, nevertheless, enjoy as great success as do the variety programs.

Program enjoyment, calculated according to the ratings, seems to indicate a great sensitivity in taste. In 1957, *Music Hall Parade*, produced by Gilles Margaritis, was watched by 94 per cent of the TV viewers and its rating was "excellent" (92). In 1959, the audience was slightly smaller—91 per cent—and the rating was "very good" (78). *Thirty-six Candles*, the great variety show produced by Jean Nohain, was regularly watched by 99 per cent of the viewers, who gave it a rating of excellent (80). Two years later, in 1959, the program had changed its title but very little of its content. It was being watched by only 78 per cent of the public and the rating was "good" (56).

Can these slight differences in "consumption" be attributed to a development in taste or to an eventual saturation with a program become too familiar, however fine and well polished it might be? An important question, but the existing data are too fragile to permit a reply.

In this same area, games like *Tele-Match* or *Big Prize* were and are followed by an audience varying between 80 and 90 per cent, with a rating of "good" or "very good," from 40 to 70. Sports reporting is equally well appreciated. Given the success of retransmissions of certain great games, for example, one may ask if the public wouldn't like to see more sports programs. It would appear that for a large proportion (70 per cent) of them, the number of hours devoted to sports is enough. Only 17 per cent would like more, 13 per cent less. These figures show that the mass of our people are satisfied with the sports programs offered, yet do not want sports to supplant other programs. One important fact should be stressed, however: TV plays the role of discoverer in the sports world. Many viewers, intellectuals and writers such as François Mauriac, have discovered through TV how interesting sports competition is.

Reactions to Productions

All films, plays, and exhibitions are obviously not *chefs-d'oeuvres*. RTF, nonetheless, does make an effort to put the public in contact with great works. For many viewers, TV is primarily a home movie. This hypothesis has been amply confirmed by a survey carried out in the rural areas of the Aisne Department. This audience plainly preferred good films to average or mediocre films; film titles they preferred are noteworthy: *The Battle of the Rails, July Rendezvous, Manon, Holiday, The Pastoral Symphony,* for example.

Documentaries, so frequently sacrificed in a commercial theater, rank among the stars on TV. The RTF survey in 1957 produced highly interesting results in this respect. Films stand sixth in the order of public preferences. Twenty-seven per cent prefer variety shows, 27 per cent theatrical productions, 7 per cent lectures or debates, 5 per cent documentaries, and only 3 per cent great films.

One reason for the lack of enthusiasm shown for the film is the fact that TV shows only films at least five years old. Though their value remains the same, the desire to see them can be blunted with the passage of time. By contrast, the possibility of making contact with reporters, explorers, and lecturers is altogether a new factor and one of the positive aspects of TV. It has been able to familiarize the public with material almost unknown to them.

According to this survey, the theater occupies absolutely first place in public preference. A rather curious phenomenon stands out in this respect in the study of rural areas: The longer the viewer has owned his set the greater value theater has for him. If, in the first period of ownership, TV represents movies at home, in the next period it is identified with the theater. The reaction of the French public to theatrical programs is particularly lively. When the plays are judged to be bad, the reactions set forth in letters from viewers are relatively more numerous and sharper than for other kinds of programs.

Replies to another question made this marked preference for the theater appear plainly. The RTF tried to find out the public's wishes for programming on Saturday evening. Only 2 per cent said they didn't care; 4 per cent asked for news reports; 17 per cent wanted variety shows; 27 per cent favored films; and 35 per cent asked for theatrical productions. Plays transmitted by TV obviously vary greatly in nature. Does the public appreciate plays commonly considered "easy" or those deemed "difficult"? The rural audience we interrogated clearly chose difficult plays. In 1954, they listed the following, in this order: *Volpone, The Annunciation of the Virgin Mary,* and *Liliom.* A nationwide survey in the same period confirmed this to be the general public judgment. Other ratings of easier plays are equally excellent, so it is hard to draw conclusions.

The recent presentation of *Andromaque* was a success, however, if we can judge by the unusually enthusiastic mail sent to the RTF as well as by the results of a random national survey by telephone and home visit the same day and the day after.

INFORMATION

The televised newspaper answers in the highest degree TV's need to be informative. If a minority of viewers accuse the news programs of not being objective enough, 88 to 96 per cent, depending on where they live, follow the news bulletins regularly and give them ratings of "good" and "very good" (61 to 74). In rural areas, people regret the fact that the debates in the Chamber of Deputies are not televised.

News coverage and social themes are also much appreciated, by the rural public as well as by the public in general. Seventy-three per cent of the public expressed satisfaction with reports on the Renault factories and Orly Airport. At the present time, *Five Columns on the Front Page*, a monthly program devoted to a number of current topics, is also having a great success. *Night and Fog*, a film by Resnais on concentration camps, although shown at a late hour (11:15 P.M.) following the news, was seen by 36 per cent of the public, an exceptional number for this sort of a program.

Reports on distant countries, such as *Voyage Without Passport*, are not only appreciated but demanded. In 1954, 67 per cent of the viewers of a national sample wanted to see more telecasts of this kind. Documentaries, often composed of various film strips, dealing with a subject or an idea, such as the *Life of Animals*, have a faithful following. In rural areas, this kind of program is as highly esteemed as the great fiction films. National surveys confirm the general approval.

EDUCATION

The line of demarcation between information and education is often most difficult to draw. Some fields make easy the spreading of knowledge through TV, for instance geography. The *Explorer's Magazine* enjoys a wide audience. While it entertains, it also informs and instructs. Likewise, the scientific programs of Etienne Lalou are very favorably received. *Science Today* attempts to introduce the public to the various questions raised by physics, chemistry, geology, biology, and so forth. In 1959, these were watched, depending on the region, by 57 per cent in the southwest, and by 84 per cent of the public at large, with a rating of "very good" (64 to 74). By contrast with the case of sports reporting, the public would like to see more programs of this kind. In fact, in 1959, only 11 per cent of the public disliked these programs and wanted fewer of them. Fifty per cent were satisfied and wanted to keep the status quo, and 37 per cent wanted to see more of them.

As far as music and literature are concerned, there are too few indications to permit any conclusions. The weekly musical program *Great Performers* is watched by only 30 per cent of the public with a rating of "good" (55). Still, this program comes toward the end of the evening and many viewers are already in bed. By contrast, on one occasion, 80 per cent of the people watched a concert given by the great RTF orchestra and gave it a rating of "excellent" (82).

Literary education is offered on *Readings for Everybody,* a program centered not on the work but on the author, who is present. It has a very special viewpoint and is followed by 26 to 32 per cent of the public. Among cultivated persons, the quality of the interviews is highly regarded. It enlarges the public for literary culture. Still, the rural public finds nothing interesting in it and the majority of the people is not reached by it. Is TV incapable of making literary culture penetrate the public at large? At the present time, an answer would be unwise. What kind of results would be obtained, for example, by a literary program along the lines of the popular book clubs, choosing a book in terms of a problem facing civilization or man today, presenting a dramatization of the text with the help of good actors, accompanied by discussion with audience participation?

This brief account of the different programs permits us to conclude that there is a great *variety* of themes dealt with. This televised culture furnished the public is heterogenous, respecting the different functions of leisure. In any case, it would be an error to assert that the public always prefers "easy" material to the more difficult (or the reverse). Ranging over the public's reaction to French TV programs, it would be difficult to distinguish categorically between a lesser culture for the masses and a higher culture for the élite.

Effects of TV on Other Forms of Leisure

Anglo-Saxon and French surveys agree on the negative effect of TV on other forms of leisure. The viewer goes out less, goes to fewer movies and plays, reads fewer newspapers and books, and so on.

But Meyersohn remarks that the present state of research does not authorize drawing any conclusions (12). In fact, what is the exact extent of these phenomena? How do they vary according to social groups? What is their significance for the way leisure is enjoyed, for the way of life or culture? A closer study makes one more sensitive to the nuances.

CINEMA

Insofar as the influence of TV on movie attendance is concerned, the trends observed in the United States and Great Britain are similar to those in France. In 1959, 80 per cent of the TV viewers in our country went to the movies less than and 19 per cent as much as before. Movie attendance declined from 411 million in 1957 to 352 million in 1959. During this period, the number of TV sets purchased rose from 683,700 to 1,368,000. We know about the serious crisis that shook Hollywood during those years and the fact that the number of American moviegoers dropped by 50 per cent between 1946 and 1959.

In the long run, however, it doesn't seem likely that the movies will be handicapped by the advent of television. In the first place, TV has brought the movies to a large number of individuals— country people, for example, who had little familiarity with moving pictures discovered them through TV (40 per cent of the French in 1958 had never gone to the movies). Film classics which used to be known primarily to the limited audiences of ciné-clubs are now shown to the people at large on TV. The movies, for their part, stimulated by this competition, had to reinvent the cinema, so to speak, and discover new forms for it. The perfecting of color films and the wide screen were technical ways to fight TV competition. In a word, this rivalry seems to have had a stimulating effect without in any way eliminating the specific features of either medium.

RADIO

At first glance, radio appears as the second major victim of TV. But here again, we believe that radio may perhaps be starting to expand in an entirely new way. In France, for the time being, the figures are rather pessimistic. One third of TV viewers no longer use their radios at all, and two thirds use theirs less—half of them were not listening more than a half hour a day in 1959. In 1948, Bogart noted that the Americans who owned a TV set listened to the radio two hours a day, while non-TV-owners listened four and one half hours a day. But examination of these few figures does not permit a valid interpretation. The functions of radio have evolved in recent years, and the advent of TV perhaps has helped hasten the change in the meaning of radio in our daily life. TV is essentially leisure activity for the family and for friends, while radio-listening tends increasingly to become an activity for individuals. The increase in second radio sets in the family has been facilitated by the relatively low cost of the new transistors. This is evidence of the new function of radio—to play an accompanying role, even becoming a way of initiating some other leisure activity during "lost" time or during the time between two other activities.

The sound-background of the radio is highly desirable to the housewife while she's doing her housework, and it extends the leisure life of the man on his way to work, thanks to the car radio. In addition, at the present time, TV programs are telecast intermittently while several radio chains broadcast practically without interruption. In France, as in the United States, the two kinds of programs most listened to are news and music.

SPORTS

Let us first distinguish between watching a sports event and actual participation in a sport, whether for recreation or in competition. Attendance at sports events is dropping rapidly. There is no doubt that in the United States the situation is worrying the promoters of these events. The example of boxing is the perfect illustration. Box office receipts at the major bouts have dropped off appreciably; the managers have recouped this loss by demanding enormous fees for the TV rights. The total of these fees is considerably greater than the box-office receipts at one of the biggest bouts in Madison Square Garden.

The meetings preparing the Olympic Games Committee of 1960 show how much sports managers feel threatened by the popularity of TV. This committee tried to impose a very high fee on the coverage by various TV networks, both East and West. The networks first offered 75 million lire; then, faced with the Olympic Committee's rejection, they offered 150 million lire. After hard bargaining, an agreement was reached finally.

The practice of sports not only doesn't appear to suffer from TV but in some cases benefits by becoming more widely known. The managers of the French Rugby Association report that telecasts of the great national and international matches is an effective means of propaganda for this sport. They base their opinion on the growing number of licenses being sought; these currently amount to about five thousand a year. This same phenomenon has occurred in Great Britain. In 1954, during the European athletic championship, we heard an English coachman credit TV athletic programs with a regrowth in interest in athletic sports among young Englishmen.

THEATER

Like the movies, the theater suffered certain counterblows from the popularity of TV. Here again, a pessimistic judgment may be premature. It is true that in 1959, 63 per cent of French TV viewers reported they were going less frequently to the theaters and 35 per cent of them were going as often. But in the United States, it has been found that the change in habits after purchase of a TV set does not last very long and that after a few years the TV viewer tends to return to his former activities (7). Still, the number who attend the theater regularly is rather small, and for the greatest number the only theater is television itself. Even in the United States, according to Bogart, variety shows seem to be giving way to dramas and situation comedies.

OUTDOOR ACTIVITIES

Television has had no significant effect on the pleasures of outings and trips. We have already seen that few viewers are sitting before their sets on Sunday afternoon. The taste for weekend auto trips is still increasing, and purchase of a TV set is in no way competitive with the desire to own a car and take the family for a drive on Sunday.

INDOOR ACTIVITIES

In the daily life at home, we can distinguish between those domestic activities that require manual dexterity and those relationships based on conversation. Inquiries made by the BBC show that in Great Britain indulgence in hobbies is highly stabilized. In the United States, the rise of the do-it-yourself market parallels the purchase of TV sets. Figures obtained in France indicate a slightly opposite trend, but available statistics are too generalized at present to permit drawing a definitive conclusion. In 1959, 23 per cent of the TV viewers, men and women, stated that they were puttering around or sewing less since they had television. But what kinds of work had they given up?

They say that "television kills conversation." Of course, it may seem that people are talking less, but conversation is difficult to measure; and we don't really know what used to be the real extent of conversation. Furthermore, we don't know what the content of this conversation amounted to. The TV program enlarges the family horizon and at the same time, no doubt, stimulates broader conversational topics. In any case, joint participation in the same activity, such as watching TV, can improve communication between parents and children. It can also lead to conflicts over the choice of programs and the turning off of the set. For the moment, we have no serious data on the different subjects of conversation as affected by television.

READING

All the Anglo-Saxon and French opinion surveys emphasize that TV viewers show a certain disenchantment with reading. The 1959 survey in France showed that 3 per cent of the viewers were reading more than before, 49 per cent as much, and 48 per cent less. Are these habits long lasting? In France, we don't yet have information on this point, but we do know that the length of time one owns a TV set is not a negligible factor in the change of habits. Bogart reports that in 1951, 51 per cent of the people who had had a set for less than two years were reading magazines and only 27 per cent were reading books, while 60 per cent of those who had had a set for more than two years were reading magazines and 34 per cent were reading books. These last percentages are about the same as for those who don't own a TV set.

We can't ignore the transformation that has taken place in

magazines and their ever-growing popularity. In the United States in 1946, 94,677,000 copies were sold every week, and in 1955 circulation had almost doubled—166 million copies sold weekly. It was noted that the public no longer expected quite the same content from their newspapers. An editor of *Life* (six million readers in the United States) stated that photographs are larger and the text itself more important. The reader asks for more substantial information in order to deepen or round out his knowledge of a subject, particularly that obtained from fleeting pictures on the TV screens.

Apparently, the existence of TV has not affected daily newspaper reading. In 1959, 17 per cent of the French TV viewers said they supplemented the news received through TV by listening to news bulletins on the radio, but 40 per cent stated they relied on "their customary daily newspaper." In the United States, the circulation of daily newspapers has grown along with the expansion of TV (10).

As we have mentioned, for about half the TV viewers the purchase and the reading of books tends to diminish. This is not a qualitative standard. Here we are approaching a complex question the answers to which may often be contradictory and difficult to interpret.

Certain programs, such as *Readings for All,* according to testimony from bookstores, do stimulate the purchase of books—even though we haven't been able to determine exactly the extent of this influence. Other programs, such as the *Explorer's Magazine,* have also brought about the purchase of books by the tele-clubs. If people read less, perhaps they read better because of the way TV serves as a reader's guide. All these comments are still hypotheses requiring proof.

Has TV definitely revolutionized people's leisure life? Its influence is profound but seemingly ambivalent. Even in the United States, where most programs are dedicated to entertainment, as Bogart has written: "Our world is still the same world, but we experiment with it in a different way."

The present state of research sociology does not permit definitive conclusions about the benefits and the evils of television; we have scarcely even begun to study the effect of television in terms of different program content and different viewing conditions; and on this point we applaud the cautionary appeal issued by Meyersohn: "The many accusations leveled against this mass communication media can neither be confirmed nor refuted in any systematic way . . . up to now we have barely touched upon the major problems of television."

Some Problems

No adequate comparison has yet been made of the public's preferences which would lead to a serious answer to these major questions. We are still practically ignorant of the significance of the public's choices and rejections in real life—culture in terms of categories, environment, or societies. When public opinion surveys indicate general approval, is that approval a sign of real approbation or rather an expression of widespread passivity? The very uniformity of these positive reactions to the most contradictory kinds of material leaves one perplexed. Different audiences from different cultural backgrounds often approve of the same program. But does this approbation derive from the same *aspects* of the production?

For example, in a sports program, a wrestling match displeases some, pleases many. Is it the same thing to all viewers? For whom is it a sport and for whom a circus number? A sadistic spectacle or an explosion of violence for some, it stands for others as a dramatic production and even as a recollection of the great celebrations related to the Myth of the Sun. Some see in the world of wrestling an emphasis on the trickster, the swindler, and the "skunk." Others see in it the victory of the good guy over the bad guy, a sort of St. George destroying the dragon; or as Roland Barthes says, "the pure act which separates good from evil and reveals the face of ultimate justice" (14). So, what is televised wrestling? Clearly, its moral impact will primarily depend on the kind of reaction it produces. T. W. Adorno quite properly introduces into the study of TV subject matter a distinction between the message sent out and the message received, between what is explicit and what is implicit (15).

Another problem arises out of the previous one: What is the *degree of integration* of all these various aspects of the TV message within group cultures? Some writers stress the importance of the influence of television, others minimize it. In the present state of research, not only in France but throughout the world, we do not know its influence generally. Nobody has focused the criteria of analysis and the techniques of evaluation on *measuring* the relative importance of TV's subject matter in relation to the totality of the cultural traits of a given social group.

Take a highly controversial example. Because of the internal logic of its audiovisual system, television has a tendency to transform problems into concrete situations, and the concrete situations into living cases, experienced by personages who easily turn into the "stars" of TV films, of games like "double or nothing," or of political interviews. What influence do these stars of the small screen have on daily life, in comparison with personages who enjoy prestige independently of TV, among the family, in the neighborhood, the company, the city, and the nation? Doesn't the variety of kinds of influence of one or another personage on TV raise questions more important than the general phenomenon of "star-making"?

Some Americans have denounced the "unreality" of TV. They see TV separating the individual from real life by a "world of shadows and phantoms" (16). Perhaps we should analyze the different aspects of TV and how the problem presents itself for each of them: A variety show is not a report on an event. Friedmann quite properly stresses that the problem of presence and absence arises in complicated ways (17) not only with respect of integration of the individual with life around him but also from the viewpoint of his participation in the totality of social and cultural life. For most TV viewers who lack the means to take a cruise to Hawaii, to attend great meetings of statesmen, or to visit scientific laboratories, TV provides an unprecedented way to be "present" in the world. "TV is the world under my roof," said a peasant in the Aisne Department. It can, therefore, also be a way to make civilization more visible, more concrete, more real in the eyes of everyone. Hence, so long as the social sciences do not succeed in determining the degree and quality of the influence that different aspects of TV may have in our culture as experienced, all the analysis of public opinion surveys will have but a limited interest.

We have seen that the dominant characteristics in public reaction to TV is not the mediocrity but the ambiguity of taste. The good—and let's admit it, the less good—from the standpoint of experts in science or art are often given equal approbation. Now, modern democratic society from the school onward is trying to eliminate inequalities in culture. By its very principles it requires stimulation of the development of everyone in a free sharing in social and cultural life.

As TV is capable of advancing leisure toward escapism, as well as toward real-life participation, the chief problem for TV programming is to find the best equilibrium among all its functions, with a view to promoting among its viewers what Adorno calls "adult reactions." Entertainment without dullness, education without boredom—these could be the slogan of a TV anxious to provoke active attitudes among the public with respect to leisure and responsibility.

How to accomplish such a purpose? Up to now, producers and researchers have rarely worked together to discover how best to do it. Producers and directors have trusted their intuition alone, guided by the opinions of their colleagues and the reactions of their generally Parisian cultural surroundings. The performer, however, faces a new responsibility, one difficult to assume. He must produce a personal performance that has quality, yet he is not free to impose his own conception, as is a painter seeking to express his truth on a canvas. The small screen is not a canvas. It is inside a home. It is watched by millions of families from every social background. The audience does not go to the performance, it is the performance which goes to the audience, and imposes itself on the audience. The responsibility of a TV producer has nothing in common with that of a painter. Many producers offer programs of high quality, but other than expressions of approval or disapproval, what effect do they have on the viewers' culture? However much of a genius he may be, what does a Parisian producer know about the problem of raising the levels of social and cultural participation among worker or rural groups? A scientific study of needs, and of positive or negative results of programs designed to satisfy these needs, is indispensable.

Inversely, studies of the viewing audience are frequently carried on without any precise reference to the problems of the producers. Public relations surveys are almost unknown to them. When they are aware of them, they willingly admit that the results are not very useful in solving their own problems. These surveys provide information about the extent of public approval or disapproval. But they do not reach the important questions we have mentioned above. They are conducted in order to keep management informed; management's own social and cultural requirements are less important than other strictly political or commercial preoccupations, depending on the system in a given country. Management is frequently more upset by twenty letters filled with moral or political protest against certain programs than it is influenced by rigorously methodical studies of the conditions necessary to any improvement in the cultural standards of leisure in the various social groups that comprise a nation.

Some opinion surveys scarcely pay any attention to variations in viewing habits as between urban and rural audiences, workers, executives, and so forth. How can a popular culture taking account of both similar and differing views be built on such statistics, if its aim is to fulfil the general needs of society considered as a whole as well as the specialized needs of society considered as made up of groups and classes? These opinion surveys pay little attention to differences in tastes within a group. They are looking for majority opinions. They emphasize the attitudes of the conformist rather than those of the innovator. Now, most of the time it would be interesting to be able to direct the production, to measure the sector of the audience from all groups that is concerned with the most difficult aspects of a program, to collect reactions, to explore motivations, and to study resistances from other more numerous and conformist layers of opinion.

Yet the greatest defect in these limited surveys of majority and conformist opinion is that they in fact help crystallize a mediocre, average portrayal of the public, which, thanks to advertising, can become a model to which everybody feels obliged to conform. "The average man," fashioned by a culture more or less insensitive to the conquest of beauty or truth, becomes an ideal man. Mediocrity is elevated to the rank of a value. This kind of superficial, static research ends up by curbing every even slightly original effort and in imposing conformist and conservative patterns.

Of course, sociology does not intend any such result, but in the form in which we have just mentioned it, it can end up by producing these results. At least, this is the diagnosis of the principal sociologists of "mass culture" in the United States, where there are more than fifty million TV sets dominated by mediocre entertainment programs. Adorno, Whyte, and Riesman have all frequently expressed this thought. TV programs should, therefore, be inspired by the search for the best balance among the leisure functions of the public. It is in trying to raise the cultural level of leisure that we will learn the powers and limitations of television.

Chapter 9

Leisure

and

Books

F<small>INALLY, WE WILL DEAL WITH READING AS A LEISURE ACTIVITY.</small>
We are here concerned with reading for pleasure of works of general
culture and literary stature. Thanks to the delights of fiction, books
can increase the knowledge and refine the tastes of a large public,
while at the same time keeping it entertained. Widespread distribution of such books in all social strata whether in town or in country
is an important factor in raising the cultural level of leisure.[1]

[1] In France, today, it is impossible to give scientific answers to these
problems. There is no Institute for Reading Research. The study of the new
cultural phenomena, such as the cinema, radio, television, and the press,
has stimulated establishment of research institutes; the same is true of the
studying of cultural phenomena that are disappearing, such as traditional
folklore or archaic civilizations. But the study of half-new, half-dying
phenomenon like book culture has not yet been so honored, at least in
France. A professor of literature of the Faculty at Bordeaux, Robert
Escarpit, however, has adopted a sociological approach to the renovation
of literary history and criticism. At the Center of Sociological Studies in
Paris, Albert Memmi is busy laying the foundations of a sociology of
literature within the framework of a sociology of knowledge. In 1954, we
and our collaborators approached the study of reading in the frame of
reference of leisure sociology and the study of book distribution, making
use of the documentary research of the Center of Economic Studies. For
the past two or three years, several book publishers and distributors, anxious
to increase their effectiveness, have been looking for new ways of knowing

In 1955, Wladimir Porché, ex-director of French radio broadcasting, told an international gathering in Geneva: "It would be
vain to close one's eyes to the fact that the book is no longer the
fundamental tool for the education of the great masses of
humanity."

Has not the growth of the mass media—radio,press, cinema, and
TV—had a minimizing effect on the book? This is a question difficult to resolve. In the first place, it is impossible to isolate these great
modern media from the entire civilization within which they are
integrated. We have seen that the survey results indicate that reading
the newspaper takes up, on the average, one half to one full hour a
day, that the movies attract the average Frenchman eight times a
year, that radio or TV sets are turned on, in every home having
one, an average of two to three hours a day. This results in diminishing the time available for reading books.

But as we have already noted, surveys of television in the United
States show that this reduction in reading affects only about half
the public, and that the time devoted to TV is subtracted mainly
from aimless pursuits and desultory conversation. Also, the time
taken up with a new audiovisual appliance often replaces time
formerly devoted to some other device—for example, time spent
watching TV has nibbled away time spent listening to the radio.
Now, around 1890, before the rise of movies, radio, newspapers,
and TV, how many people were reading books? It is impossible to
determine whether they were more numerous then than today.

Advertising in newspapers, at movies, and on radio and TV
can either damage or improve the distribution of books. It is because
of the great mass media that certain books have been able to reach
out beyond the narrow circle of the literate public concerned with
literary activities. Also, these modern media themselves are part of
a civilization other elements of which undeniably have favored the

what is happening in the book market and of forecasting what the readers'
needs may become. After mentioning this development, we shall try to
identify the problems of a sociology of reading within the framework of
dynamic research, research into cultural action.

taste for books. The general rise in the level of education is one of the most effective agents in the development of reading habits.[2]

The rise in living standards has allowed an increase in expenditures for leisure equipment in general. Books cost less than in 1910. Last, there has been an increase in free time of at least 30 per cent since the time when newspapers started having a wide distribution, and this opened up new possibilities for leisure activities, including reading books. We must, therefore, be cautious when we try to analyze the changes in the amount of book-reading over the past fifty years.

Some who despair at our era recall with nostalgia the status of reading in the nineteenth century. Yet, in the last century how many citizens actually read books and to what class did they belong? In 1850, what were the cultural leisure pursuits of the broad mass of the people, the workers and the peasants? The investigations made extensively by Varagnac (2) into traditional culture, those by Paul Delarue (3) of popular stories, and especially those by Nisard (4) of popular books and the literature sold by book peddlers provide us with some indispensable indications.

Today, the peddler has been eliminated due to new means of transportation and communication. Books are far more available in town and country than in earlier times, thanks to the spread of bookstores and libraries, including bookmobiles. They are better known because of the press, radio, and TV. Besides, the essential book list stocked by the peddler was composed of almanacs, with their rudimentary scientific and medical notions, presented under the cover of rather naïve fiction. The *Vermot Almanac* and a few regional almanacs, if we make every allowance, still preserve certain of these characteristics. Alongside these almanacs, there were a few novels by Florian or Bernardin de Saint-Pierre, some condensed (already), illustrated literary classics, and also a few good joke

[2] According to the University Bureau of Statistics, 75 per cent of today's elementary-school students in the cities continue their studies beyond the elementary level as against 15 per cent fifty years ago.

books and anecdotal material; some simple tales of adventure and travel, books on astrology and magic, advice to the lovelorn—all of which we mentioned earlier in this book.

We have reported the similar opinions of Nisard and the editors of the workers' newspaper *L'Atelier* on the quality of the popular novels and short stories of that day. Despite the quality of the research of an historian like Georges Duveau, one is astonished at the way he deals with the question of reading by the working class of the nineteenth century (5). Some admirable, self-educated men like Agricol Perdiguier, Martin Nadaud, and Gillard taught themselves during the days of the 1848 revolution. Yet how many of them were there? It is impossible to hold up the list of authors recommended to workers by Agricol Perdiguier (Robert de Lamennais, Alphonse de Lamartine, Victor Hugo) as proof of working-class culture. What, in fact, did the workers read? In 1863, Perdiguier himself went so far as to say: "Gaston, a bosom friend and one of my most hard-working students, whom I mention as a rare model for all workers, writes me from Lyon that since his departure from Paris he hasn't met a single worker who really likes to read, especially serious, instructive, and beneficial reading matter" (6).

Henri-Louis Tolain, about the same time, also stated: "You can talk all you want about the spread of enlightenment and the progress of education among the lower orders. Who is naïve enough to believe any of this? Don't mention one, two, or ten exceptions. I know one, I know them, and the exception confirms the rule. What is certain is that the mulitude is ignorant" (7). On the eve of the War of 1870, 30 per cent of the conscripts were illiterate.

Publishing

The statistics maintained in the legal book depository do not provide the number of copies of books published, but merely the number of titles. We have those figures since 1887. One fact is striking. There is no plus or minus variation in the number of titles in the periods following the appearance of the big newspapers, the movies, radio, or TV. These new media do not seem to have slowed down the publishing of books, even for a moment. The only deceleration took place during the two wars.[3]

How does French book production compare with that of other countries? In 1952, in terms of the number of titles published in each country, France is in seventh place, following the Soviet Union (37,500), the United Kingdom (18,745), India (17,400), Japan (17,306), West Germany (13,913), and the United States (11,480). Any international comparison is difficult, since definitions of production vary from country to country. India, for example, attained the high figure indicated above only because of a very broad definition of "book." By contrast, Italy is the victim of too narrow a definition. The Soviet and British figures, based on a broader definition than our own, should be somewhat lower, and the figure for Japan should likewise be reduced. It is enough to say that France is among the "big" in book production.

Studying the number of titles published per million inhabitants produces a different result. Some small, economically prosperous European countries with an educated and cultivated population come to the top of the list. In 1952, the Netherlands published 673

[3] With these two exceptions, when the number of titles dropped to about 4,000, the number has remained constant between 10,000 and 12,000 a year (with a high point in 1936 of 16,000); in 1958, it was slightly above 11,000. But how can we know the number of copies per title? We are reduced to making estimates. R. E. Baker (8), in his study of books in the world, calculated the average run for different kinds of books: novels, short stories, scholarly works, and so forth. On this basis, he estimated about 100 million copies of books were published in 1952. But French publishing circles disagree with both these figures and his method of reaching them. Pierre Monnet (9) prefers basing his estimates on the paper tonnage used for publishing books. In 1957, this amounted to a little more than 45,000 tons. As each kilogram corresponds to an average of four volumes, there were about 16,000,000 copies published in France. It is probable that this figure is much greater than the production at the beginning of this century, though we have no means of statistical verification.

titles per million inhabitants, Switzerland 649, Austria 558, Belgium 512, and France only 242.

The content of the production also varies as between countries.[4] Literary works, including novels and short stories, generally constitute the biggest category. In France, this category accounted for 31 per cent of the titles; in the United States, 36 per cent; in the United Kingdom, 33 per cent. By contrast, in the Soviet Union, it is the category covering political, social, and economic matters that is the largest, accounting for 39 per cent of the production in 1952.

One other relationship worth studying is that between book publishing and reading matter in the newspapers that has expanded so spectacularly during the first half of the twentieth century. Robert Escarpit remarks that reading matter available to the French reader in the newspapers is, by volume, about ten times greater than that in books. This is the same ratio found in most

[4] How should the titles be classified? Since 1938, the proportion of works of technical science remains rather constant. From the viewpoint of production classified according to subject matter, there are some changes, for example, an increase in works on pure science and applied science, a slight reduction in those on social sciences. In 1958, omitting 1,330 translations, there were 10,212 domestically produced works. Literature is at the top with 3,247 titles. But under this heading, besides books on linguistics, are both works of literary character (Malraux or Sagan) and cheap popular novels (*Chaste and Dishonoured*), and the like. Then come history and geography with 1,340 titles; economic, political, social, and juridicial sciences with 1,094 titles; technique, games, and sports with 1,086 titles; medical sciences with 1,019 titles; mathematical, physical, and natural science with 786 titles; religious works with 741; and philosophy and education with 437 titles.

Here, again, only the number of copies would give us the relative value of this production. We have obtained, indirectly, an indication on this point through a professional survey of publishers' activities. One questionnaire went to 769 publishing houses and brought 447 replies from houses publishing on a regular basis. Gross business amounted to about 44 billion francs in 1957 ($88,000,000 in old francs, Tr.), more than half accounted for by nineteen publishers. The five largest houses alone accounted for about 30 per cent of the total. Gross sales by the principal branches of the publishing industry were as follows: literature, 32 per cent; children's books, 12.5 per cent; classics (school manuals or scholarly works), 22.5 per cent; religious works, 5.5 per cent; technique, pure and applied science, medicine, and law, 22 per cent; art and bibliophilia, 5.5 per cent.

countries of Western Europe. In the United States, the place of newspapers and magazines is even greater, where the ratio is 200 to 1. In the Soviet Union, under the impact of a questionable but effective publishing policy, it is much less, on the order of 4 to 1.

One may ask whether works of general culture are well adapted by their subject matter, form, and presentation to the needs of the large public educated during the past three quarters of a century only in the elementary school. At the present time, is publishing resolutely aiming at enlarging the reading public for literature? The English Penguin series was the first example of a type of book of good quality, low price, and wide public acceptance. Inexpensive paperbacks appeared later in the United States, where they rapidly won considerable success.

The *Livre de Poche* appeared in France in 1953, following the American example. This collection already includes more than four hundred titles. It is spreading beyond the novel in other genres: a history series, an exploration series, a classics series, an encyclopedia series. None of these new series has yet approached even at a distance the sales of an American best seller like that excellent anthropology by Ruth Benedict, *Patterns of Culture*, which went through fourteen reprintings between 1946 and 1957.[5]

The French figures, nonetheless, are impressive, especially insofar as the novel is concerned. Each month seven hundred thousand copies from the *Livre de Poche* collection are sold—that is, about 5 per cent of the total book production. As of January 1, 1959, the total number of copies sold had reached twenty-four million. The reprint figures often exceeds by far that of the original edition; their audience is not limited to the well-educated. It would be interesting to measure this spread by public opinion surveys. Recently, in 1958, a new collection, *J'ai Lu*, in pocketbook form has been launched by Ditis. It currently offers about seventy titles. Ditis tries on one hand to provide these books at a very low price

[5] This book was translated into French under the title *Echantillons de Civilisation* in the collection *Essais,* Paris, Gallimard, 1950.

(1.80 new francs, less than forty cents, per copy in pocketbook form) and to distribute them through the most frequented sales points—bookshops, dime stores, department stores).

We are not dealing with the question of children's books directly, but it must be noted that since 1945 there has been spectacular progress in this area. Faced with competition from picture books and comics, this type of book is now spreading knowledge of the most varied and often the most difficult kind, aided by the number of high quality illustrations that help understanding the text. In 1957, these books were already accounting for about 12 per cent of the publishing business. Local surveys permit assertion that this kind of book is read not only by children and youngsters, but by all members of the family, especially in groups without any familiarity with literary works. Publishers have probably discovered in this way a formula that could have great influence not only in encouraging children in this age of pictures to read more and better books, but also to enhance the spread of books of quality among adults outside the literate elite. It is possible that this may be a new kind of adult education that could turn out to be a fruitful contribution to popular culture. Research by cultural sociology in this direction could be of prime importance.

Meanwhile, despite this progress in presenting and adapting works to the taste of the modern public, there remains this problem: If we compare the content of literary works written each year with the themes of daily conversation or in local papers read by everybody, we may ask if there are many current books that correspond to the cultural needs of this vast number of new lower class male and female readers whose grandparents were illiterate. For whom are most writers writing? Since the eighteenth century, the situation has changed very little; writers write for a cultivated public. During the nineteenth century, illiteracy was, little by little, liquidated. The entire nation learned to read and write. The successive political constitutions kept raising questions about equality in culture for all; a movement for popular culture took shape. On the whole, writers today do not seem to have become aware of this new situation. How many of them indulge in activities or think in terms that would allow them to search for, stimulate, and express the cultural needs of dynamic personalities among the common people? The latter, in spite of having acquired a basic culture, remain strangers to literature. As Escarpit says (10) in his picturesque language: "Like the great microcephalic reptiles of the Mesozoic Period, the city of millions of men has a literature in the image of a thousand."

Distribution of Books

BOOKSTORES

Change in production has been accompanied by no less important changes in the distribution of books. What does the commercial distribution system look like in France? In the big cities, there are several large bookstores with a wide assortment; they are, in a way, the "department stores" of the book. In 1945, there were about two hundred of them; after ten years, there had been hardly any change. Next there are smaller bookstores which in big cities have tended to specialize—in poetry, history, and so forth. Only a great many studies of local history could provide information on how widespread this specialization is and how it came about.

But there is another much stronger trend—toward decentralization of the sales outlets for books. Most of these are small bookshops that have grown up in neighborhoods of the city or in towns that never before had been reached. With the growth in less costly editions, book outlets have multiplied—in railway stations, at sidewalk kiosks, at tobacco counters, in all sorts of stores having stationery counters, in music stores, dime stores, groceries, and so on. It comes as a surprise to see the latest Prix Goncourt alongside an underwater hunting rifle in a tiny grocery at a seaside resort. In 1956, there were 6,273 bookshops handling trade books for publishers; that same year the INSEE counted 7,259 enterprises classified under "book business." Yet the total number of sales outlets for books is very much larger. In 1956, Pierre Monnet estimated these outlets numbered seventeen thousand. Here again, we need studies of this rapid growth in connection with leisure in both town and country, during periods of work and of vacation. Our systematic observations in a city like Annecy, compared with the findings of the INSEE and added to our findings on various trips have persuaded us that the number of book sales-points probably approaches thirty thousand at the present time.

There are changes not only in the number but in the style of bookstores. Until recently, bookstores operated according to an ancient rhythm, waiting for the customer rather than soliciting his custom. Bookstores were left behind by the renaissance in business. In the past few years, younger booksellers have launched a movement to increase efficiency in the sale of books. Modern business examines the real and potential market, makes forecasts, improves its public relations, and organizes advertising campaigns. Why should bookstores remain immune to these renovating influences? Bookselling must win a permanent victory; otherwise, forces hostile to reading may win the day thanks to their powerful publicity resources. Publishers and booksellers must use the methods of mass information in behalf of books that film producers and distributors use. This is the thinking of groups such as the Center of Bookshop Productivity established in 1956.

The Bookshop Circle has itself hired a market specialist. At the end of 1958, a new periodical, the *Book Bulletin*, was created by some newspaper men for the purpose of providing a forum for the indispensable dialogue between publishers and booksellers and of spreading new ideas throughout the publishing world. There is talk of training courses for booksellers . . . a new climate is being created. Sociological research into the conditions necessary for increasing the sale of quality books among new strata of the population is becoming possible. All these new currents, supported by a favorable economic outlook, resulted in a noticeable increase in book sales during the 1950–57 period. Based on an index of 100 for expenditures on culture and leisure in 1950, the index in 1957 was 142: "Spending on reading has risen at the same rate as the general index, namely an average of 6 per cent, with a higher rate for books than for newspapers" (1). This, incidentally, was an increase running parallel to the rise in the purchase of TV sets.

LIBRARIES

When we look at the present situation of libraries in France, we find a movement toward decentralization comparable to that in the domain of the bookstore. Municipal libraries are being modernized, public reading halls are being associated with them, branch libraries are strengthening the central library. There are an estimated five hundred municipal libraries supervised by the Library Administration.[6]

[6] In our library system, public libraries play a considerable role; a brief retracing of its history is in order. During the Revolution, an enormous mass of books taken from institutions and reading rooms of the privileged classes of the Ancient Regime were placed at the disposal of a multitude of small libraries incapable of making use of them. During the nineteenth century, the problem of conservation absorbed the attention of librarians. Erudite and welcomed by the learned societies, many of them had no interest in the people's needs. Toward the end of the Second Empire and the beginning of the Third Republic, there was a strong movement in favor of reading for all, leading to the creation of school and popular libraries. This movement did not reach its full growth for a number of reasons. Organizational efforts were spread too thin; the subject matter was poorly suited to the needs of the new public; currents favoring popular culture were weak.

At the beginning of the twentieth century, the general outlook was rather bleak (12). After World War I, American influence fortunately made itself felt — the first experiment with a circulating library in the Aisne Department; transformations in certain municipal libraries in Paris, principally the one on the Rue Boutebrie (1924), which because of its directors became the model of "Happy Hours" for children. In the interwar period, quite a few municipal libraries were modernized.

After the Liberation, the need for renovation was obvious and there were decisive changes made. The French Library Administration was created at that time. It played a crucial role. Municipal libraries were encouraged

Another typical action of great importance was the creation, alongside the municipal libraries, of a parallel system of small libraries which developed as part of the expansion of organizations concerned with recreational and cultural leisure activities. Around 1900, there were thirty such organizations in a city such as Annecy (which was three times smaller than today). In 1957, there were about two hundred actively engaged. As we have seen, the growth of these organizations reveals the intensity of a new form of local life; it activates a network of direct relationships among social strata, groups, and individuals. It seems to be a movement complementing or compensating for the growth in mass media (press, film, radio, and TV) which tend to isolate families and individuals from one another. This trend has led to the spread of small libraries with fewer books than the municipal libraries but which penetrate much more deeply into the various social strata. A survey made of 5 per cent of the heads of family in Annecy showed that about one hundred persons out of five hundred borrow books from the library. Even though the municipal library is managed by a young, dynamic director, only 20 per cent of the borrowers go there. Eighty per cent utilize other libraries. In this industrial town, where 30 per cent of the people are workers, 20 per cent prefer to use company libraries; lesser numbers use lay religious libraries, school libraries, and various libraries associated with sports, outdoor activities, cinema, and popular culture.

School libraries in France, which numbered 45,800 in 1947, are used to varying degrees. Initially, funds of these institutions were devoted not only to schoolchildren but also to the adults of the community. Yet they are often impoverished and, in 1947, only about half of them (23,500) were open to the public. The circulating

and supervised. Central lending libraries were organized in twenty-odd departments, and undertakings by both departments and private groups were supported in many areas. The Library Administration saw to it that librarians were given proper training leading to special new diplomas: higher librarian diploma and certificate of librarian aptitude. A considerable program of research was carried out on the technical level.

libraries are currently bringing about a beneficial transformation of the circumstances in which the school libraries operate in rural areas. In another domain, that of secondary education, we are seeing a favorable trend toward creating central libraries in the high schools open to both parents and children.

In the private sector, let us take note especially of the actions of two large organizations—the General Women's League for Catholic Action and the French Education League. In 1956–57, there were 1,152 libraries and 2,976 other outlets dependent on Women's Catholic Action. Of these libraries, 257 were installed in regular shops and 202 away from religious surroundings, with show windows opening onto the street. This is a total of 459 libraries in direct contact with the man in the street. These are called "Everybody's Library" and try to be open to everyone without discrimination on religious or political grounds. This is why those responsible at the national level prefer neutral premises to religious ones. During 1956–57, these libraries lent nearly six million books, an indication of their importance.

The Lay Center of Public Reading, a séction of the Education League established in 1951, has taken upon itself to encourage the renovation and creation of circulating libraries on the departmental level and to train departmental librarians. The Center has a purchasing agency. It has stimulated the establishment of libraries in many community centers. Its main activity has consisted in implanting circulating library services in thirty departments.

The most important fact for the progress of reading in the working class is the growth of company libraries. They often have access to considerable means, and they have the great advantage of locating the book distribution point on the spot most frequented in a worker's life—his company. We realized their outstanding importance in Annecy. It would be useful to cross-check this information with surveys in other localities. On the national level, we are already aware that one big business with four hundred thousand employees (the SNCF, French National Railways Company) has to its credit some remarkable accomplishments in this respect. The SNCF has instituted a "Bibliofer"—a book-car. The employees of the French National Coal Company, the French Electric Company, and certain big companies like Renault are benefiting from similar accomplishments. As there are about three thousand active company committees (out of ten thousand existing), it is impossible today to know the precise number of company libraries. B. Levaillant, labor consultant, has assembled some factual data (13) on the various types of companies—small, middle sized, and large in the Paris region and in the provinces—that show that company libraries reach between 10 and 30 per cent of the work force in the factory, a high percentage rarely attained by other libraries. In Valence, a community enterprise (Boimondau) has even proved that under the effect of social and cultural stimulation and thanks to a well-placed, well-maintained library put to good use, the percentage of worker participation can be still higher. In fact, out of 170 employees, 135, mostly workers, are regular subscribers, producing an annual borrowing rate of twenty books a year per capita.

It would be useful to be able to promote other experiments of this kind and to control the results obtained so as to evaluate the possibilities of integrating reading into popular leisure, a vital aspect in the permanent education of workers and of worker culture.

In the rural areas, the major factor is the establishment of central lending libraries. These libraries with headquarters in the main town of the department, are part of the government, and using bookmobiles make book deposits in towns of less than fifteen thousand population. These book deposits are always under the control of public authorities, mostly in schools, where the teacher acts as agent. Sometimes, the books are placed in the town hall. Twenty out of ninety departments are presently being served by circulating libraries which have placed book deposits in about ten thousand communities. Department public library services have been created in twenty-odd other departments with grants from the Library Administration. We should also remember the services provided by the Lay Center of Public Libraries which have at their disposal fewer personnel and smaller means than the central lending libraries, but which, because of the devotion of their staffs, have succeeded in circulating books in thirty-odd departments.

This progress in equipping libraries has been accompanied by advances in the techniques of book distribution and reader education. New ways have been developed to adjust libraries and group reading to the customs of a world conditioned by mass media and local organizations. Company libraries announce new books over the factory loudspeaker. Some librarians periodically put on exhibits with photographs and posters at the time of school reopening, Christmas, summer vacation, and so on. Following new methods developed by "People and Culture," thousands of cultural promoters read excerpts of great works aloud; the readings are followed by discussion. In the clubs and schools managed by the French Coal Company, nearly three thousand reading clubs were founded between 1955 and 1957. Some educators produce plays based on novels. In Nohant, George Sand's *les Maîtres Sonneurs* was staged as a play by a dramatic-art instructor, Jean Nazet, for the benefit of thousands of spectators. This example has been followed many times, using works such as *Notre Dame de Paris, le Père Goriot, les Thibault* and *Maria Chapdelaine*. Various training courses provide instruction for these librarians and promoters of popular education, and their efforts are beginning to bear fruit. We should take note of the quite recent formation in the French Librarians' Association of a section of small- and medium-sized educational libraries.

BOOK CLUBS

Another means of distributing books has been developed recently outside the bookshops and libraries—book clubs (15). Their origins go back to Germany in 1918, but their most varied and broadest development has taken place in the United States. After the Liberation, the idea took hold in France and in fifteen years became widespread. The French Book Club, which in 1946 occupied a tiny office, has taken over a building where more than one hundred employees are working today. It has about one hundred thousand members. Its success has been imitated by competitors, and members number in the tens of thousands. In 1956, the Best Book Club and the Book Guild each had seventy thousand members.[7]

Publishers and bookstore owners dueled with one another in the creation of new clubs: the French Booksellers Club, the Bookshop Club, the Publishers' Club, among others. We still don't know how far bookselling goes, but in Annecy, if the current literary output is omitted, books offered by clubs amount to about one third of the sale of books of general literature at the main bookstore. Our survey of home bookshelves in Annecy showed that 20 per cent of those who bought books were members of a book club. There has not yet been a scientific study of the reasons for the success of this formula in France. A well-documented study of book clubs by Paul Riberette, however, provides some indications of the public's attraction to the beauty of these book-objects, well bound and well illustrated (14). "Cultivated people who loved good books and whose taste ran to beautifully bound and handsomely jacketed books were attracted to the book clubs, since repeated devaluations of the currency and the cost of handmade book-binding had not always permitted them to create a choice library," Riberette reports. The solution they found was the book club.

Such an explanation would probably fit only a portion of the public. Young people seem to like the book club because it represents a modern technique of expression, using modern art, advertising innovations, and movie-montage. Thereby the book is transformed, and new attributes of our picture civilization are conferred upon this traditional vehicle of knowledge. Another advantage of the club derives from the fact that it encourages the feeling of belonging to a group.

In selecting a club, each individual chooses a style of literature

[7] The Readers' Digest Club is somewhat different but it is supposed to count more than three hundred thousand members.

and of presentation. Some book clubs are more classical, others more modern. In presenting their books, some show moderation, others audacity. In joining a club, everyone links himself with an editorial team in whom he has confidence. The *Club Bulletin* (or *Club News*) plays the role of a literary review that is not a slave to the moment and that makes judgments and reaches decisions after due consideration.

The member, faced with the mass of information that pours in on him from the newspapers, radio, and movies, often feels lost, disoriented, and incapable of making a choice on his own. The club frees him from the need to choose. The reader feels encouraged to buy the book because he believes the club's choice is a guarantee of the quality that agrees with him.

RESISTANCES TO BOOK DISTRIBUTION

In spite of advances in quality book distribution made in our country since 1900, there remain cultural obstacles and social barriers. First, the Booksellers' Productivity Center is still far from putting pressure on bookstores to improve selling conditions. Most small- and middle-sized bookstores use old-fashioned sales methods. They have no urge to conquer new markets. Frequently, they are isolated from the local institutions that exist to improve the cultural level of all groups, especially that of the mass of the people. When the booksellers themselves are cultivated persons, they are often uninterested in attracting a new clientele. The best of them sometimes are opposed to modern sales methods because they seem incompatible with the nobility of the profession.

As for the others, who make up the bulk of the managers or owners of the seventeen thousand bookstores or book outlets, they are often lacking in education and culture. They are incapable of giving advice to the cultivated élite and they are ill-suited to provide education to the general public. They sell books as they would sell tobacco or groceries. The question of the social, cultural, and technical qualifications of the modern bookseller has never been asked.

Although there may be illegal practice in medicine, there is no practice that is illegal in bookselling. Sell what you can; too bad for the public.[8]

As for the librarian: Is he always well qualified for his job as promoter of popular culture? Like the bookseller, he has a great responsibility for the attraction and guidance of readers. M. Jean Lemaire, control librarian of Beauvais, has made some systematic observations of the attitudes of those who come to him. The largest majority of the readers have no precise idea of the book they will choose. These visitors place confidence in the librarian as a guide, rather than as a salesman. How many librarians are socially, culturally, and pedagogically qualified to assume this difficult responsibility in such a variety of cases?

Many professionals have a solid technical education but hold a conception of their mission that is a trifle dogmatic. They have a legitimate concern with "quality," but too often they remain on the sidelines of popular life. They may have good techniques of presentation, but sometimes they take no interest in developing permanent contacts with recreational and cultural associations which could serve as intermediaries between themselves and the various local publics. Although highly cultivated themselves, they are, perhaps, not adequately trained in the use of modern techniques of promotion among the people.

As for the voluntary librarians who are at least twenty times as numerous as the professionals, if the figures from Annecy are representative, their social, cultural, and pedagogical training has

[8] About two thirds of the inhabitants of Annecy never, or practically never, buy a book. Among their suggestions for improving this situation: Out of 423 replies, we found 156 related to economics (books ought to cost less), 63 to psychology (booksellers ought to put them at their ease, help them find books, and give them more advice or be more literate themselves), and 23 to technical matters (booksellers ought to increase their advertising, pay more attention to the public, for example). These replies reveal a serious gap between the behavior of the bookseller and the expectations of a certain number of those who still have never bought a book.

never been systematically organized, beyond a few courses that don't reach more than one hundred persons a year.

The physical appearance of bookstores leaves a great deal to be desired. Many are unattractive to the public, when compared with a modern grocery or dime store. Cultivated persons go into them, but others are not attracted. Even when the shop is modern, the display window will be designed for the sole purpose of attracting literary connoisseurs, those who enjoy literary pursuits. Likewise, most bookshops are located in streets that workers do not frequent—in the center of town, in the business section, in the finest neighborhoods. By contrast, the small bookshops located on the edge of town or in the suburbs where workers do go, primarily display books that perpetuate the sentimental and melodramatic tradition of the popular novel.

We are not saying that there are two circuits, so to speak, one for the cultivated and the other for the common people. We do say that extension of book distribution beyond cultivated circles runs up against the incompetence of many booksellers and the unpreparedness of bookshops to spread quality books among all segments of the population.

Libraries likewise lack proper equipment. The Library Administration runs afoul of the widespread lack of comprehension of municipal and public authorities for whom library development is not a major concern.[9]

Few city libraries have adequate equipment. In some great cities, organization for public reading is still embryonic, although the number of city libraries (five hundred) is almost equal to the number of towns with more than ten thousand inhabitants. The surburbs

[9] Our study of five hundred homes in Annecy reveals that the city library is far from satisfactory to meet the needs of the population. The number one desire is for the library to have many more modern books; second, they want easier access (the city library is on the top floor of the city hall); third, they want the library to organize book clubs and to educate the public; fourth, they want the library to stay open after work hours; and fifth, they want the library to advertise.

are as lacking in libraries as in bookstores, and the program to provide rural bookmobiles has not been pushed at the same rate as it was after the Liberation.[10]

The library situation in France is worse than that in many foreign countries, such as Australia, Canada, Denmark, the United States, England, and Sweden, where the number of books lent per year by public libraries is higher than the total number of books published in one year! In France, the situation is reversed. Even though the Library Administration may not have been able to determine the over-all statistics on book-borrowing, one can estimate by cross-checking partial information that the number of books borrowed from libraries is far smaller than the one hundred and sixty million copies of books published annually in France. In comparison with the rest of the country, Paris is relatively well served. Yet the Paris city libraries lend only about one book a year per inhabitant, while British public libraries lend eight a year per person (this is a national average that takes local imperfections into account, the average in cities being higher).

It should be noted that the English are not, for all that, depriving themselves of the delights of the movies and TV.[11]

The social groups reached by libraries are not at all representative of the nation as a whole. We have no nation-wide survey of this subject, but several monographs give indications. They all cross-check on this point.[12] The middle classes, and in particular the

[10] It is estimated that about two thirds of the villages in France remain without service. Only 23,500 school libraries out of 45,800 are really open to the public. In the Seine-et-Oise Department, according to P. Breillat, director of the central lending library, out of 1,095 schoolbook libraries enumerated in 1951, 723 were exclusively for school usage, only 372 really provided for lending books to adults, and these were those served by the department library.

[11] In fact, the English go to the movies on the average twenty-nine times a year, the French eight times (17). In France there were about 1,800,000 TV sets in 1959, as against 10,000,000 in Great Britain.

[12] The Departmental Circulating Library in the Dordogne, which reaches 8.4 per cent of the population, reaches only 6 per cent of the farmers and 5 per cent of the workers, although the total of these two categories amounts to 42 per cent of the population (18). In Paris, in 1957, the municipal

white-collar employees and bureaucrats, are the classes relatively most often reached by libraries; schoolchildren and other students, those without employment, and retired persons are also very numerous.

The Readers

Given the present state of production and distribution, by turn favorable and unfavorable to progress in book-reading, how many Frenchmen read books and to what social categories do they belong? Are the regular customers of a bookstore or the subscribers to a library the only readers there are? Various surveys have shown that a purchased or borrowed book is read on the average by three persons. Benigno Cacérès (19) is correct in stressing these "hand-to-hand" circuits, which may be more important than all the others. It would be interesting to study them in terms of the network of social relations that surround each individual, at his job, in his home life, during his leisure activities. Meanwhile, we can grasp the over-all effect of all these purchases, borrowings, and exchanges of books only through surveys of the extent and frequency of reading by the public.

Reading books is not solely the apanage of the cultivated élite. The facts are much more complex. A survey by the IFOP of a sample of Frenchmen living in cities and in the country established that sixty-two out of one hundred read books at least once a year (2). In 1948, in Auxerre, two thirds of those interviewed were reading books.[13]

library in the Twelfth Arrondissement served only 9.6 per cent of the manual workers and craftsmen there; in the Seventeenth Arrondissement, 6 per cent; in the Eighteenth, 11.5 per cent. About 10 per cent of the readers in the Rouen city library are workers; the percentage in Annecy is a little less, while the percentage of workers in the population is 35 per cent. All these figures agree.

[13] Since this chapter was written, the results of a big investigation by the National Publishers' Syndicate of a representative national sample have become available (1961): Forty-two per cent of the French read books.

While many educators are talking about a decline in book-reading, nobody really knows if these percentages are greater or less than they were at the start of the century. From a survey of older people in Annecy, it appears rather that there has been an improvement. Whatever the situation may be, it is not just the élite who own home libraries.[14]

The cultivated élite is estimated at about two million; they are the ones interested in literary life, who follow the competition for literary prizes, and who, periodically, by taste or snobbery, buy modern books. But the group of those who continue to read books regularly or intermittently after leaving school can be estimated at about twenty million. This public reads less but is ten times more numerous.

It will be said that 60 per cent of French readers belong to the upper and middle classes. Do the workers read books? The IFOP survey shows that the percentage of workers who read at least one book a year, while lower than the general average, is, nonetheless, 53 per cent (as against 42 per cent for farmers) (2). And in Annecy, we have seen that two workers' homes out of three possess books. Are we to conclude that equality in culture has now arrived? Far from it. Even limiting ourselves to the summary criterion of how many books are kept in the home, there remain inequalities that call

About 25 per cent stated that at the time of the interview they were in the process of reading a book. To a comparable question asked of representative samples in other countries, 21 per cent of the Americans, 33 per cent of the Swedes, and 55 per cent of the English replied in the same way as the 25 per cent in France.

[14] In fact, 65 per cent of the homes in Annecy have books; 55 per cent have a small library with at least five books (omitting children's schoolbooks), and about half have more than twenty-five books in their library.

 9% of the homes had from 1 to 5 books.
19% of the homes had from 6 to 15 books.
10% of the homes had from 16 to 25 books.
24% of the homes had from 26 to 75 books.
13% of the homes had from 76 to 150 books.
 6% of the homes had from 151 to 250 books.
10% of the homes had from 251 to 500 books.
 4% of the homes had more than 500 books.
 5% of the homes were uncertain.

for intensifying all sorts of economic and cultural actions in order to diminish them. In Annecy, for example, salaried employees own libraries proportionately more than do workers (from three out of four homes as against two out of three). We found not a single home belonging to an industrialist, executive, or member of a liberal profession without its library. An instrument of culture or of national prestige, the library, in these circles, is as indispensable as the *bachot* (baccalaureate) or the automobile. When one confines himself only to libraries having at least twenty-five books, the percentage of workers' homes falls from 50 to 20 per cent. Inequalities, therefore, do persist, to the disadvantage of the workers, especially the less skilled and unskilled ones.

What do these readers from all classes and levels of education read during their leisure time? What kind of published works are most likely to reduce the social and cultural distance between the cultivated public and the people at large? Do there exist books originating in cultivated circles that are widely read by the general public? Or is the general public so busy reading minor works that quality literary productions can't reach them?

We have assembled a documentation[15] based on a variety of sources relating to the biggest sales of books during the years 1945 to 1955. In this period, only one hundred and fifty titles out of about thirty thousand sold more than sixty thousand copies. Some publishers claim their sales have increased since the last war. By how much? Only by research into several old publishing houses could we obtain the figures. Georges Charensol's opinion of their quality is clear: "Most books that have enjoyed very large sales since the Second World War are of excellent literary quality." We have come a long way since the novels of Clément Vautel, Maurice Dekobra, and Victor Margueritte who at one time used to beat all records.

What are the reasons for the success of these bestsellers? Charensol points out that books winning one of the four main

[15] Especially the data published by Georges Charensol (24).

literary prizes[16]—Goncourt, Renaudot, Fémina, and Interallié—
which receive vast publicity in the press, frequently sell more than
100,000 copies: *Weekend at Zuydcoote* (260,000), *The Mandarins*
(85,000), *The Happy Valley* (120,000), *The Banks of the Syrtes*
(115,000). In addition, when the movies adapt a literary work to the
screen, a new audience two, three, or even five times greater is
created.[17]

Of course, many books that have not won great prizes have still
attained enormous sales records—for example, *Bonjour Tristesse*
by Françoise Sagan. Literary success may be the basis for cinema
success. This was true for *Don Camillo*, which sold about one
million copies; the publisher estimates that the film increased sales
of the book by about 50 per cent. So, the action of various mass
information media, far from harming the sale of books, on the
contrary, makes an unprecedented contribution to it.

Literary successes occur among a variety of books. Some are of
a political order, such as *I Chose Freedom* by Victor Kravchenko
and *Zero and Infinity* by Arthur Koestler (500,000 and 450,000
copies each). Some are religious, such as *Jésus et son temps* by
Daniel-Rops (more than 300,000 copies). Others have a social
character: *Les Hommes en Blanc (Men in White)* by André
Soubiran (300,000) took the place of *Corps et Ames (Bodies and
Souls)*. Others deal with private life, like *A Certain Smile* by
Françoise Sagan. Some deal with sporting achievements—a whole
series of fictional accounts like *Le Grand Cirque de Clostermann
(Clostermann's Great Circus*—550,000 copies) and *La Grande*

---

[16] Note that there are about six thousand literary prizes given each year
—that is, nearly three times more than there are great and minor novelists
published. Why?

[17] Before being made into a film, *Le Salaire de la Peur (The Ransom of
Fear)* had sold only 40,000 copies. After the success of the film, more than
75,000 copies were sold in one year (1954). *Cela s'Appelle l'Aurore (That's
Called Dawn)* had sold 50,000 copies. After the film, and thanks to the help
of popular editions and book clubs, its sales exceeded 150,000. *Le Journal
d'un Curé de Campagne (The Diary of a Country Priest)*, *Barrage contre
le Pacifique (Pacific Barrier)*, and the *Bridge on the River Kwai* (20,000 sold
before the film, 112,000 afterwards) are similar examples.

Crevasse by Henri Frison-Roche (350,000 copies) as well as a dozen others of the same kind.

Other best sellers owe their fame to poetry—*Le Petit Prince* by Antoine de Saint-Exupéry (400,000 copies) or *Paroles* by Jacques Prévert (more than 300,000 copies)—or else to humor—*Major Thompson's Diary* by Pierre Daninos (350,000) or *Don Camillo,* already mentioned.

What are we to conclude from all this? We will really know nothing about this subject until serious studies of readers' motivations have been made. For the moment, we may note that books of the most opposite kind but endowed with a certain literary quality are finding ever greater acceptance outside cultivated circles.

In spite of everything in Charensol's investigation that is interesting, it is not complete enough to clarify all the possible ways there are of raising the level of literary culture of twenty million French readers. In fact, these readers do not all live at the pace of the present day—far from it. We would also have to add in figures on the recent sales of the works of the principal modern authors before 1940—Malraux and Colette, for example, as well as the figures on reprints of the main classical authors, since we know, from the IFOP survey, that the French are as interested in reading the classics as they are in new works (22 per cent in each category) (20). Inversely, it would be useful to know about the best sellers whose success stands in the way of quality works. We will try to complete Charensol's investigation by using figures on sales of mediocre novels which are, in fact, obstacles to the spread of the general culture among the public at large. Some of these lesser kinds of books are undergoing a decline—for example, the dull novels of Delly and Max du Veuzit. Thanks to their obliging publishers, we know that since 1928 the works of Delly (twenty-five titles) have sold about three million copies, but since 1945 the sales curve has shown a constant drop. The same is true of the twenty-five books by du Veuzit, of which 2,500,000 copies have been printed since 1931 (21). Another type of mediocre literature that is at least at a stationary level, if not undergoing a decline, according to the publishers, is the "little library" series published by Ferenczi, Fayard and Del Duca and selling at prices ranging between 75 and 175 francs (15 to 35 cents). These little books sell about thirty thousand copies, with some exceptional sales exceeding one hundred thousand.

By contrast, two types of books are expanding in sales: the photonovel and the detective story. We do not have the figures for the sales of the first type, which is benefiting from a tremendous publicity and promotion effort by Del Duca, but a recent study of the detective story provides some interesting details. There will be some who will be astonished that we give such importance to this kind of literature. Because of the richness of their observations and the quality of their style, the detective stories of Agatha Christie or Georges Simenon may attain a high literary level, but, on the whole, this type of production is generally second rate. When it furnishes supplementary reading for the tired or nervous intellectual, it does not have the same significance as when it is the sole nourishment of a reading public. In the latter case, the detective story is all too frequently an obstacle to the discovery of quality books. That is why we mention it here. We need to be aware of the fact that the monthly production of detective stories amounts to about two million copies (22), representing, so far as we can determine, about one third of the literary output per month.

Such statistics give us figures on the amount of production, but they say nothing about the literary tastes of the various segments of the population. To our knowledge, few bookstores have made any systematic study of their various customer groups by interrogating a representative sample of their clientele.

Besides, a special sense of professional secrecy often prevents them from furnishing precise data on these matters, as if giving out such information might ruin their enterprise. By contrast, the statistical observations of certain librarians shed light on the taste of readers at various social levels. There ought to be a study at all levels of the size and growth of the minority that likes nonfiction; this group prefers travel books, biographies, and historical and geographical works. Fiction is everywhere the favorite of the majority (60 to 90 per cent of the borrowers).[18]

Each social group has a different appreciation of authors and types of novels. At the Limoges municipal library, which is used by a well-read urban public, these are the preferences: Colette, A. J. Cronin, and André Gide; then Balzac and Hugo; Mauriac and Zola; Dumas, Dostoevski and Saint-Exupéry. The choices in the rural area served by the Department Circulating Library in the Haute-Vienne are somewhat different: Hugo and Dumas are far and away at the top of the list, followed by Colette, Cronin, Balzac, Delly, Duhamel, George Sand, and Zola.

The effort at the Boimondau community to raise the cultural level of a worker group that is already alert because of the special conditions in which it works is well known. At this library, the authors most in demand during the 1951–55 period were, in descending order: Maxence Van der Meersch, Colette, Cronin, Pearl Buck, Thyde Monnier, Emile Zola, Mazo de la Roche, Honoré de Balzac, Frank Slaughter, and Anatole France.

Such surveys give us useful indications. They cause certain differences and resemblances in taste to stand out as between the countryside and the city, between the middle class and the common people. But the number of papers written on this subject is still too limited to permit drawing any over-all conclusions. And besides, the library public represents but a tiny fraction of the population.

How can we find out which books the general public has in its home libraries? Only intensive and systematic surveys of representative samples of all types of families, rationally chosen from significant local groups, can bring forth any adequate response.

We began this work in Annecy, a town of forty-thousand

[18] In hospital and public assistance sanatorium libraries in 1958, 421,000 novels were borrowed out of a total of 580,000 books lent. At the library in the Boimondau company, at least 80 per cent of books borrowed are novels.

inhabitants, using a sample of one twentieth of the population. A nation-wide survey of reading conducted by the IFOP permits comparison of our findings with those of the nation as a whole (20). What is striking at first glance is the variety in kinds of books contained in Annecy family libraries.[19]

We sought to find the differences between men and women (heads of families) in the use of these books. We found no significant difference between them with respect to picture books, major and lesser novels, classics, children's books, and dictionaries. But there are significant differences for the men with respect to detective stories, technical books, and scientific works. These findings were confirmed by the IFOP nation-wide survey. The novel is preferred by 72 per cent of the women, as against 51 per cent of the men; the detective story was selected by 13 per cent of the men as compared with 4 per cent of the women.

What about working-class homes? Is their library limited to the Larousse dictionary? An important development has taken place. There are to be found in workers' homes all the kinds of books listed in the general family library, and in the same proportions, except for essays, travel books, classics, and literary novels.[20]

The anomalous mélange on workers' bookshelves is the first thing that strikes one: a novel by Delly next to *Le Petit Prince* of Saint-Exupery; a minor novel beside a volume of Balzac. . . . The writers most frequently found are Henri Frison-Roche, Gaston Rebuffat, and Maurice Herzog, rather than Hugo and Dumas. Contrary to what we find on the bookshelves in the homes of the

---

[19] Dictionaries in 285 homes (57 per cent); literary novels in 206 (41 per cent); technical works in 167 (33 per cent); classics in 103 (21 per cent); lesser novels in 94 (19 per cent); children's books in 89 (18 per cent); travel books in 80 (16 per cent); detective stories in 75 (15 per cent); scientific essays and books in 46 (9 per cent); and photographic or picture books in 18 (4 per cent).

[20]

	In Workers' Libraries	In All Home Libraries
Essays	7 per cent	15 per cent
Travel books	15 per cent	25 per cent
Classics	15 per cent	30 per cent
Literary novels	40 per cent	60 per cent

lower middle and middle classes, in working-class home-libraries, there are no Goncourt Prize winners, no books by Françoise Sagan. More usual are titles like *Les Hommes en Blanc* or *Corps et Ames.* Modern literary titles most often found are likely to be books translated from English: *Forever Amber, The Keys to the Kingdom, The Citadel, Gone with the Wind,* as well as earlier titles such as *Jane Eyre, Wuthering Heights,* and *Typhoon.* This selection, along with fictional tales of escape, is the same as found in the home libraries of all categories of the population.

Are we to conclude from this that, in spite of differences within each group, the distribution of literary works is the same at all social levels? This would be a hasty conclusion. First, our survey would have to be subjected to statistical treatment and to systematic interpretation; we plan to do this later. When we go beyond trying to find out which books are on which bookshelves, and seek to determine the dominant type of book on each shelf, disparities and inequalities appear, to the detriment of working-class home-libraries.[21]

These are the current trends and dimensions of the production, distribution, and allocation of books, particularly literary works, according to the various social categories. In spite of the growing influence of the press, cinema, radio, and TV, and often because of it, reading of literary works is advancing among ever more numerous social groups. This advance, however, is encountering many cultural and social obstacles, and the actual situation is still far from the ideal that we expect from a democratic society based on equal rights to culture.

The ambiguities in the content of popular leisure directly affect

---

[21] The literary novel is dominant in 30 per cent of the bookshelves in Annecy. (The IFOP survey shows that 32 per cent of the French have libraries composed essentially of novels.) The novel is predominant in only 15 per cent of working-class homes. Including popular detective stories in the category brings this figure up to 26 per cent of the family libraries in Annecy (29 per cent in the IFOP survey). But the proportion is not the same in all groups: 37 per cent workers, as against 12 per cent white-collar employees; 14 per cent businessmen as against 15 per cent executives.

the reading matter of the masses, just as they affect the movies and
TV among the masses. We come back once again to the same basic
question: What are the best conditions for and the most efficient
ways of raising the level of general culture during the leisure time
of the various social classes? Often, the practitioners have an
intuitive awareness of how to find these answers. Bigger libraries
are one of these urgent necessities, but not the only one. Is book
writing itself perfectly adapted to the new needs of the masses?
What are the best radio, movie, and TV programs for developing
active interest in reading? What types of books are most likely to
increase interest in reading in the average home? What relationships
should be developed between libraries and the thousands of
recreational and cultural groups in the city as well as the country?
What are the best school courses and methods for spreading a
lasting and spontaneous taste for reading in free time? So many
questions the practitioner's intuition alone cannot answer.[22]

[22] The recent establishment (October, 1961) of a Book Study Group in the
General Planning and Productivity Commission has made possible a joint
undertaking with the Leisure Sociology and Popular Culture group in the
Center for Sociological Studies. We hope they will do research along the
lines we have suggested.

Chapter 10

Leisure,

Education,

and the

Masses

J EAN FOURASTIE EMPHASIZES THAT THE PASSAGE FROM THE
traditional to the postindustrial way of life has already been marked,
and will increasingly continue to be marked, by the "entry of the
average man into intellectual life" (23). After formal schooling,
what does cultivation of the mind consist of in the popular leisure
of our society? If we move from the occasional reading of books to
the continuous growth of knowledge among the mass of people, we
encounter an even more difficult problem. How can a spontaneous
taste for learning be expanded into the various social strata? Does
"intellectual adolescence" ignore social barriers? Some say that
the cultural subject matter of our society tends to be uniform everywhere and that the chances for cultural improvement are equal on
all levels. In contrast, others claim that there is nothing to this and
that the divisions between categories and social classes persist in
the cultural domain as in all others. Here again, we see the need
for some broad and basic sociological investigations, as much in
terms of scholastic reform as of the development of cultural action

including the school and prolonging the school while renovating it.[1]

This research is needed for the orientation of the country's cultural development in relation to its economic and social development. It alone will permit posing the question of popular culture in terms of a modern, democratic society. We will limit ourselves to presenting here the first results of a questionnaire that asked three questions of a sample of heads of family, chosen by lot, one out of twenty, from about five hundred individuals in our Annecy study.

The first question was aimed at discovering the attitudes of the self-educated: "Are there any subjects about which you have obtained or tried to obtain substantial knowledge, by seriously collecting facts on a regular basis or otherwise? If so, what are they?"

Topics of Interest to the Self-Educated

First, the outstanding trait of our sample is *indifference*. We tried to measure this indifference—slightly more than half of those interviewed could not indicate any real subject of interest in any of twelve subjects out of the fifteen submitted to them. In general, more than 60 per cent simply abstained from answering. Only three kinds of subjects managed to escape their indifference: practical matters, technical questions, and geography. Analysis by socio-occupational categories will clarify this. Certain groups show a veritable lack of cultural vital energy (atony) by the poverty of their interests and the number of their nonresponses.

Even in the groups where dynamic attitudes toward learning are manifest, the subjects chosen are few in a sizable proportion of the sample. As we shall see, there are only two subjects of interest selected by more than one fourth of the people interrogated—their work and geography.

[1] Cf. *People and Culture, Planning and Popular Education,* No. 56, 1960, Social Science and Popular Education, No. 581, 1958.

Yet, in every different social group, a minority shows a real appetite for learning. Here is a list of preferred subjects in which more than 15 per cent of those interviewed showed an active interest:

Subjects	Number	Percentage of Persons Interrogated
1. Geography	140	28
2. Your job	128	26
3. Medicine	113	23
4. History	100	20
5. Hobbies	97	19
6. Education	96	19
7. Mechanics	96	19
8. Cooking	94	19
9. Travel accounts	91	18
10. Mathematics	91	18
11. Art and literature	90	18
12. Gardening	89	18
13. Economic and social issues	84	17
14. Philosophy and religion	84	17
15. French or a foreign language	84	17
16. Ethics and the art of living	83	17

a. First, we note the preferred topics are connected to *utilitarian* preoccupations, answering a need for information about matters affecting daily life. As one would expect, one of the chief concerns of a man is the kind of work he does. Of course, he wants to improve his skills; it is hardly surprising that he should attach such importance to it. It helps us realize the tremendous importance of paid-time-off for study. Knowledge of mechanics is essential to those who work in a factory, and interest in this subject is mainly connected with practice of a particular trade or line of work. We shall see by what follows that mathematics itself is selected mainly because it is indispensable to improving one's competence on the job.

Elsewhere we shall consider the important role of these preoccupations in other activities of everyday life. Medicine and education affect family life in the highest degree. Hobbies, cooking, and gardening are practical occupations whose immediate usefulness is clearly apparent. In short, we must remember the interest in practical and technical questions—categories, incidentally, that prompt the fewest nonresponses.

b. Now let us classify the fields of knowledge mentioned on the form handed to the persons being interrogated, using a different criterion. Besides practical and technical knowledge, we can distinguish scientific subjects: mathematics (arithmetic), physical sciences (physics and chemistry), life sciences (medicine and natural sciences), disciplines relating to the humanities (geography, history, economics, politics, education, and psychology), means of expression (art, literature, and language), and problems of human destiny (philosophy, religion, and ethics).

With the exception of psychology, social sciences interest a great many people. In a day when the world is changing rapidly and opportunity for travel is increasingly available, geography seems to enjoy the most widespread interest of all the subjects of general culture. Finding one's place in space is felt as a daily necessity. The Frenchman is no longer "that gentleman who knows nothing about geography." This interest is shared by people from the most varied backgrounds. Geography thus seems to be a vanguard of a more open common culture. History also is widely esteemed, although interest in this subject is less widespread and uniform. Man feels a need to situate himself in time almost as much as in space.

The timeliness and the essential quality of these two traditional disciplines make them stand out in the minds of adults. This is indicated by the vogue of certain popular magazines and by the interest shown in this kind of publication in bookstores and libraries.

Economic and political questions also interest a sizable number of individuals. Problems of education, which have an immediate impact on family life, attract more interest than does psychology;

those from certain social backgrounds are quite indifferent to this subject.

Means of expression and problems of human destiny interest a significant minority of people. By contrast, it is astonishing to note to what extent both pure and applied sciences are rejected. The natural sciences are nineteenth on the list of subjects, with 71 votes; physics and chemistry fare very poorly (57 votes). Only *medicine* escapes this relative disrepute. As it is of immediate interest, medicine is esteemed by people from every walk of life. We all know the popularity of the novelists who make use of medical themes—Cronin, Slaughter, and André Soubiran.

At a time when science is playing such a considerable role, one may ask why scientific subjects attract relatively few people. Certain groups show an interest in technical problems and the arithmetic needed to deal with them that does not carry over into an attitude favorable to the experimental sciences as a whole, probably because they are considered too remote and too difficult.

Differentiation of Subjects According to Social Backgrounds

To what extent is there a growing cultural homogeneity? Do the various social groups share equally in this culture, or do they have cultural traits peculiar to themselves? Analysis reveals a considerable differentiation in the terms of social background; culture is far from uniform and standardized.

A double fact stands out. On one hand, the choices of persons in certain social categories are much less numerous than those in another. Indifference, in some cases, is considerable. On the other hand, those who are most indifferent and least curious also show less diversity of choice; their interests are chiefly in practical and technical matters.

If we consider the average number of subjects chosen per individual, we see that the smallest number is chosen by technical

Percentages of responses in relation to the number in each category[1]

	MEN IN GENERAL	WORKERS[2]	WHITE COLLAR EMPLOYEES	EXECUTIVES[3]	CRAFTSMEN	BUSINESSMEN
Puttering around, hobbies	19	21	29	15	13	15
Your Job	29	26	29	34	47	25
Mechanics	23	27	22	18	29	19
Mathematics	20	23	33	14	21	11
Physics and Chemistry	13	7	18	23	13	6
Medicine	22	16	29	24	23	31
Natural Sciences	15	5	22	23	18	19
Geography	29	24	35	36	23	31
History	22	13	22	32	21	25
Political economy	18	11	13	29	13	25
Education	19	12	22	26	16	23
Psychology	14	6	13	25	10	17
French and Foreign Languages	17	13	20	18	16	15
Art and Literature	17	6	15	33	16	17
Ethics	17	8	24	24	18	19
Philosophy and religion	17	7	16	28	21	17

1. We have not presented all the categories in the population, and in each category there are multiple responses.

2. Workers : foremen, skilled and semi-skilled and laborers.

3. Executives : includes professions, higher executives, teachers, middle-rank executives and bureaucrats.

workers (6, 8,) and this in spite of many possible choices in the practical and technical series (more than one third). Craftsmen and small shopkeepers make an average number of choices (8, 4 and 8, 2 respectively). The number is larger among middle-range executives (14, 4), a different group with diverse preoccupations. A comparative analysis of responses and nonresponses gives similar results.

If we study the variation in the number of topics of interest selected by over 20 per cent of the members of each category, we note significant gaps. Thus, twenty-two subjects are selected by more than 20 per cent of the middle-range executives as against only four by more than 20 per cent of the semi-skilled workers and laborers.

Analysis of the list of subjects selected by over 20 per cent or more of each sociooccupational category shows clearly this variation in interests.

Industrialists and big businessmen are interested in practical and technical matters. Business is in first place, along with mechanics. Gardening is seventh. But the diversity in interests is significant. Political economy, the natural sciences, philosophy and religion take precedence over history and geography. This group appears to have a vast and abundant curiosity.

Craftsmen are predominantly interested in their trade, far more than in any other subject, as well as in technical matters (mechanics and motors). Certain subjects of general culture—such as geography, history, philosophy, religion, and medicine—are also represented among their choices.

Small businessmen have a noticeably different attitude from that of the craftsmen. They are less interested in technical subjects. For them, geography, history, medicine, and education constitute the subject matter of general culture, along with economic and political questions.

Practical and technical questions that excite a very strong interest in certain groups, notably the workers, are practically ignored by members of the liberal professions. For them, the dominant concerns are history and geography, art and literature; also science, economics, and education.

The higher executives are greatly interested in their business, very interested, too, in political economy and psychology. Their culture approaches that of the liberal professions. The interests of teachers are close to those of the two preceding categories. Middle-range executives exhibit a particularly original behavior. They are interested in a great number of subjects and make up the smartest and most inquisitive group. They are the only group showing a lively interest both in science and in art and literature. Practical and technical questions take second place.

The behavior of white-collar employees is somewhat similar to that of the workers. Practical interests concern them—arithmetic occupies a place of honor. Nevertheless, their culture is broader, approaching that of the executives. Besides history and geography, they like medicine, education, ethics, and natural sciences.

Foremen have multiple interests, particularly in practical and technical matters. They are interested in their work; they seem to want to go deeply into all its various aspects. They show concern about certain subjects of general culture. Skilled workers are interested, essentially, in the practical side of daily life (fishing, hobbies, gardening), technical subjects (mechanics, electricity), and arithmetic (useful on the job). Their interests, then, are not very diversified. Geography is the only subject of general culture they favor to any extent. Other subjects—such as medicine, sports, history, and economics—are sometimes mentioned. They show little interest in science, art, literature, or philosophy.

Semiskilled workers and laborers have a similar but much thinner culture. Only a few practical or technical interests are evident. Arithmetic occupies an important place. In the area of general culture, only geography and history engender any interest.

Service personnel (waiters, maids) are interested in arithmetic and languages—both subjects needed in a job involving human relations—practical matters, medicine, history, and problems of human destiny. Geography is missing from their list of interests.

A reclassification of categories permits major conclusions to be drawn. The behavior patterns of workers and executives are quite different one from the other. Workers are more interested in practical and technical matters and in arithmetic. An appreciable number also mention geography and medicine. By contrast, there is little interest in science, psychology, art, literature, and problems of human destiny. Executives show about five times as much interest in art and literature as do workers. The behavior of craftsmen, shopkeepers, and white-collar employees falls about halfway between that of workers and that of executives. Craftsmen and clerks are close to the workers in their interest in technical matters. General interests are more developed, especially among shop-keepers, without, however, attaining the level of the executive group.

Unquestionably, cultural differentiation is associated with social stratification. There are also noticeable differences between masculine and feminine culture. Among women, interest in the household arts corresponds to the interest of men in knowledge affecting their work. In both cases, one's daily work is the dominant preoccupation.

Medicine is in fourth place on both lists, but many other medical subjects appear on the women's list. The woman who has responsibility for family life is concerned with health problems.

While history goes along with geography on the man's lists, women lean more toward art and literature. They are more interested in psychology, less in economics and politics. Is this culture, the main characteristics of which we have just outlined, in the process of developing rapidly? Can we see new and renovating tendencies among the younger generations? Do they take more part in the main currents of contemporary culture? Contrary to what one would expect a priori, analysis of the results indicates that the chief interests in self-improvement *do not vary much according to age.* Older persons (fifty-one or over) seem to be more interested

Centers of Interest in Which More Than 15 Per Cent of the Men and Women Are or Have Been Interested

	MEN (TOTAL 415)		WOMEN (TOTAL 75)	
	Subjects	Number	Subjects	Number
1.	Your work	123	Cooking	37
2.	Geography	120	Sewing	36
3.	Mechanics	95	Household arts	31
4.	Medicine	92	Medicine	21
5.	History	91	Geography	20
6.	Arithmetic	86	Arts and letters	19
7.	Puttering	81	Education	18
8.	Travel accounts	81	Puttering	16
9.	Gardening	80	Dietetics	16
10.	Education	77	Hygiene	15
11.	Political economy	74	Cancer	15
12.	Ethics	74	Psychology	15
13.	Philosophy and religion	72	Medicine through plants	14
14.	Art and literature	71	Surgical discoveries	13
15.	Languages	71	Languages	13
16.	Fishing	65	Philosophy and religion	12
17.	Accounts of exploration	65		
18.	Natural sciences	63		

in puttering around; people between thirty and forty are more concerned with economic questions; young adults (under forty) seem to be more interested in art and literature than are older people. These facts merit careful study, but they aren't as important as the main finding—the relative homogeneity by age group. Is this a fact peculiar to an average town where attitudes change only gradually? Or is it a confirmation of the popular belief that "people learn at every age"?

To what extent has the schools' influence affected the self-improvement attitude of the adult? Are adult interests merely an extension of studies that he wishes he had learned more about at school? Or, rather, does he want to fill in some gaps in an education that no longer meets the cultural needs he finds in life?

There is only a rather remote connection between what interests adults and what is taught in school.

The subjects to which the greatest amount of time and importance are devoted in school are not those that have the greatest interest for adults. French and mathematics are less interesting than geography and history. Very few are attracted by science, but many are interested in economic and political questions and a whole series of subjects like education, medicine, and so forth. These subjects are given little attention in the primary school, or even in the secondary. Should they receive more attention in school? Or should they be left for adult education?

Adults seem to be aroused by two considerations: (1) a better understanding of the world in which they live; and (2) an effort to solve the many problems they confront in their daily life. It is doubtful that the schools have fully prepared them for this task. In any case, schools have far to go if they are to succeed in creating in the various social circles the common outlook that was intended to result from sharing a common culture among all the citizens of the country.

The percentage of workers interested in art and literature is five times smaller than that shown by executives. The commitment of French education to equality is well known. Prolongation of mandatory school attendance, from this viewpoint, is essential for the progress of a common culture that would reduce the imbalances (the interest in mathematics is much higher among white-collar employees and workers than among executives and the liberal professions).

Each job makes its demands, but the different evolution in each social group implies a difference in training which, in certain cases, could be compensated for. Sharing in popular culture would then become a life-long acquisition.

Knowledge of the adult's real interests permits specifying the basis for training in popular education. Education for adults must be adapted to their preoccupations and must especially take into account their marked interest in thinking about the activities of their daily life. For them, popular culture primarily consists in thinking about the problems of everyday living.

Interest shown in certain subjects may be cultivated with a view to enlarging what is felt to be an overly narrow culture.

Geography, now widely enjoyed, may be a way to introduce other historical, economic, political, literary, and artistic subjects. Interest in medicine could lead the individual into the field of life sciences. At the present time, these areas of interest are relatively underdeveloped in popular education.

How Is New Knowledge Acquired?

SELF-INSTRUCTION

In our interviews, we asked the following question: "How do you prefer to get at the facts in a serious manner?"

A large majority replied "by reading"—68 per cent, of which 53 per cent mention reading in general and 47 per cent mention books or periodicals. Other sources of knowledge are scarcely mentioned. Practical lessons are considered of little importance; only 12 per cent prefer them. People acknowledge they learn through practice, especially in the area of manual training and education. Is conversation alone, without actual practice, regarded as a means of getting the facts? Only 7 per cent mention this as a means. Lectures, courses, study circles using school formats are rarely used. Only 8 per cent of the responses mention them. This traditional method of transmitting knowledge is clearly preferred by only a minority. The preferred method appears to be personal study—that is, reading. Audiovisual methods, which are currently developing so rapidly and which are so powerfully insisted upon for this purpose, have almost no influence. Five per cent mention them.

Among those who prefer reading printed matter, 59 per cent mention periodicals as against 41 per cent favoring books. The daily newspaper is a relatively important source of information, even in this area: special columns, special departments, special reports (only 25 per cent mention periodicals). For adults, the schoolbook still plays an active role. It is used, or reused, especially in the study of languages and mathematics, as well as for history and geography. In these areas, it is *the* indispensable reference work. For the future, research probably ought to give increasing attention to this function of certain schoolbooks, not only in the education of children, but also in the on-going education of the family.

CULTURAL COURSES

Evening classes are highly popular in the Soviet Union, as much as in the United States and the Scandinavian countries. In France, they are not widespread. By contrast, intensive and short-term courses seem to be ever more popular. The law of July 22, 1957, providing twelve days of unpaid vacation, applies only to trade-union education; a recent expansion of this law offers new possibilities for self-improvement in various areas of popular education. It was interesting to learn to what extent people were attracted by this provision and wanted to take advantage of it, in cases where it would be accompanied by a remuneration. The question asked at Annecy was: "If a paid study-vacation of twelve working days (in addition to regular paid vacation) were offered in order to train you for administrative work in a union, political, sports, or cultural group or to prepare you for an examination, or to increase your knowledge of a subject of your choice, would you accept—or not?"

Thirty-four per cent of the working men replied affirmatively. Those who rejected the offer gave various reasons we shall analyze later: lack of interest or time, age believed too advanced, among others. Interest varied according to socio-occupational grouping. This variation was in direct relationship to the number of those in each group interested in self-education.

Sixty-one per cent of the executives wanted such a "sabbatical." This is a comparatively high percentage, related to the fact that this is the category with the greatest curiosity and the most education. Generally speaking, it is the industrial and administrative executives who most favor this approach. Forty-six per cent of the higher executives and 43 per cent of the foremen would like to enjoy its benefits. Those in the liberal professions and white-collar group, respectively, were 37 and 42 per cent in favor.

The following groups seemed reticent: craftsmen, shopkeepers, and workers. Only 13 per cent of the craftsmen were interested. This indifference contrasts with the relatively high approval shown by shopkeepers (31 per cent). Skilled workers (35 per cent) show more interest than semiskilled or manual workers (23 per cent). These results corroborate our earlier analysis that showed the cultural passivity (atony) typical in certain social groups.

One would like to think that young men, anxious to enlarge their knowledge and endowed with minds still open and supple, would show a more pronounced interest in a paid educational sabbatical. And this is the fact, although less obvious than would have been expected. The highest percentage of those favoring a sabbatical is not in the under-thirty group (46 per cent in favor), but among those between thirty and forty (51 per cent favoring between ages thirty-one and thirty-five, and 53 per cent between ages thirty-six and forty). The percentage drops rapidly thereafter: 25 per cent of those between forty-one and fifty, 16 per cent of those over fifty.

What subjects would they like to study during these educational furloughs? The largest group (40 per cent) want vocational improvement. We have seen earlier that a man's work takes precedence as a major, central interest. The same number of men (18 per cent) are interested in scientific and technical questions as are in economic, social, and political matters (18 per cent). Twenty-six per cent of the responses indicate a desire to increase one's general culture.

Mass culture is not limited to entertainment. At all levels of society, there are people who have not lost the taste for serious study, for learning about various subjects that require greater knowledge and better aptitudes. Concern for job, family, and social responsibilities seem most frequently to lie at the origin of the demand for knowledge.

Despite the enormous effort exerted by the great mass media— entertainment, book distribution, audiovisual instruction—it must be emphasized that the means most used by the public for increasing its knowledge is still reading. In contrast to the feeble interest shown in lectures and courses, the formula of sabbaticals appears to answer a real need. This need is felt primarily between the ages of twenty-five and forty; does this not suggest an important formula by which to advance knowledge through popular education?

Do all levels of society show an equal appetite for knowledge in the same subjects? Can we speak of a unification of our culture? Despite the differences in social background, the percentages of those interested in the same subject vary within quite narrow limits, rarely in a ratio of more than 2 to 1. The job, geography, mechanics, and medicine occupy the front ranks of preferences in almost all social classes. Between executives and workers asked about sabbaticals for study of the same subjects, the differences in attitude may vary from 1 to 3. Of course, there are variations in preferences depending on the particular culture of each group. We must remember that artistic and literary concerns are proportionally five times stronger among executives than among workers. Cultural disparities as among social classes are far from having been liquidated.

We have evidence, therefore, that in our present social context indifference to learning is the dominant public trait. Should not the school blame its curriculum and its organization? Is it enough to prolong school attendance for all? Should not school organization take account of the educational needs at different stages in life? Should not there be a new balance among the functions of entertainment, information, and education provided by the great mass media? Should not the activities of the educational associations be strengthened and new legislation advanced to provide study-vacations for all who need to improve their function in society?

We have tried to show that the culture experienced by the mass of the people is profoundly affected by the multiple and ambiguous ways leisure time is spent, the extent, the prestige, and the value of which are constantly increasing. Are not present-day societies, even the most liberal ones, if they are to avoid incoherence and

impotence, obliged increasingly to face up to the effect of the
cultural content imposed by the school and offered by private
associations and the great public and private mass media during
free time? The institutions are diverse but Man is one. For him
each of these three types of cultural action agencies has a different,
even though comparable, responsibility. The democratization of
culture is a right encouraged in our Constitution; *it is also a problem
which has not been solved.* In an ever more complex and more
rapidly evolving society where cultural development cannot stop
with childhood, the school, even reformed, will not be able alone
to solve this problem. What to do? A long and difficult research
program is required in order to find the optimum relationship
between cultural action by the school and after school, by private
groups and by public and private telecommunications. It is possible
that the growth of leisure will oblige the Ministry of National
Education to undertake new forms of continual or periodic, mandatory or permissive, semifree or free intervention in order to
spread a general culture that is both life long and renovated and
better adapted to the changing needs of society and to the spontaneous interest of individuals ranging in age from six to forty. This
is, perhaps, the future condition of what Bachelard calls "continued
culture." It will be continued after formal schooling for an increasing number of individuals from all walks of life only if it identifies
itself at least in part to the complex functions of leisure as it is
experienced. Yet these ideas are hypotheses that the sociology of
leisure has defined without having been able yet to prove them.

What Methods Have You Used in Order to Keep Yourself Informed, Seriously and Regularly?

	Practice	Conversation	Lecture and Study Center	Movies	Radio	Daily Newspaper	Technical Magazines	Other Magazines	School Books	Other Books	Dictionary	Literature	Reading in General Books Included	TOTAL
Practical, technical questions	150	50	38	14	9	22	55	28	3	35	4	1	134	543
History, geography	19	6	14	14	9	13	11	25	23	14	3	5	115	271
Medicine	11	13	7	2	5	16	12	15	3	13	5	0	77	179
Education	31	12	18	0	0	6	15	11	2	16	2	0	50	163
Physics, chemistry, natural sciences	12	8	10	4	2	7	12	21	6	13	3	1	67	166
Psychology, morals, economy	9	16	27	1	18	23	15	25	0	22	2	2	82	242
Philosophy and religion	1	7	18	0	0	3	6	15	0	14	1	1	77	143
Art and Literature	5	7	12	14	4	4	6	13	0	12	1	4	74	156
Languages	6	11	13	0	2	1	3	8	19	9	5	2	61	140
Arithmetic, geometry, Algebra	9	3	13	1	0	1	2	6	22	6	2	0	41	106
Miscellaneous	9	9	6	5	6	8	1	5	5	4	1	3	4	66
TOTALS	262	142	176	55	55	104	138	172	83	158	29	19	782	2,175

Chapter 11

Dynamic Attitudes
and
Style of Life

Dynamic Attitudes

AFTER DEALING WITH THE DIFFERENT KINDS OF LEISURE-TIME behavior—vacations, television, movies, books, and self-improvement—we should now clarify the concepts of activity and passivity that we have used so often. What is terrifying about leisure in our mechanized age is that it is liable to develop and maintain a generalized passivity. In company with other authors, we have emphasized that the key problem for leisure civilization lies in the possibility of promoting dynamic approaches to the use of free time.

Friedmann speaks of active leisure; some years ago Riesman ended his critical study of our civilization with an attack on conformity in American leisure and an appeal for the "autonomous man." Recently, Max Kaplan was insisting on the need to define, through research, the standards of leisure necessary for the growth of man in our civilization (2). In the United States, as in Europe, all research workers cry out against this danger of passivity, but this unanimity itself is based on ambiguities from the minute the terms *passivity* or *activity* are attached to a particular leisure activity. When is leisure active, when passive?

For some, watching a movie is passive, while attending a theatrical performance is active. Many movie experts have analyzed the spectator attitude as a form of hypnosis. But for Pierre Francastel "the mind of the spectator is as active as that of the producer." For others, attendance at any kind of show is passivity, whether sports, theater, or movies. For them, to derive an educational benefit, a man should practice a sport or act in a play or make a movie.

Some theoreticians of the youth movements establish a contrast between activity and intellectual games. Working with material, handsome or ugly, useful or not, is said to be "thinking with one's hands"—this is considered "active leisure" par excellence. For still others, active leisure requires reflection, especially after much reading. The book, for them, is even more than an instrument of learning, it is a mythical mind-generator; while the audiovisual media are merely the cause of widespread passivity.

It would be easy to prolong this list of differing conceptions of active leisure. They include partial truths but seem to be too "systematized." Their partial truth becomes an absolute that avoids experimental verification and excludes a priori any other conception.

To begin with, it is not the leisure activity itself that is active or passive, but one's attitude toward it. Furthermore, the active and the passive attitudes are not opposed to one another in an absolute sense. It is more a matter of relative predominance varying according to individuals and situations that ought to be measured in terms of scale of intensity. After all, value criteria ought to be general enough to be applied with a flexibility that takes account of the different requirements of each group and each individual. In this way, an *optimal* dynamic attitude can be empirically determined in terms of both social and individual needs. Agreement may then, perhaps, be reached between those who are active in cultural pursuits and those who are observers of the effects of this action on the public in terms of three fundamentals.[1]

1. The dynamic approach implies a conscious and voluntary participation, at least periodically, in some form of *social life*. It is opposed to social isolation or withdrawal, what Durkheim called anomie, normlessness. It does not consist of a conformist adaptation to the cultural norms of a social group, but of a willingness to assume at all levels a varying degree of responsibility in the life of a group, a class, or a society, while at the same time being determined by them. This participation involves the family, the company, the union, the community, and all groups and classes.

2. It involves a conscious and voluntary participation in *cultural life*, at least periodically. It is opposed to submitting to the routine practices, the stereotyped pictures, and the ready-made ideas of any group. It stimulates efforts to feel, understand, explain, or utilize the products of technology, science, art, and, if necessary, invention, in order to add to their enrichment through creativeness.

3. It always involves free *personal development* through a search by the use of free time for balance among relaxation, amusement, and continuous and harmonious growth of the personality. This balance will vary with each individual.

In this way, the dynamic approach or the active attitude represents *a combination of physical and mental attitudes capable of assuring the optimum growth of the personality through an optimum participation in social and cultural life.*

How may we observe in a given group and for a given activity the various types of dynamic approach? Here we will limit ourselves, in illustrating what we mean, to an anlysis of certain dynamic approaches to the movies.

---

[1] This is our hypothesis: We seek to confirm it in accordance with the Thurstone principles through a committee of experts representing all the existing trends in cultural activity and research in our own country and in several European nations of differing cultural tradition, economic level, and political regime.

Active Spectators

What is an "active spectator"? There are *a hundred ways* to react to a film, depending on one's background, the situation, and the individual. It would be unwise to try to deduce from analysis of film criticism the cultural patterns of the whole population, without taking into account the specific cultural habits of the various social groups. Without underestimating the considerable bearing that criticism has upon the esthetic appreciation of film productions, it mustn't be forgotten that criticism, generally, is the work of intellectuals who are scarcely familiar with the conditions and growth processes in the cultural levels of various audiences. By contrast, in a given group it is important to observe the reactions of the most critical spectators, those of the various types of people who have educated themselves about movies, especially those who play the social role of opinion leaders (3).

When there are innovating groups, such as the ciné-clubs, it is interesting to observe the reactions of the organizers and analyze what attitudes they are seeking to inculcate in their worker, white-collar, or executive audiences. They have an intuitive awareness of the explicit or implicit ideal and real cultural patterns that are created in ciné-clubs (when they avoid the estheticism of a coterie) and in an educational-film group (when it avoids moral dogmatism), and also of the evolution of the public from passive into dynamic attitudes.

The number of weekly admissions in the five movie theaters in Annecy amounts to about ten thousand (children and adults). The number of members of ciné-clubs and educational film groups (including children) is about two thousand. A qualitative study of the patterns of these clubs and of the cultural behavior of their leaders has led us to this first analysis of the dynamic approach toward the movies. It is rare to find all of these traits in the attitude of the same individual. They are to be found primarily in the different ways people approach a film.

From these patterns, we learn that the dynamic attitude is above all *selective*. The spectator does not go to the movies solely for lack of anything else to do. He doesn't go just because the theater is nearby or because it's Saturday evening. He chooses such and such a film and rejects another. He does not choose it just because of the movie star's name. In France, only 62 per cent of the movie-goers make their selections on the basis of the star's name (4). Our spectator pays attention to the quality of the work, its subject matter, and its form. He attaches importance not only to the star but to the actor, the director, and the production team. He chooses his information sources. In the last twenty years, use of the press and the radio to aid in the choice of a film has made much progress. Twenty-six per cent of the public use this approach. For 33 per cent, word-of-mouth criticism is the determinant. The active spectator seems to choose his informants more carefully. He is not content with rumors; he seeks advice from competent persons in his local area.

In what respect does the active spectator's approach to the film itself differ? First, he is *sensitive* to the pictures, to the action, the words, the sounds—the totality of the film. He tries to get rid of ready-made notions, moral or social prejudices which could atrophy his immediate sensitivity to the production. The dynamic attitude consists first of all in creating a state of total detachment, in order to live the imaginary life in full, to liberate completely the mechanisms of projection and identification, without which there is no effective participation. This is the moment of the "awakened dream." Intellectuals are not the only ones who run the risk of depriving themselves of this capacity to receive. Often, workers who regularly attend the movies, guided by standards irrelevant to the film, will laugh or whistle at the wrong time and will react to some detail without being affected by the general meaning of a given scene. In this case, the spectator missed his rendezvous with the film because of lack of sensitivity or because of too much conditioning. Like intelligence, sensitivity can be passive or active. It is also capable of improvement and refinement.

Next, the active spectator seeks *understanding*. Each film has its specific language—its vocabulary, grammar, and syntax—which our spectator tries to decode during or after the show. Not only does he appreciate fine language, but poor language prevents him from appreciating the story, the scene and its feeling or idea. His understanding pierces to the roots of the film. He makes distinctions between likelihood and unlikelihood. While he won't weep at all the melodramas of Margot, he remains sensitive to all the human verities.

After the show, he more or less analyzes the meaning of the action and the characters he saw, the underlying artistic or philosophic conceptions, at least when the film intends a message. To sum up, he tries to capture the esthetic, psychological, social, or philosophical meaning of a production in accordance with the producer's intentions.

Assembling his sensations and impressions, he re-creates the making of the film, transforming "the picture into feeling and the feeling into idea." But understanding the film in itself is not enough for the active spectator. He pulls back from it in order to *evaluate* it. He compares this film with others. He compares it with reality. Morin properly emphasizes that realism itself "is not the real thing but the picture of the real thing." Does this picture represent reality or not? Which parts of reality have been retained and which eliminated? What is the place, the value, and the meaning of the film, on the one hand on the screen, on the other in real life? One of the functions of the cinema is to visualize dreams, but our spectator is careful not to mistake these dreams for reality, the performance of the star for the life of the "eternal feminine," the world of "spirits and ghost" for the world of everyday.

The phenomena of identification with movie stars and of projection into situations on the screen are part of the game produced by

the magic eye. If these phenomena last only briefly, they are conducive to a good equilibrium; prolonged too long, they may bring
about social maladjustments. The influence of movies on delinquency is highly controversial, but it does seem possible for such an
influence to exist if the young person is unable to separate fantasy
from reality. From this point of view, greater censorship seems less
important than training movie-goers to develop critical faculties
that will make it possible for them to leave the movie theater and
face up to situations in real life. For the active spectator, the degree
of reality expressed or lacking is the ultimate test of the film.

The active spectator is looking for the meaning. He doesn't
limit himself to evaluating the strengths and weaknesses of the
production. He is trying to find out the reasons for them. The work
is the product of an artistic conception: How is it related to the
art of the producer? This conception frequently derives from
psychological, social, or philosophical ideas. What are the producer's ideas? These ideas can be accounted for by the
producer's personality, his family and his social background, and
the period when he made the film. For the active spectator, the film
may be the point of departure for a fascinating study of culture,
society or men, as is evidenced by the works of Bazin or Morin.

It is in this way that the movies may provide the occasion for
refining one's taste or for stimulating one's understanding, one's
critical mind, one's knowledge, or one's own social and cultural
activities. While providing entertainment, the movies may become
the means by which the cultural level is raised, as is shown by the
evolution of part of the public during these past fifteen years. Under
certain conditions, the audience may reach out to the producer, as
the producer is reaching for the audience. The active spectator is
he who assembles all the resources of his sensitivity and his intelligence in order to place himself, to the greatest extent possible, in
the producer's shoes.

The active spectator does not keep all he has learned from the
film to himself. He *shares* it with others. He spreads word of the

film to his friends and family, on the job, in his neighbourhood, or even beyond. It is through the leaders of opinion that the group develops. Intermediaries establish the meaning of the film; their action may be more important than the direct action of the film itself. They thus contribute to changing public attitudes and to preparing a climate that can influence the producers themselves.

Style of Life

In all kinds of leisure, dynamic attitudes should be studied and analyzed without dogmatism. Their general effect would tend to constitute a style of life for each group and each person. One's style of life may be defined as the personal manner in which each individual conducts his daily life. As we have seen, the inviduality of many a person is best asserted during his free-time activities and less and less during the work that he has to perform. Through these activities, the individual has time and means for developing his style of life, even with respect to his work. Seeking and realizing a style of life give leisure its greatest significance.

We must state the idea of originality precisely: the American ethnographer, Ralph Linton, studying the relations of the individual to the culture of his background, distinguishes four categories: (1) the universal—beliefs and attitudes common to every normal member of the society; (2) the special—beliefs and attitudes differing according to type of job, sex, and so forth; (3) the alternative— ways each one thinks while doing what the others are doing; and (4) individual peculiarities.

True originality does not consist only of one's individual peculiarities. It is also found in the ways by which each person experiences the norms of his group, his class, and the whole society to which he belongs.

Initiating a style of life begins by promoting an awareness of these norms and their determinants. It is a matter of understanding everything in the freest part of daily life—leisure activity. From this clear awareness can flow a valid choice among alternatives and the most complete realization of each one's individuality, at one and the same time as adjusted as necessary and as autonomous as possible. There is no sports technique in itself, no way of traveling in itself, no film interpretation in itself. There is first a common way of behaving, in the way one uses one's body, in the way one travels through an area, in the way one looks at a movie. It is in relation to this behavior, and not by ignoring it, that the worker or the farmer may acquire an original art of living during his leisure time.

Search for a style of life, then, is inseparable from an awareness of the problems of social life—that is, of the conditioning that must be overcome. Behavior is, therefore, not the mechanical result of conditioning. It makes use of the resources of the environment in terms of the needs and aspirations of the personality. It is not a matter of a fastidious attempt at life-long self-education. Each person becomes concerned about his own balance between relaxation, entertainment, and self-improvement along the stream of everyday occurrences. This choice leads each one to establish a *hierarchy* in his physical, manual, intellectual, or social activities, to strengthen every day the autonomy and the structure of his personality, while at the same time increasing his conscious and voluntary participation in the life of society.

Defined in this way, the search for a style of life leads to "raising to the highest point certain of our natural qualities while at the same time maintaining an equilibrium among them all . . ." (Paul Valéry). It is an attempt to organize free time and orientate thinking on the basis of a preferred form of leisure—a hobby, an Ingres-playing-the violin, voluntary social work—without forgetting the others. Such an effort implies revolt against everything one is forced to submit to and an option for everything that expands life. A style of life is a riposte against a conformist and depressing background. This is why our urban, industrial civilization is also a civilization of the outdoors and the return to nature. This is why our "ready-made" civilization of assembly-line work is also the civilization of puttering around, of the amateur mechanic, of the inventor or creator. The counterdeterminants of the contemporary world are thus in part created by the leisure that this world itself has made possible.

In this perspective, leisure time appears as the framework of an attitude that is by no means marginal, but that is a mediator between the culture of a society or a group and the reactions of an individual facing situations in daily life. This mediating role is also carried out in connection with leisure activities and with other activities, on or off the job. At the same time that leisure is pleasure time, it also becomes a time of apprenticeship, of attainment, and of integration quite different from the aggregate feelings, knowledge, patterns, and values of the culture, and also from work activities in which the individual is involved. Leisure can become a breaking-away in two senses. It is a stoppage of activities required by the job, or family or social responsibilities, and at the same time a sharp questioning of the routine stereotypes and ready-made notions resulting from the repetitiveness and specialization of day-to-day responsibilities.

By making this double-breaking-off possible, not only for the privileged classes but also for the people at large, leisure carries with it the chance that a revolutionary change in the culture itself may be brought about. By becoming a possession of the people, culture might once again undergo a metamorphosis. The aristocratic origins of our culture presuppose a man "a fine man" who is doing nothing. In its frigid nobility it may be uninterested in the humble daily life of work. A democratic reaction to this asserted itself during the nineteenth century: Work was exalted. From Marx to Mannheim, reformist thinkers claimed that work could and should be the basis of a new culture that would no longer be set aside for a few idlers, but would be open to all who work. Other thinkers from Condorcet to Jules Ferry sought to accomplish a democratization of culture in another way. They imposed on all the children of the "people" a time free from productive work, an ever longer period of schooling, without calling into question the very foundations of the culture they were propagating, a culture inherited from the past.

Today, the possibility of extending and improving leisure for the mass of the people forces us to ask ourselves questions under new conditions. These conditions are not contradictory to the preceding ones; they place them in a different perspective. The fact is, the "man of leisure" does have and will have more free time, like the humanist of the sixteenth or seventeenth cntury. However, belonging to the mass of the working population, he continues and will probably continue to stress *activity*, whether manual, physical, or intellectual, as the basis of a living culture. Instead of emphasizing work activities alone, he may see in leisure activities a mediating factor between the general culture and the totality of his activity. These leisure activities provide the time necessary for discovery, attainment, and free creation. It may well be that, henceforth, the relationships between physical culture and intellectual growth, between serious activity and fun, will change profoundly in a culture experienced by the mass of the people in a civilization ever more characterized by leisure.

It seems to us that one of the most important goals both for humanists and for sociologists of contemporary culture is to follow this new culture, which is more alive than classical culture, more unselfish than "polytechnical" culture, more intimately linked with the dynamic attitudes of the Man of Leisure toward travel, sports, movies, TV, reading for pleasure, and voluntarily participating in social life.

Chapter 12

Tentative
Conclusions

So, DURING THE PAST HUNDRED YEARS LEISURE HAS BEEN BORN, has grown up, and has taken on significance. It is in full flower. While enjoyment of it is still limited by misery, disease, and ignorance, it still stands there, like an imperative demand or a latent value in every social group, especially in the younger generation. In every industrial society, what was a class phenomenon in the nineteenth century has become a mass phenomenon in the twentieth.

It is not a by-product of present-day civilization, but central to it. With the rise in individual income, more free time is for most men perhaps their basic outlook. Work is not performed as an end in itself, but as a means.

Modern nations, however, have not yet become aware of the general problem of leisure. Leisure is still experienced in fragments, in diverse activities. Analyzing their interdependence and arranging them in balance to form a style of life is difficult. By turns, leisure is vacation or volunteer work, idleness or sport, a good dinner or a musical show, a game of love or a game of chance, reading a newspaper or studying a *chef-d'oeuvre*, gossip or study circle, hobby or group organization. All these leisure activities, however, are circumscribed within free time. They show no sign of necessity nor duty. They do not aim at making money; they are carried on in between responsibilities owed to family, society, politics, or church. They can be complete in themselves, serve to counterbalance one another or to substitute for one another in accordance with personal or group patterns. They are undertaken freely for the purpose of obtaining some satisfaction. Most often, they are ends in themselves. Whatever their content, these activities have for individuals and for society much more similar significance than would first appear (1). Free time is time when every form of human decadence or human growth is authorized.

In its multiple forms, leisure stands forth as a challenge to all utilitarian moralities, all community-minded philosophies, all taboos inherited from a traditional civilization dominated by misery, ignorance, fear, and the restrictive ritual of the group (2).

It requires these moralities, philosophies, and taboos to readjust the application of their principles. A hundred and fifty years ago it was said that "happiness is a new idea in Europe." Today this statement may be repeated. This search for a new *joie de vivre*, this new "rage for life," is not only part of a *nouvelle vague*, but of a new civilization. It is deeply rooted in the conquests of the machine age, but at the same time opposed to all the physical and moral constraints born of this age. Leisure activities are its privileged zone of accomplishment, and the values of leisure are among its most widespread and attractive components.

Most of our present-day systems of interpretation, coming down from the past century, stand defenseless in the face of the expanding phenomena covered by leisure. Many philosophies of work still consider leisure as a complementary or compensatory aspect of work. Most consumer specialists treat it as an element in the "miscellaneous" items that go into the budget for food, clothing, shelter, and health. Almost all family experts hardly ever trouble even mentioning its name. The organization of leisure is never a consideration in present-day studies of family functions.

When young people assert their confused but powerful yearnings for gang activities or for destructive and delinquent acts, 99 per cent of which are carried out during free time, these phenomena are analyzed merely in terms of laws broken, failure of education, searching for a new community or a new mystique . . . almost never in the light of the new demands of a civilization that stresses the preferred age for leisure: youth—and which has not yet found its ethic, its philosophy, or its law. To this day, no French author has drawn up an analysis in the slightest degree comparable to that of "muscular delinquency" by Daniel Bell in his *The End of Ideology* (3).

While absenteeism at union or political meetings is mentioned, it is not related to the evening or Sunday activities that take their place. It is analyzed only in terms of the crisis in political or union ideologies. The content and the form of political participation in a leisure civilization are excluded from the field of study. When sociologists of religion study the increase in the pleasure-seeking aspect and the decrease in the ceremonial character of holy days, they do so mainly in terms of traditional community ideology.

The crisis in culture, the divorce of art from the public, and the ambiguities of popular culture are most frequently criticized from the viewpoint of an intellectual or sensual philosophy of culture or from the viewpoint of a democratic or aristocratic philosophy of the age of the masses, but almost never in terms of the possible content of the free activities of repose, entertainment, or self-improvement, which may *really* embody for the mass of the workers their own cultural effort.

Almost all national education reformers deal with the new needs of agriculture, business, and industry and try to compensate for the misdeeds of specialization through general culture, but, in most cases, the preparation of children for a balance between the functions of leisure in the world of tomorrow occupies a minor, if not a nonexistent, place. All these reformers are thinking solely about addition or subtraction with respect to a system the over-all structure of which has scarcely changed since Napoleon and Jules Ferry.

To sum up. We tend to measure new facts with an anachronistic ruler. Leisure, however, has already the force of an independent fact. It must be considered primarily on its own terms, with its own dynamic, next in its one-to-one reciprocating relationships with work, family, politics, religion, and culture. All the systems connected with these great ideas of civilization must be expanded to include the ensemble of characteristics and factors of leisure civilization. Leisure is the expression of a whole collection of man's aspirations on a search for a new happiness, related to a new duty, a new ethic, a new policy, and a new culture. A humanistic mutation is beginning. It may even be more fundamental than the Renaissance. It has advanced slowly, almost imperceptibly, "on doves' feet," since the end of the second half of the nineteenth century when, for the first time, labor unions demanded not only a raise in wages but a reduction in hours of work. It is the logical outcome of the democratic and industrial revolution of the past century. It is one of the major components of the "giant test with uncertain results" that constitute the application of the Promethean inventions of Man on the scale of Humanity. This is the central hypothesis that emerges from our sociological investigations and in the critical study of the works of our European and American colleagues concerning leisure.

Has the world really entered upon a civilization of leisure? Tremendous disparities exist among individuals and social groups. A large number of people are still overwhelmed with work.[1]

Many people are still attached primarily to their work. For them, the technique of work is less important than the atmosphere of the shop and its friendly relationships. For others, work is a

---

[1] In France, two thirds of the workers earn less than 58,000 old francs per month (about $116, Tr.) and half of them only 39,000 francs a month (about $78, Tr.), according to tax authorities, published in the *Statistical and Economic Study Bulletin* in 1960.

privileged occupation that imposes a discipline that they need; it is this factor of equilibrium that Freud insisted upon. For a certain number, work invades their free time—pleasure-work, extra jobs, moonlighting. We have already spoken at length about this as much with respect to France and Yugoslavia as to the United States.

Of course, we all know that the slums and inadequate housing create problems requiring solutions far more urgent for a vast number of individuals than the question of knowing how to spend their leisure time. In France, half the homes should be reconstructed. In the underdeveloped countries, leisure problems are secondary to the struggle against hunger or ignorance. Two thirds of the people of this world do not eat enough; the half who don't know how to read or write are incapable of taking their own destiny in hand. First things come first.

However, we think that from this point on, to a greater or lesser degree, the problem of leisure is there, to be dealt with at the heart of industrial civilization, whatever may be the degree of technical development and the kind of social structure envisaged. Not only is it already present; it is reacting to the other economic, social, or cultural problems at the same time as it is being acted upon by them.

Obviously, it is the country that has attained the highest living standards and the shortest workweek (on the average barely forty hours, with some industries having a regular workweek of thirty-two hours) that the problem is most acute. Outside the 5 per cent who are permanently unemployed, and the 20 per cent who are relatively poor (having an income no greater than that of a little French clerk), all Americans have plunged in the race for consumption of objects which often satisfy less a personal need than a need for conformity or prestige.

If one has kept a car for two years, he will keep the next one a year and then buy two at the same time, and so forth. The race seems endless. According to Riesman, the overcongestion of the market that causes this permanent and anarchic pressure by advertising on the consumer can in the long run lead only "to complete

madness." It is in the area of leisure that this race runs the danger
of producing the most frightful effects on the social and cultural
aspirations of the mass of the people. Many organizations that could
encourage popular participation feel discouraged. Two thirds of
the Americans show no interest in them (4). Adult education efforts,
although increasing since 1950, (the number enrolled rose from
twenty-five to fifty million) are running into countercurrents. And
only fourteen states out of fifty provide subsidies. Most Americans
go to school up to the age of seventeen, and 30 per cent go on to
college, but their surroundings stress other values in a brutal
manner. TV programs of real intellectual or artistic quality are
restricted, crushed under a mass of mediocre comedies and variety
shows which are simply vehicles for obsessive advertising. Sales of
biographies of scientists, writers, and philanthropists are declining,
overwhelmed by life-stories of the stars of Hollywood and other
places. In spite of authors and innovators capable of improving mass
tastes and ideas, a thousand distribution channels impose the conformism of the average customer, the common man, as the image
of the ideal life.

"We don't have any institutionally organized ways of channeling
our abundance into grants for the improvement of both the quality
and the substance of our daily lives."² Urgently seeking to reform
the content and style of sales, Riesman concludes that it is easy to
foresee in the coming decades a great expansion in the number and
the activities of avocational counselors, the absolute necessity for
whom he shows in all sorts of shops and clubs that distribute leisure
goods or services to the mass of the people: fishing, sports, movies,
reading, and so forth. It is obvious that a great number of the
social and cultural problems in the United States depend on a
human rearrangement of the civilization of comfort and leisure.

Isn't it already the same for countries that have not yet reached
the production levels of the United States? We have seen throughout
this book that a European country such as France is already running

² David Riesman, "Work and Leisure," in *Mass Leisure*.

up against some of these problems in work, in family life, and in culture. In all the European countries with a capitalist structure in which a comparable survey of leisure was carried on (from 1956 to 1959), we have come up with the same findings. Leisure has such prestige that in each country all classes, even the workers, tend to imitate the middle classes to a large extent. We are aware of the phenomena of *embourgeoisement*, or standardization.

People around the world tend to look to the richest nations. The American way of life, in which leisure plays so great a part, has an undeniable influence. Whether it be a taste for automobile driving or worship of the "movie stars," present-day models are being dispatched by powerful media to the four corners of the earth.

They reach into the slums of Belleville as well as into the mansions of the Sixteenth Arrondissement, into the backcountry shacks of North Africa and into the villas of Algiers, into the shanty towns of Latin America and Africa as everywhere else. In the film *Moi et un noir*, by the ethnographer and movie-maker Jean Rouch, the young people of Abidjan are nicknamed Eddie Constantine and Dorothy Lamour. Of course, there still exist large isolated areas protected by surviving traditions. Sometimes, organized resistance to this cultural invasion is successful; but it is a fact that in former times the culture was above all the superstructure over the local institutions and customs, while today there is a changed situation. With the prodigious growth in communications, the planet has become very small indeed. Cultural models are transmitted from one end of the world to the other.

Patterns of leisure especially are being determined less and less by local experience alone, and more and more by messages coming in from the civilization that appears to be the strongest, the richest and the most prestigious. There is found the pole of propagation for a civilization that is tending toward universality, a *tele-civilization*. Henceforth, a dangerous social mimicry will threaten to determine the cultural life of every country, each one imitating today or tomorrow the beneficient or malignant aspects of leisure *à l'américaine.*

So it seems quite essential that we now focus our attention on those nations that have reached the stage of industrial civilization. Each country must anticipate its own evolution, both economically and culturally. It would be wrong to limit cultural action to the opening of schools to combat illiteracy or to the lengthening of compulsory school attendance. Ten years from now, what role will the school's influence be playing? Educational policy must be supplemented by a broad policy involving the institutions of recreational and educational leisure for the whole population, young as well as adult.[3] Tomorrow it may be too late to provide leisure in industrial civilization on the scale of Man.

Is the importance of leisure any less in countries having a socialist structure? Does the imperious need for leisure appear there only as an artificial stimulation originating in the capitalist system, without organization and without a collective ideal? In a recent article on "the cultural progress of society, an essential precondition for the achievement of Communism," a Moscow academician, G. E. Glezermann, recalled that according to Marx, "the true wealth of communist society will be the productive force developed by every individual; then the measure of wealth will no longer be the amount of time devoted to work but that devoted to leisure" (5). Did not Marx go so far as to evoke an idyllic state where, work having been reduced to a minimum, leisure activities themselves would become the essence of life? This would be a society "where no one is haphazardly assigned to some specialized task, but where everyone would perfect himself in any branch of activity that suits him. Society would take over the general management of production and thus permit the individual to do one thing one day and another tomorrow, or even to hunt in the morning, fish in the afternoon, and

---

[3] We have noted with pleasure that in UNESCO the old concept of basic education for underdeveloped countries has yielded to the much rarer concept of life-long education in entertainment for the whole population.

work on literary criticism after dinner, just as he pleases, without ever becoming hunter, fisherman, shepherd, or critic."[4]

The Soviet Union has not waited for this happy era to create a vast system of leisure institutions for the masses. All observers agree that the Soviet Union has been the most successful of all countries in organizing mass sports. Since Russia's first appearance at the Olympic Games in 1948, it has made constant progress. At the 1960 games, Russian teams carried off by far the greatest number of trophies. Recently, another Soviet academician mentioned in a French magazine the breadth of the cultural achievements of his country on behalf of the masses (6). However, some questions need to be asked.

Will an organized system of education like this be able to satisfy the aspirations of the newer generations, once the Soviet standard of living approaches that of the Americans? Won't the question of what to do with free time then cause even more complex problems? Even today, do not certain latent needs remain unfulfilled, in spite of the censorship of leisure activities and of culture? The first study of leisure in Russia, one having seemingly limited purpose, has already revealed that a great many people do not accept this planned policy (7).

In other socialist countries, whether dependent on or independent of Moscow, such as Poland or Yugoslavia, where we have participated in investigations in various localities, it is apparent that despite the environmental pressure in behalf of cultural development, large parts of the population pay little heed to the educational leisure-time institutions or take only a pro forma part in them, through either snobbery or conformism. In Yugoslavia, where socialist education is carried on under much more flexible conditions than in Russia, the problem of leisure has become so important in terms of its positive or negative effects on popular participation in labor union or municipal activities that it became in 1960 the subject

---

[4] Karl Marx in *The Holy Family*, mentioned by David Riesman in *The Lonely Crowd*.

of a debate on the occasion of the most important meeting about the country's political and ideological life (8).

To sum up, all countries, whether capitalist or socialist, are faced with major problems arising from the growth of leisure. One side employs a development policy for the masses that is too narrowly authoritarian; the other suffers from an absence of any policy at all, which permits a commercially based anarchy of entertainment to flourish. Both of them at different levels of technical development and with differing or opposing social structures, already find themselves in the grip of the central question of leisure civilization. This question may be formulated as follows:

How can a civilization in which leisure has become a right for everyone and is tending little by little to become a fact for the mass of the people, help each individual, whatever his birth, wealth or education, to achieve an optimum *balance* freely chosen from among the needs for repose, for entertainment, and for participation in social and cultural life?

In our view, there is no problem more important for the future of man in industrial and democratic societies. The stakes are enormous. The objectives of economic and social development are relatively clear. But what are the objectives of cultural development at the stage of a society's growth when the mass of the people gradually begin to reach out for leisure? There is talk of the institutions required for the progress of economic, social, political, and educational democracy, but such progress presupposes participation by the citizenry. Their participation implies that they are interested in the corresponding knowledge and values, that they use part of their leisure time to learn about scientific, technical, and artistic matters. The democratization of power, organization, and decision-making is obviously inseparable from the permanent democratization of learning. It is not enough to maintain that management by society of consumption and production is essential if a "gadget civilization" is to be avoided. The theories of post-Keynesian writers like Galbraith are necessary, but they are inadequate for the creation of a more human civilization. It is equally necessary, but also inadequate, to include a broadened educational program among the list of social objectives. The fact is, the promotion of leisure for the mass of the people has forced upon us the vast problem of *cultural democratization* in this second half of the twentieth century. It is just as important as economic, social, and political democracy. It is conditioned by them and in turn conditions them in large part. We are unable to cope with it, because it is so new, at least when taken in its *totality*.

Today, the cultural development of our mass society is enveloped in incoherence and impotence. In France, there is a certain amount of cultural action in all classes. Cultural action may be defined, in relationship to social and economic action, as the method by which public or private agencies intervene into the interests, information, knowledge, patterns, and values of the people, both in groups and in society as a whole, in terms of their standards of cultural development. These standards exist, consciously or unconsciously, but they are generally incomplete and poorly defined with respect both to ends and to means.

It is not enough to think that such uncertainties are caused only by the powers that be. The more or less permanent boards that are elected for the purpose of choosing, improving, or applying these powers are themselves in the greatest confusion. The Higher Council on National Education, for example, has never been able to decide upon the kind of scholastic education that ten million students should have or to fit it into the general framework of the life-long educational process proposed for the whole population. Its idea of the power of the great information mass media or the cultural institutions and associations is oversimplified. The effects of their cultural action on those of the school or the university has never been subjected to any scientific research. The Council has not even been able to surmount the minor squabble between the traditionalists and the modernists within the teaching world who argue all year long, not about the school's contribution to a cultural development appropriate to the leisure time of the mass of the people, but over whether to add or subtract an hour of Latin, mathematics, or French in the school curriculum. All the efforts at reform, however timid, that are aimed at exposing the teaching profession to the demands of "continual culture" have been smothered.

The Higher Council on Popular Education is on the whole more receptive to the problems we have raised. But today it suffers from the greatest confusion as it tries to establish standards of approval and subsidy for the so-called popular educational associations.[5]

Today, new types of associations are being formed to link popular educators not only to school educators but also to industrial and union instructors (who are involved in the cultural activities of the company committees), to social workers (sociocultural promotion in the new housing developments), to journalists (TV programs on the sciences of today or *Science and Life* in its new format), and to interesting researchers or inventors (associations of science writers, and the like). New groups concerned with the problems raised by today's cultural development for the public at large abound—in isolation from each other, without much publicity, and without significant help from the public bodies whose own responsible officials are poorly informed about these complex and changing needs.

The industrial sector, itself plagued by new problems of training its personnel, is hesitant about what direction to take. The need for developing a general culture among industrial managers is increasingly felt.[6]

What is the content of such a general culture, linked as it is both

[5] The Council instructed a committee to study standards of approval and subsidy in this new context. It has been waiting two years for the results. Today, the heads of this committee, though highly competent, acknowledge that their conclusions have already been left behind by events. Could it be otherwise, given the current state of information and research?

[6] The Institute for Practical Training of Managers, which includes representatives of almost all the training services in industry, organized its 1960 session around this theme: "General Culture and Industrial Training."

to leisure problems and to work problems? A recent report on social progress by the Economic Council (1962) included a long chapter on the necessity for cultural progress. But how are they related to one another? What should be the content of each, in relationship to economic development, social progress, and the free flowering of man in his leisure time? This is another presently obscure matter requiring research.

If we turn to the ways in which the great mass information media are involved, the disarray is just as great. The Higher Council and the program committee of Radio-Télévision Française are working under a good motto: "To amuse, to inform and to instruct." Yet, to what extent is the third purpose actually achieved? The public relations department does not have the ear of those in charge of programs. It is not itself equipped to be a service for studying the manifest or latent cultural wants of the various social categories that make up our society. Why, for example, don't we use more excellent dramatic or scientific programs, entertaining without dullness and instructive without boredom? Their reception could be prepared for in the schools, the universities, and the innumerable recreational and cultural leisure-time groupings? Afterwards there could be discussions on their content.

Why is the liaison between the RTF and the school or university so incomplete, so uncertain, and so obscured by misunderstandings over little matters between those responsible for one or the other? Could not the interchanges between the RTF and the whole mass of national, regional, and local institutions and associations for leisure and culture be less sporadic and less chaotic? What a waste of time, money, and talent, to the detriment of effective free-time cultural development for the whole people!

Two examples. One grant-in-aid group tends to favor quality films and literary productions that would never be produced in a business system based on supply and demand. This is an interesting form of intervention, but what standards govern its choices in either field? Assisting a de luxe edition of Mme. de Staël or an art film on plastic materials can both be justified. But why these productions instead of others? Such decisions should be made in accordance with an over-all policy of cultural development for the different categories of the population.

The situation with respect to censorship of artistic production gives evidence of even more serious intellectual poverty. In fact, the board can ban a film for a year and then authorize it two or three years later, at random, at the whim of a meeting. The censors make decisions by deducing from their own reactions those of millions of individuals, without seeking the slightest serious research into the real effect of the film, without paying the least attention to the question which, since Aristotle, has remained unanswered: the relationship between mimesis and catharsis. The question is posed by the movies, literature, and all the arts. Does Werther's revolver shot drive the reader to suicide or does it prevent him from really committing suicide by offering an opportunity to kill himself through an imaginary proxy? Or does quite another aspect of the book remain in the reader's mind and penetrate into his feelings?

In short, all these forms of positive and negative intervention, to ban or to stimulate intellectual and artistic productions by the positive or negative action of the RTF or the censorship board, are evidence of a profound crisis in standards of cultural development in our democracy.

It is, of course, desirable that there be differences between the contents and the performers of cultural action. Democracy can only be pluralistic; otherwise it is self-denying. Let no one, however, speak of "freedom" where there is only incoherence and impotence. In most cases, what results is the most humiliating kind of dictatorship—conformism, the mediocrity of cultural products so easily sold to the mass of people who are sufficiently educated to be interested but not educated enough to demand better entertainment or information.

The social sciences cannot yet formulate and clarify the alternatives for social decision with respect to these problems. But we do have the right and the responsibility to raise these questions in terms better adapted to today's new situation. Only an alliance between creative imagination and scientific rigor can help us get through the present crisis of cultural democracy. It would be vain to hope that action, even planned action, can bring about a solution, given the present state of thinking on this topic. A vigorous program of bold achievements in cultural action for the whole population in all its segments, allied with a strenuous effort at basic research, is imperative.

We know this is the hard way. We don't know of any others capable of helping us escape the current verbalism in which it asserted that "each citizen in a democracy has a right to culture," while at the same time it is accepted that technical knowledge is the privilege of the technicians, administrative skills that of the administrators alone, and intellectual and artistic learning that of intellectuals and artists isolated from the mass of the people. For us, it is not merely a question of describing the most spectacular characteristics of a "mass culture" fabricated in certain commercial dispensaries. We must study cultural situations that exist, but also situations that could exist; not merely behavior but needs. We will repeat for the last time that cultural sociology should prepare for a conversion in attitude similar to that which political economy has recently undergone, in becoming far more concerned with trends and with forecasts. Like the study of economic development, that of cultural development ought to bring about in every great modern country the creation of new research institutes which would work in close cooperation with the planning and forecasting organizations and with all the agencies of cultural action: schools, training units, mass information media, leisure-time institutions and associations . . .

The findings of this research into cultural action should be widely diffused by the various agencies among the public at large. This kind of educational work is the democratic liaison between creators, specialists, and the people. It is the basic condition of cultural democracy. It is normal for democracy to pay the price for this dynamic research and for the continuous diffusion of its findings. There has been talk of the social cost of democracy; there should likewise be talk of its cultural cost. Increasing the school budget, we have said, is necessary, but not enough. What must be envisaged is the cost of all forms of spreading the knowledge, in school and out, needed if cultural development in a mass society is to be on a par with *the values of democracy and the powers of technical civilization.*

We lay stress upon the "values" of democracy. The most miraculous progress in the social sciences will never replace the need for a choice among values. The social sciences can and should illuminate this choice. In the realm of action, the social sciences can and must avoid any spirit of dogma and system that associates these values with dubious mystiques, supernatural myths, or techniques of doubtful effectiveness. The social sciences will never replace a philosophy of values. There is reason to fear that cultural action could be inspired by totalitarian values incompatible with the freedom of the individual conscience. Pluralism within the great currents of ideas is co-existent with any complete democracy. On the other hand, we know that a society must possess a minimum of common values if it is to live and progress, if it is not to destroy itself. We may assume after a cursory analysis of our public and private cultural action, that a common minimum culture does exist among institutions and groups that otherwise are widely separated from one another. In order to see this more clearly, and to identify better the standards of cultural development that will respect the differences of each individual, it seems indispensable to call together all those responsible for private and public cultural action into a *cultural council.* This should play, with respect to the various cultural forces in our country, a role comparable to that which the Economic Council or the High Commission on Collective Bargaining Agreements play with respect to the various economic and social forces.

Would such a vast convention of ideological forces concerned with mass leisure-time cultural development not be the best bulwark both against totalitarian propaganda and free-enterprise incoherence. Would it not be the best basis on which to build our cultural democracy?

Critical Notes
on the Literature
on Leisure and Popular Culture
in the United States

Eric Larrabee and Rolf Meyersohn (eds.), *Mass Leisure*
(Glencoe, Ill.: The Free Press, 1958).

T HIS BOOK IS INTERESTING NOT ONLY BECAUSE OF ITS CONTENTS,
but because of its very existence. The very fact of the appearance
of a book dealing exclusively with the problem of leisure indicates
the importance given to this problem. Larrabee and Meyersohn
have tried to present as complete a picture as possible of the present
state of research in this area.

Their selection of articles represents, on one hand, one of the
first attempts at studying leisure in the largest sense, and, on the
other, an effort at analyzing its components (leisure activities) from
the standpoint of their mutual relationships, as well as indicating
some of the great social and cultural problems—leisure in industrial
civilization, time off from work devoted to leisure, the effect of
leisure on the various social classes, and the consequences of
automation for leisure in the near future.

[1] The critical study of this book and of the one by Max Kaplan was done
with the collaboration of Aline Ripert.

Leaving aside certain classic articles, such as the theories of play by Piaget and Huizinga or the famous "right to laziness" of Lafargue, there are a number of interesting ideas in this book. Martha Wolfenstein in "The Coming Fun Morality" shows how a kind of pleasure ethic is supplanting the traditional morality of work. Clement Greenberg, in connection with work-leisure relationships, denounces the negative concept of leisure considered as the opposite to unsatisfying work. He wants work and leisure to be integrated into an "authentic culture" capable of promoting the full flowering of Man in the industrial age.

A chapter of a book by George Lundberg dating from 1934, *Leisure, A Suburban Study,* gives us the first findings of a study of leisure-time budgets. Interesting data, collected from reliable sources, show the extent of the extraordinary growth of the "do-it-yourself" movement. Larrabee shows how the idea of the "hobby," so widespread in industrial society, includes quite different, even contradictory phenomena that require calling the whole thing into question. At the end of a nation-wide study, Charles Wright and Herbert Hyman state that participation in organized activities is relatively less important than it used to be, as shown by sociological studies before World War II.

Riesman predicts that leisure will facilitate adaptation to the modern world and to technology, but he speaks of a new kind of leisure, one liberated from the social constraints that foreshorten and deform its potentialities, whether in traditional society or in today's American society. This precedes the fascinating investigation by Harvey Swados of the city of Akron, where the workweek in the rubber industry is thirty-two hours, and where for various reasons, including escape from idleness, nonwork may lead not to increasing leisure activities but to a search for a second job.

Despite the real interest of all these articles, the lack of methodology and the paucity of conceptualization must be regretted. The whole is interesting, certainly, but not adequately coordinated.

The large bibliography stresses the importance that American authors give to leisure problems. But the limited choice of references of all kinds (philosophy, essays, economics, history, as well as sociology) unfortunately makes it rather difficult to use as a working tool.

Bernard Rosenberg and D. M. White (eds.), *Mass Culture* (Glencoe, Ill.: The Free Press, 1958).

In a recent edition of the *Public Opinion Quarterly,* Bernard R. Berelson gives echo to the crisis that the sociology of "mass communications" is undergoing today in the United States. He shows that research into "communication" along the lines of Lasswell, Lewin, Hovland, and Lazarsfeld has reached an impasse. To escape it, they are attempting a revival through a combination of the following different approaches: comparative international studies, economic analysis related to psycho-sociological studies, sociology applied to business affairs, study of the masses, and study of popular culture.

This collection of articles on mass culture is part of the growing stream of research into the great mass media. It had a great success in the United States. Completed at the end of the summer of 1956, it was published in 1957. By 1958, it was already in its third printing. It is a very well-constructed anthology, much better, in our opinion, than *Mass Leisure,* which was published a year later by the same Free Press. It brings together articles of general import concerning current commercial and cultural output; popular reading-matter, soap operas, songs, radio and TV programs, slogans and advertising gimmicks; and in this way it presents the main, if not the only, subject matter of what the publishers call mass culture.

The two editors, Rosenberg and White, explain that they have had some difficulty in pulling together and matching sociological articles on so vast, and paradoxically so new, a subject for American social scientists, in spite of thirty years swarming with empirical

research projects of all sorts, large and small. Fifty-one collaborators were called to the rescue in order to build this 561-page
structure. Between Berkeley and Columbia are there fifty-one
sociologists of popular culture? Obviously not. The authors
acknowledge it humorously in their preface. But they have gone
beyond the artificial barriers of academic distinctions, and this takes
them a long way. They have called upon first-class sociologists and
also on others. They have rounded up psychologists, literary critics,
art critics, and journalists. The one trait all these writers have in
common is not a passion for social science but a real interest in the
effects of the great mass media upon the culture of the mass of the
American people. What results from this focusing on curiosity?

It is fascinating, even though disconcerting. This book constitutes a disparate whole, and the divergences in viewpoint provide
the stimulating charm of an uninhibited forum. All the contrasting
aspects of mass culture appear, even in the preface. In fact, the two
authors warn us that their book will be a very special one, "perhaps
unique in its genre," since they are not at all in agreement even
with one another.

In the first two articles, Rosenberg plays the role of Dr. All's-for-
the-Best with respect to mass culture, while White plays the part
of Dr. All's-for-the-Worst. Each makes it a point of honor to play
according to the usual rules for great radio and TV debates; each
makes a slight caricature of himself so as to stress the antagonism
of his views to those of his neighbor, as if he were performing
before an audience whose mind had been somewhat brainwashed
after years of mass culture.

While some of the writers have, nevertheless, avoided the oversimplified picture of popular culture, we don't feel it is a betrayal
of the polemic stance of the book to put the virtues of mass culture
on one side and the evils of it on the other.

The virtues occupy a highly limited space. Thanks to the mass
media, learning and good music are reaching the public at large.
TV offers Shakespeare's works to one hundred and fifty million

spectators. Pocketbooks have made great literature available to everybody. Since 1920, sixty million Mozart records have been sold (White); the blues have disseminated among the public at large a feeling for sincerity in both music and words. They draw a distinction between most of the other popular songs, which are mediocre and false (Hayakawa), and authentic jazz, which has graduated from jazz combos to the school and the university (Berger), and so on.

On the other hand, the evils. TV broadcasts silly entertainment 75 per cent of the time. Americans are absorbed by this eighteen hours a week (Meyersohn). According to Berelson, not more than one fourth of the adults read even one book a month. During the war, the American people (one third of them adults) consumed ten times more comics than the number of books published by the two largest publishing houses (Bogart). The American people are becoming more infantile. America's symbol should really be not Uncle Sam but Peter Pan (Donald). The mass media disseminate stereotypes that put thinking to sleep (Adorno). Intelligent subject matter is eliminated because it won't be understood by everybody. The same is true for any topic that could divide opinion, such as racism.

It follows from this that the mass media cultivate social conformism (Lazarsfeld and Merton). The commercial plug must reach the greatest possible number of customers. Advertising aims at the most common and lowest tastes of the people (Van den Haag). It is the end of great art. There was a time when the best-seller was Dickens; today the best-sellers are crime novels by authors nobody ever heard of. In other times, the idols were political personalities. Today, they are movie stars (MacDonald). The true artists in the United States are unknown to the general public. They count for much less than in the Soviet Union, despite the advantages of not being subjected to any "line" (Seldes). Finally, the public infantilism in acclaiming Frankenstein and King Kong could develop into a taste for the horrors of fascism or Hiroshima (MacDonald).

What is the cause of this menace? For some it is capitalism, for others democracy itself. The anthology includes the comments of de Tocqueville on the dangers of democracy for the arts and of Ortega y Gasset on the effects of the revolt of the masses who threaten the rule of the elite to the misfortune of all. For still others, who feel even more threatened, the cause is perhaps a certain system of private-property control over the media (Lazarsfeld and Merton; Seldes).

The solutions? They are not worked out in this anthology; nevertheless, in the final article Seldes asks if the existence of the English or Russian noncommercial radio and TV does not create a problem for the American system. Is an excessive commercial freedom in the control of the content of these media acceptable? Should there perhaps be undertaken an educational campaign and a structural reform aimed at awakening dynamic attitudes in the public which would become aware of its own responsibilities for popular culture.

If this digest helps one to read the book, it is perhaps faulty in being too structural and schematic. Reading the full 561 pages would afford many nuances and emendations. Still, it seems too long, too repetitive, and, above all, too uneven. There are seven or eight excellent articles that we intend to translate for the French public: Riesman's on popular music, Berelson's on reading, Lazarsfeld and Merton's on mass media, popular taste, and social action, Adorno's and Meyersohn's on TV, and Lowenthal's on the historical perspectives of popular culture. The rest of the articles are confusing because of the oversimplification in their hypotheses, inadequate documentation, and indifference to evidence worthy of the name.

We wonder why certain important articles by Riesman, Wolfenstein, Lipset, or Lazarsfeld concerning popular culture were omitted. Was it because of a desire to publish only one piece by each author? That would be a rule of sociological courtesy scarcely favorable to the scientific quality of the book. But if this rule was deemed inevitable by the editors, why sacrifice major texts like those of

Riesman in *The Lonely Crowd* or of Lazarsfeld in *Personal Influence*. Are they supposed to be already so well known?

The editors warn us that sociological studies of popular culture are something new in the United States. We have no difficulty believing them. First, the research field itself seems to be poorly delimited. The working definition of popular culture implicit in the articles selected seems questionable. Why eliminate the amateur theaters or the Sunday painters so numerous in the United States? And why limit mass culture to the products of the mass media? We do not understand, for example, why cultural organizations are classified under leisure (in *Mass Leisure*) while card playing is taken as an example of mass culture. The distinction between leisure and culture does not seem to be quite clear in the minds of the editors, let alone the authors. Would it not be more accurate and more practical to consider as leisure activity everything done away from one's job, family, or social obligations, and popular culture (at least in part) as the cultural content of this activity?

Thus card playing, reading a book, attending a course, or watching TV would, in the first instance, be regarded as leisure activities, and then the cultural content of each leisure activity could be studied.

So, this fascinating compilation has sketched out some questions of method. They will be decisive for the advance of the social sciences concerned with popular culture. We must attack them seriously. We have greatly appreciated the allusions to this matter made by Riesman and Lowenthal. For Riesman the problem of methodology is presently the most important if the sociology of popular culture is to escape from metaphysics and make a systematic inventory of the contents of popular culture along the lines of Lasswell's principles. "Who says what to whom to what effect?" This is a well-known line of research, worth following in depth.

Lowenthal makes a convincing plea for applying the historical method to the study of popular culture in order that the cultural reality of today be neither praised nor condemned in terms of metaphysical or personal criteria of the needs of society in a given period. In a remarkable statement to the Fourth World Congress of Sociology on "popular culture, a humanistic and sociological concept," Lowenthal deepened this method by completing it with a sketch of a research operation into the very concept of popular culture. The sociology of popular culture will probably make its surest progress along the route laid out by Lowenthal.

Max Kaplan, *Leisure in America*: A Social Inquiry (New York: John Wiley, 1960).

The ambiguity of leisure on the conceptual plane in the United States is complicated because of the language itself. The terms used to analyze leisure are numerous and frequently interchangeable (leisure, recreation, play, entertainment, and so on).

From the first pages of his book devoted to studying leisure in the United States, Kaplan faces up to these difficult conceptual problems. He shows clearly his desire to distinguish between the over-all concept of leisure and that of recreation so frequently used in the past. For him, leisure can from here on no longer be reduced to any one of its components. The meanings and functions of these related concepts of leisure are put in their proper place. The over-all concept of leisure borrows from each of these partial concepts that which belongs to it. The analysis of these components, which are barely sketched in by Kaplan, should be pushed much further.

The idea of an over-all concept of leisure has led the author to classify the different leisure activities and to integrate them within this concept. This attempt is so important that it should be extended and perfected by more rigorous research into the different criteria that would permit regulating, even hierarchizing, the whole of leisure activities and bringing the structure of the concept into view.

In a general way, this summary of the book indicates the intent of the author. Leisure is studied in its relationships with the various social factors—work, family, social class, religion, sociability, and so forth. Each chapter is testimony to the desire implicit in the author—never to isolate the problems of leisure but to study their interactions within the social and cultural environment.

On the other hand, leisure's right to autonomy is asserted. It is no longer a matter here of considering leisure as only compensation for work or as the "negative" of work. At the same time, the problem of the relationships of leisure and the whole of the activities of daily life is clearly set forth. "Leisure is more and more an end in itself, its own life. As with all human goals, leisure is strongly linked to morality, ethics, systems of thought, and all the institutions of society."

Insofar as the relationships between work and leisure are concerned, Mayo as early as 1929, had noted the influence of leisure life upon work attitudes, during an investigation carried on in the plants of the Western Electric Company. But since then, most industrial sociologists have instead sought to analyze the influence of work on leisure. Kaplan once again insists on the opposite. He does not hesitate to assert that work is increasingly judged according to the values of leisure life. It is this life that provides the new standards for judging activities on the job.

Sociology has never clearly separated the functions of leisure from those of the family. Kaplan's interest in the family system is in terms of leisure's place in it. According to him, the role of leisure activity is highly important, since it allows the family to regenerate itself through increased connections with the world outside. In particular, the increase in leisure time has contributed to the growth in the number and importance of local associations. These do not only constitute a new link between society and the family, they are veritable training centers for various activities. In an urbanized society, the association offers isolated citizens new possibilities of integrating with the life of the city.

The author properly criticizes the strictly economic approach so often employed in studying the household budget for leisure goods. He shows the inadequacy of inventories. He wants a study of consumer goods from the onset of the desire and the motivation for the purchase all the way through to the specific functions each object purchased fulfils in each kind of family life. Possession of a tennis racket, for example, would be examined through the various stages of its purchase and utilization (desire to play tennis in order to meet friends, purchase in such and such a shop, actual use for Sunday amusement, and so forth).

The cleavages among the various social classes are the result not only of differences in income but also in the kinds of life that are enhanced by the growth of leisure. Kaplan also criticizes the concept of social stratification by classes. He claims that the most important criteria are not the objective standards of status but the subjective criteria of awareness. He goes so far as to assert that the individual situates himself in society primarily by his awareness of his kind of life. Starting with Pieper's book on leisure and certain works on Jewish theology, Kaplan goes on to maintain that in a time when leisure is highly valued, religious thinking, whatever the faith, tends to accept free time as a potential period of spiritual growth. Work is no longer considered the basic or exclusive factor in human growth. This is bringing about a change in the Puritan work ethic which marked the period of the rise of capitalism as analyzed by Max Weber.

For the author a new system of values is attached to leisure. He offers a number of criteria by which a leisure of quality might be determined—the only kind, he says, capable of allowing man's fulfilment in our society. The criteria are these: Successful leisure promotes belonging; it helps one differentiate oneself from others; it may fulfil several functions for the same individual; it is as useful to society as to the individual; and it has no objectively measurable evil consequences.

Valid leisure, that is leisure meeting these standards, provides not only personal satisfaction but also the means for developing new forms of sociability. The example of peer groups studied by Riesman illustrates the way by which leisure has permitted young people to associate with one another. The importance of this kind of association goes beyond the specific framework of the limited group, since the association, in fact, becomes a training ground for social relations, particularly in the vast urban housing developments.

There has grown up during leisure time a whole swarm of sports and games that tend to furnish models in areas outside these activities themselves. Kaplan indicates that social workers in exercising their profession promote apprenticeship in leisure values. In fact, values drawn from the world of games and sports are increasingly applied to life at work, and even more broadly in the whole of daily living.

In this respect, the author pays special attention to the problems raised by sports and games. He introduces a difference in meaning between *play,* which is free and gratuitous, and the *game,* which emphasizes performance and the will to win. Besides, he seems to regret that in sports, the game aspect is ever more tending to win out over the play aspect. The taste for competition leads to the need for specialized champions, who in turn provoke an increasing professionalism, an imbalance to the benefit of the display and to the detriment of the game as played by everybody.

The relationship between art and leisure is not neglected in *Leisure in America,* but art is treated solely as an activity. This new situation of art integrated with leisure permits reconciling both its esthetic and its social role. In this respect, Kaplan stresses the cultural and artistic explosion that has taken place in America since the war, due to local and federal assistance to greater democratization of art.

In this same connection, the author underlines the importance of the mass media, especially television. But he warns against studying the impact of these media in terms of standards of activity or passivity, for the same activity and the same content may fulfil quite different functions, depending on the individual. The same activity may also fulfil several functions for the same individual.

In a chapter devoted to comparing the phenomena of movement and immobilism, Kaplan contrasts travel with television, the two most widespread forms of free-time activity in the United States. After describing travel in terms of the latest studies, he takes up the tourist's motivations. He insists particularly on the existence of two types of tourists: the "ethnocentrist" who is his same self wherever he goes and the "emphatic native" who identifies himself with the country he is visiting. Travel having become a mass phenomenon, Kaplan deplores the fact that the tourist industry has not understood the new wants of the middle class and is still guided by the tourist patterns of the upper classes.

After confronting the problems of leisure with those raised by social control and the growth of the personality in a technological world, he terminates his analysis with a short study of leisure as a source of values for "adaptation and creativity" in industrial society.

The problem posed by leisure becomes critical in a society approaching the era of affluence, yet the principal goal must be to find a way of promoting a veritable leisure aristocracy among the constantly expanding middle classes.

Despite the brevity of his analyses and the simplicity of his methods, Kaplan's study has the merit of attacking the general problem of leisure in American society. It is a sign of a theoretical renovation that is in the process of taking place in the empirical sociology of leisure in the United States.

Appendix B

Methodology

I. *Leisure Sociology and Action-Research Models*

AS PRIVATE AND PUBLIC ORGANIZATIONS BECOME EVER MORE
aware of the ambiguous power of leisure, they are seeking to
influence its conditions or contents; in democratic societies leisure
tends to reflect a threefold need that our entire inquiry has
emphasized.

a. Maximum participation in leisure must be encouraged
among all classes and categories of people and all individuals in
their social, family, or work life; otherwise family or social organ-
isms, even in a democracy, will be managed by specialists or techno-
crats isolated from their group.

b. Democratic societies need to develop participation by everyone in cultural life, and in the appreciation of, and even the production of, technical, scientific, and artistic works; otherwise higher
culture will become the privilege of a minority, while the mass of the
people, despite the influence of the schools, will be relegated to a
state of cultural underdevelopment and have to be satisfied with a
lesser culture.

c. In democratic societies, everyone must adhere to this policy; each individual must be challenged to choose how he will balance his leisure time among relaxation, entertainment, and personality development through participation in sociocultural activities.

In order to satisfy this threefold need, each society imposes upon leisure or through leisure—in an authoritarian manner (legal or moral constraint) or in a liberal manner (pressure and persuasion), in a unitary style (countries of the East) or a pluralistic style (countries of the West)—activities for protection, orientation, stimulation, regulation, organization, or planning. This aspect of sociocultural evolution seems to confront leisure sociology with the most important problem of today and tomorrow. With respect to leisure, the blind, anarchic, and unorganized sociocultural modes of conditioning must continue to be dissociated from the purposeful, conscious, organized, even planned modes of sociocultural action, for the group and by the group itself, so it can raise its own level of culture. The purpose of sociology, as we conceive it, is above all to compare the conditions, the processes, and the results of these two kinds of different or antagonistic modes. We are not thinking of I-know-not-what sort of black-or-white voluntarist sociology that would find all evil in the first modes and all good in the second. Our attitude is *experimental*. If man has a chance to intervene in the interplay of sociocultural decisions, it is especially by stressing voluntary, organized, or planned action by groups themselves, and by instituting scientific control over the results of that action. The content of such and such an action raises the first problem: What is its effect on leisure, whatever may be the means of communication used to disseminate it?

To study its effect and efficacity, it is wise to regroup all the partial concepts created by theories of communication, advertising, information, apprenticeship, group restraints, and social relationships into a more complete and more dynamic concept of *sociocultural action*. We know the practical interests of this analytical sociology, but experience has also shown that these concepts often overlap in reality and that it is impossible to make the experimental study in a real situation without reclassifying them in one way or another. If the content is really of greater importance than the channel of transmission, reclassifying the partial concepts itself provides experimental sociology with as many practical and operational advantages as it does theoretical and conceptual advantages.

Finally, the comparative study of the types of modern or traditional communications media, of telecommunication or direct communication, seems to us less important than studying the different types of organization and structure in which the contents of leisure at the micro- and the macrosociological level are worked out and disseminated. The study of the variations incident to or provoked by the content, linked with different structures and organizations, as well as their effects on the functions of leisure in industrial and democratic society, appears to us, all things considered, to be the over-all perspective in which we should place our experimental study. Sociology in small pieces provides small comfort for true knowledge.

1. REMARKS ON ACTION RESEARCH

Yet we often find ourselves defenseless when confronted with such a proposition. We depend on overformal distinctions between theory and doctrine, between research and action: Research presents the problem, action provides the solution. This is a misleading distinction. In reality, there is no separation. In the very way the problem is presented, an action is implicit, and in the way the solution is provided, the problem is presented. Because of this false separation, scientific knowledge often ends up merely presenting obvious problems with clarity, while the difficult or hidden problems are posed—or handled—by men of action, blindly, through sheer intuitive awareness, as we have already said. Following the recent example of political economy, which is becoming increasingly a science for improvement of living standards, and that of social psychology, which has produced an experimental science of group dynamics, leisure sociology should orient itself more and more toward experimental study of the conditions and the processes required to raise the sociocultural levels of leisure. It is not yet there, but thanks to the increasing development of means of orientation, organization, and education on the scale of either limited or larger groups and even broader units, it is tending to take shape around action research.

It is possible to stimulate and control changes. Of course, action research tends toward experimentation brought about by the researcher himself. But that is the final stage. Action research very much tends to be research *through* action (controlled), but it also is research *into* action. It is not a question of applied research limited by its external imperatives, in contrast to basic research freely developed through its internal imperatives; it is a matter of research into a situation *whose elements, whether favorable or not from the viewpoint of sociocultural needs, are always studied with respect to a real or possible action aimed at best satisfying these needs.*

Hence, it is a matter of a simultaneously or alternatively *critical* or *constructive* sociology that should allow research as permanent as action itself into the needs and the processes of satisfaction, which in their turn make new needs appear. To us, the best means of knowing a society is to explore its schemes for *intervening upon itself.*

The problems of action research call for an appropriate methodology. If the investigations are to deal with the most important of these questions relating to research and action, sociology cannot be satisfied with some hypothesis produced by itself. It is illusory to think that one has merely to pull together the "objective data" on which the man of action will be able to exercise that creative imagination which Claude Bernard so strongly insisted upon and which C. W. Mills has just recently rehabilitated in sociology. From the *very conception* of action research, the researcher must assimilate the intuitive awareness of needs that men of action have, that they intend to satisfy, and of the results they achieve or think they are achieving. This is a point of departure indispensable if we are to unite intuitive and scientific knowledge. Thus, the researcher must indicate his absolute independence by *criticizing* the action criteria through sociological reflection and observation. On these bases, he should elaborate bit by bit and *construct theoretical models* for observation, explanation, and transformation of the situation, starting with *explicit criteria*. For him, there is no question of normative or dogmatic assertions; on the contrary, action research is an attempt at verifying models common to both action and research, through rigorous techniques of control (refutation of invalid hypotheses, scales of measurements, ways of isolating variables, and so on). The most important point, perhaps, is to renounce the absolute distinction between causes-consequences and ends-means. In fact, one can consider (a) the purpose of an action (raising cultural levels) as an anticipated result, a level anticipated from the situation by comparison between the starting and the final levels, and (b) the means of the action (a film or a study group) as more or less determinist forces among others shaping the situation.

Thus, an action destined to change a situation rests upon a hypothesis of transformation (end and means) that we can verify by a hypothesis of explanation (cause-consequence). If the final level has approached, reached, or exceeded the anticipated level, and if our means of control allows imputing this change to the forces set in motion by the action, the hypothesis of transformation is verified. Everything happens as if the absence of this action explained the difference between the initial level and the anticipated level in the situation. If not, other hypotheses must be sought in order to verify. Hence, every situation can be approached from the viewpoint of a real or a possible action, all the while dealing with it with scientific independence and rigor. What are the models required for such action research into leisure sociology? We will speak of mathematical or nonmathematical structural models, located between great, unverifiable theories and petty, insignificant hypotheses. They are composed of a combination of disjointed elements and regulated by a system of hypothetical relationships such that it may be possible to construct a field whose properties permit experimental study of whether the system of relationships is verified or under what conditions it is verifiable.

2. DESCRIPTIVE MODELS

A. First, leisure is described as a social and cultural *situation, not* as an isolated compartment. In this situation, the individual lives according to his social and family status, his age and character, in a culture whose features form a *structure*. The study of leisure behavior is less important than the content revealed by this behavior. It is important to treat these behavioral acts as signs, the significance of which we will analyze in relation to a frame of reference which may serve as a code. The contents of different leisure activities can be related to one another or to those relating to other activities—family, job, civic work, and so on. These varied contents relating to different activities may arrange themselves according to culture *sectors*. With these sectors are associated interests, performances, norms, and values that determine cultural *levels*. These are differentiated according to types of knowledge—practical, technical, scientific, artistic, philosophic, and so on—whence cultural types. Finally, for each type there are corresponding degrees of participation in the products and minor, average, or major works of civilization, from the viewpoint of explicitly chosen criteria. Whence the determination of cultural *levels* of leisure. Such an analysis oriented through such a frame of reference permits us to *connect* the problems of leisure with those of culture. It is primarily structural and its licensed method is a variety of semantic analysis (Charles Morris would say semiotic).

B. This content of leisure is fixed in time. It is studied as a segment of a process of the permanent or semipermanent evolution of a *series* of events. The present period was produced by the past period and the present period is producing the future period. This future period (*in statu nascendi*) seems to us the most important to grasp. History and sociology must cooperate in this prospective research. The sociology of the growth of leisure and the development of its contents will be biased in order to be anticipatory.

C. The big problem is to know if these tendencies (actual or potential) are or are not meaningful needs of the society and of individuals.

a. It is important to study the needs of society, of its classes and groups (family, enterprise, neighborhood, and so on), through leisure. Observation of the phenomena of maladjustment and of non participation in the social and cultural life of a group in relation to the content of leisure is basic to learning, through *objective* observation, about the negative or positive functioning of a group, about social needs in matters of leisure.

b. The cultural level of the group often develops through the conscious action of the formal or informal dominant or opposition opinion leaders. It also evolves through the active attitudes of *innovators* who are the agents of development. The dynamics of cultural needs cannot be satisfied by a study of average behavior; it will also have to be based on an objective analysis of the influence of the leaders (promoters, leisure organizers) and the power of the *innovators* (the self-taught, the creators) in their relations with members of the group and with the group itself.

c. It is also important to detect among the average population not only needs that have been satisfied but also *latent* needs that are not being satisfied under present conditions—whence the interest in varying the leisure situation actually (comparative method) or fictitiously (filmed situations, projected or conditional questions, for example) in order to reveal these latent needs to the utmost. Calm comparison of the results of this threefold objective and subjective approach can result in an awareness of needs that will be more precise than the usual vague assertions about "human needs" or the "human factor" in leisure sociology.

These objective investigations into needs allow especially for determining the ideal or potential cultural levels of leisure in each situation, and measuring the difference between these levels and the actual levels from the standpoint of the action intended to reduce this difference.

3. EXPLANATORY MODELS

A.   Leisure in this way is integrated into a social and cultural situation endowed with an over-all character. Description of the contents of leisure as they evolve or could evolve would not be enough. They must be studied as a *result*. In fact, they are the product of a *quasistationary equilibrium,* of a play of social and cultural forces; knowing their totality is important in order to throw light on the act of choosing between possible means and discovering points of resistance to success. From this standpoint, it is easy to understand that a simple opinion survey or a mere study of attitudes is not enough. Action research needs to analyze the environment of the forces that come to bear upon the individual. A *morphological* study of the means provided, the relationships, the organizations, and the structures is indispensable.

B.   In this general view, it is proper to distinguish and to compare the positive or negative value (Lewin would say the "valence") of these different forces with respect to the means of action demanded by the situation. Special attention must be given to the forces that influence leisure directly: (a) the great mass media, (b) the institutions and associations of leisure (cafés, clubs, and so forth), and (c) free-time social relationships (spontaneous relations, influence of leaders and educators, and the like).

To avoid a formal sociology quite useless in action, it is essential to study the content of these different systems, the social and cultural stratification of the social groups they affect (workers, peasants, managers) and the social structure in which they operate (commercial or noncommercial, capitalistic or cooperative regimes) . . .

C.   Special attention will be paid to the results of innovations brought about by society and its groups for the purpose of raising the cultural levels of leisure of their members (laws assisting cultural action, dissemination of *chefs-d'oeuvre* by film, TV, or association). Research has scarcely started into the impact of the various types of leisure organizations connected with the job, the school, the church, or activities of a sports, touristic, museum, or social character. There are, however, some conscious and intentional efforts by the community to play a role in the sociocultural evolution of leisure; the results have not yet been seriously evaluated on a large scale. Here is a gap between research and action that should be closed.

Of course, the isolation of one group of forces from the whole is not easy. It can be brought about by the kind of retroactive experiment (ex post facto) performed by Chapin and others. It is in this sense that action research should perfect its explanatory models.

4. EXPERIMENTAL MODELS

Naturally, the preferred method of learning in action research is experimentation itself, whether incidental or brought about.

A. Each time a change in situation takes place in a negative or positive sense, from the viewpoint of the criteria selected, the sociologist must try to set in place a control device. This is the most appropriate means of learning about the possibility of changes in the phenomenon, and the conditions and the process of this change. In the field of leisure, the increase in devices for social and cultural orientation in differing capitalist or socialist *contexts* should allow for progress in experimental sociology: Organizers and educators who are concerned with leisure should learn not only to know each other better, but to work out together a research program of a new sort. It is not easy, but certain devices for controlled action can become the apparatus of on-going research (samples of terrain, observation, control of intervention techniques, evaluation of spot results, among others).

B. Then we will be able to elaborate bit by bit the conditions and the process of experimentation stimulated by the dynamics of the research itself. It is not only a matter of making investigations and communicating their results to the interested parties, in order to bring about a feedback.

The techniques of intervention that result from this are often oversimplified and lend themselves to justifiable criticism by experienced men of action, above all when they originate with young laboratory sociologists or psychologists ignorant of the elementary rules of real action (politics, administration, or teaching). On the contrary, experimental research should go into the *very norms* of action for the purpose of finding the *sociocultural optimum* of an organization of leisure, relating it to the nature of the situation and to the needs of the individual and of society. From this viewpoint, leisure sociology must take the greatest interest in the progress of the planning sciences and, in a more general way, in operational research that tends to bring within the field of science not only information but decision. As Guilbaud says, "We are beginning to glimpse the possibility of scientific thought nourishing and coordinating various techniques whose very purpose is human action, action and decision seen from within, that is from the viewpoint of the responsible agent himself." We should not add— actual potential.

II. Lippitt, Watson, Westley, *The Dynamics of Planned Change, A Comparative Study of Principles and Techniques* (New York: Harcourt Brace, 1958).

The subject of this theoretical essay is planned change, taken in the broad sense—that is, change brought about by the will to better the situation or the attitude of individual groups. This comparative study aims at clarifying the major experiments of *controlled* action (upon the person or the group) and the principles and techniques of planned change. The authors analyze some one hundred controlled interventions (1947–58), principally those of the

National Training Laboratories. They go even further. They take up the great ideas of Kurt Lewin on the necessity of uniting the *democratic and the scientific attitude* so that societies can effectively improve the human condition through a rational process of action and of evaluation of the results of action. They try to formulate the concepts that underlie the scientific experiments of social dynamics and to relate them to the general idea of democratic progress through a theory of planned change.

This essay evidences a new effort of conceptualization that should greatly interest the specialist in group dynamics as well as the expert in on-the-spot social and cultural experiments. Certain insights may even interest those who think, as we do, that sociology can renew its hypotheses and its methods by approaching the new problems of social and cultural planning connected with economic planning. The change brought about is studied, successively and systematically, in what the authors call four "dynamic systems"— the personality, the group, the organization, and the community. The problems of sociology in local planning are touched upon. The implied thesis of the whole book is that, to a certain general degree, planned change poses similar problems, whatever may be the size of the social and cultural units.

According to the authors, research into change should not be limited to a scientific study of problems; it should attack the study of solutions. For them, the preferred level of study is what they call the "level of problem-solving effort." It is less important to study what *is* than to search for what *could be* (the potentialities). Spontaneous, fortuitous, unplanned change is of less interest to research than the change brought about, the need it reveals, the effects it has. The controlled interference by professional agents of change is essential for rational progress in what the authors call the "client system," but also for the progress of knowledge about *both* desirable and possible transformations.

The authors' general research orientation can be of the greatest importance not only for social psychology but also for sociology.

In our area, present-day sociology is neither dynamic enough nor experimental (interventionist) enough to attack scientifically the problem of *raising cultural standards,* as economics has recently attacked the problem of raising standards of living. This book will help researchers (sociologists and social psychologists) better to appreciate the scientific possibilities of controlled action, as well as specialists in sociocultural action (educators, cultural promoters, social workers) better to understand the practical possibilities of research. It can encourage a dialogue between them about concepts and techniques. Such a dialogue is an indispensable condition for achieving what we call action research. It alone can lay the scientific basis for an on-going, conscious, and intentional creation of cultural democracy.

One may ask, however, if the authors have not yielded to the temptation to generalize too quickly about the conclusions of their specific research. It is regrettable, in the first place, that among the four systems envisaged, the last one, that of communities, has been studied far less than the others. When the authors stress the need for change, they are right. The concept of *need* has been dropped by certain static, conservative, or scientistic trends in sociology and psychology, although it is of primary importance in sociology, as in economics, for any progress in action research.

But in this work, the problems of the scientific analysis of needs are not considered. The authors are content to show that the ends of the controlled action correspond to a certain *good* and a certain *evil* (what causes pain, what is ineffective), defined solely and vaguely in psychological terms. In diagnosing sociological determinants, the authors pay attention only to the variables in organization, leaving aside the variables in structure and in culture, as if they were of no importance. The result is the analysis of the causes for success or failure in a planned change seems altogether too superficial.

The experimental models in this book seem more interesting than the explanatory models. Lippitt and his collaborators feel strongly that the current concept of "feedback" is inadequate. The experimenter must have a *creative imagination.* "Social invention" must produce complex models to be verified by action. The authors also stress that the mobilization of innovating energies in the group is necessary and that intervention by the agent of change must assist this. But they are not very explicit about the political and pedagogical problems that such an attitude creates with respect to work; it is thus regrettable that the theory of planned change is here rather oversimplified. This theory was born, in the first place, out of experiments in social psychology. It has remained stained with psychologism, while extending itself into the domain of sociology. It would be interesting to start it again on a broader base, for social units of varying size while respecting their specific differences. In this work, the resemblances among the four systems are emphasized, while the basic differences between a city and a little group of ten persons are underestimated.

Lippitt alludes several times to national and international planning in order to show that planned change can be practiced and studied in social frameworks of any dimension. We think so, too. But planning by a nation or a group of nations perhaps raises special problems. In our opinion, the weak point in Lippitt's generalization lies in an *absence of serious confrontation between the concepts of social psychology and those of sociology and history.* This first theory of planned change opens up a road rich in promises for the social sciences. It is on this road that sociology could close the gap between it and political economy conceived of as a science for planned raising of the standard of living. But this theoretical research must be undertaken through an interdisciplinary confrontation of researchers who are concerned with work on organization and planning; such researchers must be not only social psychologists but also historians, economists, demographers, and sociologists.

III.   C. Wright Mills, *The Sociological Imagination* (New York: Oxford University Press, 1959).

Mills wants a rebirth of "sociological imagination" which in our time has been narrowed by "false theoreticians" and by the technicians of "bureaucratized research." Sociological imagination is first of all the aptitude for situating the social structure of a society with respect to a great variety of other social structures belonging to other societies of the past, the present, and even of the future. "Social worlds in which men have lived, are living and might live." He attaches particular importance to two methods: the historical and the comparative. Empirical studies don't seem to him of any more interest for the progress of sociology than reflection upon the classic works of sociology. He advises students to get along without them as much as possible.

This book is a polemical essay against the tendencies of American sociology which, under the pretext of technical *exigencies,* puts aside the great problems raised by those whom Mills calls the classics of sociological analysis—Veblen, Marx, Weber, Durkheim, Spencer, and others. According to him, whatever may be the system of values with which their works are connected, these social thinkers raise three sorts of questions:

1.   What is the structure of the particular society, taken as a whole?
2.   How is this society situated· in human history?
3.   What kinds of men and women emerge in this society and in this period, what kinds are prevailing?

Taking off from this standpoint on the social sciences, Mills launches an attack that is, in turn, pertinent and excessive, against the two currents that presently dominate American sociology: the

Great Theory and "abstract empiricism." In the first, he is aiming primarily at Parsons and, in the second, especially at Lazarsfeld.

For Mills, the great theory amounts to studying "the nature of Man and Society" by associating and dissociating the concepts for analyzing a "social system," without regard for the most important problems raised by the social structure of the total society. Mills shows no tenderness toward this "Well-Worth Considering Theory." One gets a notion of his moderate tone from the last question that Parsons' work inspires in him: "Is this merely verbiage, or is it also profound? My answer is this: only about 50% verbiage, and 40% commonplaces. The remaining 10%, as Parsons himself would say, I am happy to leave to the results of your empirical investigation. . . ."

He deals with abstract empiricism less fiercely. Nevertheless, Mills deplores the fact that it achieves only minor results, because the questions of social relations of small groups of representative samples that it studies are generally *abstracted* from the great problems raised by the global social structure. The author violently criticizes the tendency to compare the models of social science with those of the natural sciences. He derides the alleged "gap" between the former and the latter. For him, it is a matter of two categories of science, each independent of the other. Mills lets fly at the tendency to deal with techniques in themselves, independent from theories, and he regretfully takes note that research is tending to become solely the work of "technicians without imagination" working in the organized teams of a new bureaucracy. According to Mills, this technocratic orientation is accentuating the tendency to remove research from the great problems of social structure. This ends up in conscious or unconscious servitude of the researcher to the existing structures. The tradition of classical sociology is betrayed.

What does Mills propose? Return to tradition; continue research into the social structure of societies, taken as a whole; explore the best ways of securing progress for liberty and reason in the politics of nations. For Mills, the progress of democracy is threatened by two types of approach: to take note in a passive way of "what interests man" and to decide in an authoritarian way "what ought to interest man." One is opportunistic, the other dogmatic. One is limited to recording interests produced, often by chance, accidentally, or else intentionally by forces that are the negation of democracy. The other, even if it is based on the best of intentions, can end up with quite contrary results. It can bring about the triumph of interests that violate democratic values. The best chance ("I believe the only chance") for the progress of democracy is to start with observation of the troubles of individuals and the issues before society as a whole or in its parts, and then to transform them into and to deal with them as problems of social science.

The great merit of this book lies in raising real problems that are fascinating for the future of sociology. It makes up for the many articles and books reaching us from the United States that prove obvious facts or require us to reflect upon commonplaces. But, still, why adopt this polemical fervor, often expressed in ways detrimental to rigorous sociology? He takes up in a most promising fashion the evolution of the social sciences in the last forty years and then leaves us disappointed by an overschematic analysis. In particular, this growth in the empirical attitude applied to large or small samples ought to be treated primarily as a social fact. It would be good if in another essay Mills would apply the historical and comparative methods he favors to this *social fact*. It is not possible to interpret empiricism in sociology without distinguishing between different types of empirical research at different times, in the United States itself, then in European countries having capitalist or socialist structures. The current vigor of these sociological practices, particularly in Poland and Yugoslavia, would be worth including in such a historical and comparative study.

2. Mills properly denounces, it would appear, a heavy increase in studies into relationships and small groups that claim to derive from the one and only possible social science. Of course, the influ-

ence of social psychology, while often beneficient on the level of method, has frequently been disastrous on the level of theory. A psychologist sometimes forgets the effect of historicosociological variables. But why replace the imperialism of microsociology with that of macrosociology? There have been psychosocial or micro-sociological studies that have unquestionably advanced the science of relationships and groups within the framework of an over-all social structure. To a certain extent, one can even claim that they have provided a scientific awareness of the partial effects of the over-all society on its various member groups and the various net-works of their social relationships, and so forth. We would like to see Mills thoroughly examine the conditions, the *limits* (whether conceptual or methodological), under which this "microresearch" might provide a real contribution to a scientific analysis of the components of the over-all society, as well as those conditions without which this same research would falsify and betray this analysis.

3. Last, we willingly acknowledge that the problems set forth by Mills are of the greatest importance for the future of sociology. We approve his idea that theory and method must not be separated and that they form a whole. The question remains whether, if Mills wants to create a social science and not a social philosophy, he ought not to study, like any researcher, two instances of research that imply two different attitudes of mind—that of the concept of hypotheses and that of their verification. In almost all his book, the author deals with the first moment of research and then under-estimates the second, to which he devotes only a few brief pages. How does he resolve the problem of proof in the historical and comparative method?

If he rejects the model of the natural sciences, what does he propose? How to get around the methods born about 1920 to avoid sociological dogmatism without bringing it back into the discussion? Here is the problem. Our appetite is aroused. We strongly want Mills' sociological imagination to turn itself toward both the deepening of problems and the perfecting of ways to deal with them. This book should have a great influence upon the progress of sociology.

III. *Organization of International Research*

A. International Group for Leisure Social Sciences[1]

In 1954, an international meeting took place at Wegimont in Belgium under the aegis of UNESCO among sociologists and popular educators on the general problem of social sciences as applied to raising the cultural level of social groups through various forms of orientation and organization of leisure. Our group fitted into this general perspective.

Its organizing session was held in Amsterdam in 1956, as part of the World Sociological Congress. Its first study sessions took place in France, at Annecy, in June, 1957. Since then, there have been five sessions. The last was held at Stresa before the opening of the Fourth World Congress. It lasted four days.

The aim of the group is the comparative study of the problems of leisure according to different technical levels and different social structures in industrial civilization. Its immediate objective, obviously, is more limited. First, a coordinated study of the sociography of leisure as it bears upon average-size agglomerations of an industrial character in various European nations—Belgium (Pierre Clemens, Ugla), Finland (Y. Littunen), France (J. Dumazedier), Italy (Alesandro Pizzorno), Poland (S. Zajanjowski, W. Wyrobkowa), Yugoslavia (R. Bonac and Vito Ahtig), Federal Germany (Erwin Scheuch). Other projects are in preparation or in

---

[1] A brief technical presentation of these various research projects appears in Volume III of the *Annals* of the Fourth World Congress of Sociology (1959). Since then, this group has been integrated with the International Association of Sociology as the subcommittee on the sociology of leisure and popular culture.

process: Austria (Leopold Rosenmayr), England (R. Tropp), Israel (R. Smilansky), Switzerland (Roger Girod).

Our investigation is related to certain American research (Rolf Meyersohn, Sebastian DeGrazia, Max Kaplan, Jack London, Harold L. Wilensky) and certain Soviet studies (G. V. Ossipov and Prudenski).

The study of cultural sociology in a city is conducted in accordance with principles and techniques worked out or accepted in common.[2]

It involves, first, sounding out the leisure practices and needs of a random sample of a magnitude of four hundred out of fifteen hundred persons, using questions partly in common. Second, a morphological study of the sociocultural environment, especially of the recreational leisure groups, based on a common study plan. Third, a *quantitative* and *qualitative* study of the effect of popular educational organizations in accordance with relatively comparable criteria. Fourth, whenever possible, a *historical* study of the evolution of these phenomena over the past fifty years as affected by the repercussions of local, national, and international events. What counts is the study of evolutionary trends rather than the present state of leisure.

This study is rounded out by an inquiry in the same countries into the evolution of leisure within a rural community in the process of development and through statistical documentation of the state of cultural equipment on the national scale.

The most far-reaching ambition of the group is to prepare for cooperation between specialists from the social sciences and specialists in cultural action for the purpose of elaborating, on an experimental basis, different models of the cultural orientation of leisure in terms of the needs of the individual and of society at the level of a locality, a region, a nation, or a group of nations. We pro-

---

[2] An analysis of the work of the group by R. Hennion is to be found in the special number of the *International Bulletin of Social Sciences,* "Aspects of Leisure," UNESCO, December 1960.

pose that our work contribute to research into the democratic conditions necessary suited to sociocultural planning in industrial societies.

For the period 1959–60 the coordinated research on leisure in cities was part of the great UNESCO project on "the social consequences of technical progress."

B. *Contribution of the Social Sciences of Leisure to the Development of Popular Education: Training Leaders for On-going Research* (Communication to the International Congress on Popular Education, La Louvière, Brussels, July, 1958).

1. For Durkheim, education is "the action of adults upon the young." This is an old-fashioned idea that sometimes limits present-day thinking by directors, administrators, and technicians in the Ministry of National Education. Of course, the problems of children's education are the most important. They have been so poorly solved in present-day France that any criticism, however excessive, is understandable. They properly call forth a demand for reform of school and university education—it's an emergency! But the long-term view is confused with the short. The same principles inspire both, and that is the danger. All modern sociological work shows that the educative function of modern societies has been transformed and is in the process of being transformed rapidly. Spontaneous changes respond temporarily to new cultural needs resulting from technical and social evolution. Education's public is changing. News tends to spread from individuals to groups. Public relations raises new problems. The economic, social, and technical services of the public and private sectors are increasingly preoccupied with information, training, and improvement. The educational function tends to become an integral part of the whole social function.

Over and over, during the same generation, adults are induced to add to or revise their knowledge, their attitudes, and even their values so as to adapt themselves to the new styles of life that are coming about on the farm, in the enterprise, at the office, at home, or in the neighborhood. A growing number of professional economic, social, and cultural leaders from every walk of life, regardless of background, are taking courses or joining cultural institutions and associations, in spite of difficult conditions, lack of equipment, and absence of any really stimulating legislation. This continuing education will become even more important. Little by little, education is extending itself from an initial unproductive period of existence into a productive, life-long experience. This is the fundamental fact about what we call "continuing education."

For the country's education, the problem is and will be how to divide up all education into periods of full-time instruction for children (up to sixteen, seventeen, or eighteen years) and periods of improvement or supplementary instruction, full time or part time of variable length—a week, a year, three years—for working adults. Public opinion is familiar with the idea of obligatory "military service periods." It will gradually become familiar with the idea of *postschool periods,* voluntary but encouraged by financial and other persuasive measures.

It is wrong to think of childhood or adolescence as the best period for everyone for every kind of background to learn. The first works of Soviet, American, and English researchers into this topic reach differing conclusions. For some subjects (economics, social questions) and for a great number of individuals (think of the hundreds of thousands of the self-taught, the "self-made men") the best period for acquiring knowledge of certain subjects is between twenty-five and thirty-five years. It is right to want to prolong formal schooling, but it is not certain that its systematic prolongation for everyone is the most humane solution for individuals and the most profitable for society, when a certain basic cultural level has been reached throughout the nation.

In France, the relative importance of adult training and improvement through the nation's educational system is dangerously underestimated. Neither the 4 per cent budget (170 million new francs) granted to the Youth and Sports Administration (1958)[3] nor the recent law relating to nonpaid twelve-day vacations, are adequate answers to a problem that henceforth will permanently affect all adaptation to technical progress, social participation, and the healthy moral, cultural, artistic, and social equilibrium of a nation undergoing total transformation.

In Sweden, in 1956, it was estimated that there were about one million members in study groups (out of seven million inhabitants). How many teachers know that in the United States, according to a 1952 study carried out by three university professors on behalf of UNESCO, there were twenty-five million adult students registered in evening courses, study groups, and cultural organizations?[4] At the last World Sociological Congress in Amsterdam in 1956, from solely the viewpoint of culture linked with work, M. Kutnetzov, Director of the Economic Institute of the Academy of Sciences in Moscow, asserted in his report that more than five million out of ten million minor executives were given training after having finished school, through clubs, groups, lectures, correspondence courses, and the like.

In the face of the widespread technical and social confusion that is occurring or will occur, the National Education Ministry ought to envisage in the next ten years a bold plan of continuing education and training for the benefit of every worker, whether adolescent or adult. We are constructing—no more and no less—a fifth order of national education. Continuing postschool education of adults should be as new and as important an accomplishment of the twentieth century as schooling for children was for the nineteenth century.

[3] Today this same budget exceeds 250 million new francs, and the law on nonpaid study-vacation has been extended from the training of union leaders to the training of promoters of youth movements and popular education.

[4] A recent nation-wide sampling of opinion in the United States (1958, U.S. Bureau of the Census study) revealed that about nine million adults were taking at least one course.

2. But this new form of education raises the most difficult problems, because of the fundamental ambiguity of the social reality that can make it possible or impossible: leisure. No obligation, no supervision of parents or teachers, few diplomas, few curricula, and so forth, and competition with all the other possible activities during free time. These are the hazardous conditions surrounding the development of this form of education.

The cultural ambiguity of leisure is well known to the educator. But is he always sure to understand it in its true sense? At the level of choice of content, the educator tends to distinguish between what is valuable and what is not, what is cultural and what is not. Very well. But in the name of what "value," what "culture"? For the man of action, the development of popular culture is a way to help expand the individual's active participation in social and cultural life, whatever may be his social status or level of education. Popular education tends to become the way to resolve a continuing double imbalance between (a) the cultural needs objectively required by technical and social changes and the manifest or latent cultural aspirations of society, on the one hand, and (b) the distances or the tensions that separate the various groups, categories, and social classes that compose the society on the other. Have educators left a large enough place in their personal culture for serious study of these phenomena? Can the solution of this double imbalance really be found in leisure activities, behavior, and attitudes? For example, under what conditions can a stock-investment group attract a part of the public away from a variety show?

At the level of the choice of means, comparative research on the effects and the efficacity of information and training media for adults has shown the importance of active group participation and of the leaders' action on spontaneous or organized groups. But what will be the chances of adult education groups in comparison with leisure groups related to the job, the home, and age bracket, people of the same background, intellectuals, and so on? Are these group activities possible without an enlightened use of the major media (magazines, films, radio, TV) for really promoting popular culture? Isn't it necessary to re-examine from top to bottom the relationship between action in one and action in the others, between tele-communication and direct communication, between reflecting upon words and reflecting upon plastic pictures or sound tracks, between spectacle and reading?

Here again the a priori ideas of the "ancients" and the "moderns" usually take the place of clear awareness of the basic questions about the most appropriate means of stimulating approaches to the use of free time.

What should we conclude from this? We have said that educators have to solve the most difficult question in the whole history of education: *the constant improvement of the levels of culture of all layers of society in terms of ever more complex needs for development and by means of the most ambiguous activities, those of leisure.* Only a common front of professional educators, popular leaders, information specialists, and social service workers can master this problem. We are pleading for a renovated national education open to people of all ages. In the face of this problem, research attitudes should be adopted that are both inventive and experimental.

As early as the spring of 1954, a UNESCO conference at Wegimont (Belgium) brought together educators and sociologists for the purpose of promoting just such an experimental approach. The seed was planted. Some French administrators have already understood its importance. Since 1956, under the aegis of three international social science institutes on youth and education, under UNESCO, sociologists of a dozen countries (as varied as England and Yugoslavia, Federal Germany and Poland, Denmark and Italy) have been cooperating in this new science of raising the level of culture of social groups. We hope that all educators and information specialists will become acquainted with the sociocultural dynamics of leisure.

3. EXPERIMENTAL ACTION TASK FORCES

The study of leisure within the perspective of improving the cultural level of social groups presupposes an increasing control of all positive or negative changes, whether incidental or intentional. This control requires constant collaboration between the person undertaking sociocultural action and the specialist in leisure social science. This was suggested as early as 1954 by the International Congress of Sociologists and Popular Education organized by UNESCO at Wegimont.

But such an experiment in active collaboration, systematically carried on in France since 1952, has convinced us that any cooperation would be impossible or sterile if the researchers were ignorant of the conditions and theoretical processes of short-term and long-term research work.

All those working with the leisure-study group at the Center of Sociological Studies carry on participative observation in leisure institutions, cultural groups, and professional meetings of journalists, movie-makers, and TV specialists.

Likewise, administrators and educators who take part in research must receive practical and theoretical training as psychosociological observers. To carry on our work on a national scale, we find it useful to form research auxiliaries among men of action at three levels of cultural activity.

a. At the ground level, activist observers are chosen and trained with a view to assigning them to the management or control of experimental undertakings in accordance with the needs of the research. Their work allows verification of the broad statistical data from administration investigations by local cross-checking, either through systematic selection or at random. For an action research group, they tend to be permanent correspondents of a kind differing from those in public opinion polls or market studies. They bear a double title: as pedagogical activists and as sociological auxiliaries.

b. At the executive training level, the groundwork activists are trained as interns or in schools by instructors and professors. We are trying to introduce the scientific principles of a sociocultural dynamic into the training of these instructors and professors. Monographs on leisure are produced by these future teachers and groundwork activists in cultural leisure organizations. In several youth and cultural groups, nationally trained teachers are now introducing elements of psychosociological training into their management training courses.

c. At the level of regional and national administration, it is a matter of creating a new attitude in the public and private agencies on which depend the organization of leisure. A certain number of administrators should receive sociological training which would give greater precision to their administrative inquiries.

They will become more capable of

1. Giving a true sociological value to a part of their administrative documentation.
2. Stimulating and guiding local and regional research projects.
3. Bringing about cooperation between continuing education and administrative sociology.

References

for the

Individual

Chapters

Leisure and the Social System

THE CHIPS ARE NOT DOWN

1. Rougemont, Denis de, *L'Ere des loisirs commence,* in: *Arts,* 10 avril 1957.
2. Caillois, Roger, *Les Jeux et les Hommes,* Paris, Gallimard, 1958.
3. Villermé, *Tableau de l'état physique et moral des ouvriers et des employés dans les manufactures de coton, de laine et de soie,* Paris, Renouard et Cie, 1840, 2 vol.
4. Stoetzel, Jean, *Les Changements des fonctions de la famille,* in: *Renouveau des idées sur la famille,* Cahier no 18 des *Travaux et Documents,* PUF, 1954.
5. Monographies d'Ecole normale d'instituteurs sur Aumale, Saint-Jean-de-Neuville, sous la direction de Jean Ader, 1958.
6. Fourastié, Jean, *Machinisme et Bien-être,* Paris, éd. de Minuit, 1951.
7. Chombart de Lauwe, Paul, *La Vie quotidienne des familles ouvrières* (Recherches sur les comportements sociaux de consommation), Paris, CNRS, 1956.
8. Lafargue, Paul, *Le Droit à la paresse, Paris,* 1883.
9. Wolfenstein, Martha, *"The Emergence of fun morality,"* in *Mass Leisure,* Larrabee and Meyersohn, eds., Glencoe, Illinois, Free Press, 1958.
10. L.E.G.E., *Dépenses et distractions, vacances, éducation,* etc., in

Enquêtes sur les tendances de consommation des salariés urbains : *Si vous aviez 20% de plus, qu'en feriez-vous?* Commissariat au Plan et IFOP, 1955.

11. Moscovici, Serge, *Reconversion industrielle et changements sociaux. Cahiers de la fondation nationale des Sciences politiques,* éd. Colin, 1961.

12. Giroud, Françoise, *Enquête sur la jeunesse de 18 à 30 ans, l'Express* 1958. *La nouvelle vague. Portraits de la jeunesse,* Paris, Gallimard 1958.

13. *Informations sociales,* numéro sur les familles en vacances, mai 1960, n° 5.

14. Arzoumanian, *Paupérisation absolue,* in *Economie et Politique,* octobre 1956.

15. George, Pierre, *Etudes sur la banlieue de Paris,* essais méthodologiques, Paris, 1950.

16. Enquête INED, *Trois conquêtes sociales* in *Population,* 1952.

17. Desplanques, *Consommation,* n° 1, 1958, *La Consommation* 1952.

18. Gounod, Philippe, *Les Vacances des Français en 1957,* in *Etudes et conjonctures,* 1958, 13, 7.

19. Friedmann, Georges, *Problèmes humains du machinisme industriel,* Paris, Gallimard, 1955.
Friedmann, Georges, *Le Travail en miettes,* Paris, Gallimard, 1957.
Friedmann, Georges, *Où va le travail humain?* Paris, Gallimard, 1953.

20. Larrabee, E. *What's Happening to Hobbies,* in *Mass Leisure, op. cit.*

21. Ripert, Aline, *Les Sciences sociales du loisir aux U.S.A.,* 1960, document dactylographié.

22. Riesman, David, *The Lonely Crowd : A Study of the Changing American Character,* New Haven, Yale P. 1950, and *Individualism Reconsidered and Other Essays,* Glencoe, Illinois, The Free Press, 1954.

23. Havighurst R. J. et Frigenbaum K., *"Leisure and Life-Style,"* in *American Journal of Sociology,* LXIV, 4, January 1959, pp. 396–404.

24. Bize, Dr. P.-R. et Goguelin, P., *Le Surmenage des dirigeants,* causes et remèdes, Paris, éd. de l'Entreprise moderne.

25. Lefebvre, Henri, *Critique de la vie quotidienne,* Paris, l'Arche, 1958.

26. Morin, Edgar, *Le Cinéma ou l'homme imaginaire,* Paris, éd. de Minuit, 1958.

27. Swados, Harvey, *"Less work, Less leisure,"* in *Mass Leisure, op. cit.*

28. IFOP, *Sondages 46–48, Jardinage.*

29. Huizinga, J., *Homo ludens, a study of the play-element in culture,* Paul Kegan, London, 1949.

30. Nisard, Charles, *Histoire des livres populaires ou de la littérature du colportage depuis le* XVᵉ *siècle jusqu'à l'établissement de la commission d'examen des livres du colportage,* Paris, Amyot, 1864, 2 vol.

31. IFOP, *Sondages* nᵒ 3, 1955, *La Presse, le Public et l'Opinion,* nᵒ spécial de la revue *Sondages.*

32. Escarpit, Robert, *Sociologie de la littérature* (Que sais-je? nᵒ 778), Paris, PUF, 1958.

33. Bachelard, Gaston, *La Formation de l'esprit scientifique,* Contribution à une psychanalyse de la connaissance objective, 3ᵉ éd., Paris, Vrin, 1957.

34. Varagnac, A. *Civilisations traditionnelles et genres de vie,* Paris, Albin Michel, 1948.

35. Benard, Jean, in *Population,* avril 1953.

36. I.N.E.D., *Enquête sur l'opinion publique à l'égard de l'alcoolisme,* in *Population,* 1954, nᵒ 1.

37. Wright, Charles and Hyman, H., *"Voluntary Association Memberships of American Adults,"* in *Mass Leisure, op. cit.*

38. Lewin, K., *Psychologie dynamique,* Paris, PUF, 1959.

WHAT MADE LEISURE POSSIBLE? WHAT WILL LEISURE BE?

1. Vauban, Sebastien la Pretrede, *Projet d'une dîme royale,* Paris, Guillaumin, 1943.

2. Fourastié, Jean, *Machinisme et Bien-être, op. cit.*

3. Pollock, Friedrich, *L'Automation, ses conséquences économiques et sociales,* Paris, éd. de Minuit, 1957.

4. Naville, Pierre, *La Vie de travail et ses problèmes, Cahiers de la Fondation nationale des Sciences politiques,* éd. Colin, Paris, 1954.

5. Barrau, P. *Conseils aux ouvriers sur les moyens d'améliorer leur condition,* 1864.

6. Duveau, Georges, *La Vie ouvrière en France sous le* IIᵉ *Empire,* Paris, Gallimard, 1946.
   et Chevallier, L., *L'opinion populaire,* in *Classes laborieuses et Classes dangereuses,* Paris, Plon, 1958.

7. Macé, Jean, cf. *Jean Macé, fondateur de la Ligue française de l'Enseignement,* par Prosper Alfaric, éd. Le Cercle parisien de la LFE, 3, rue Récamier, Paris.

8. Coubertin, Pierre de, *Leçons de pédagogie sportive,* Lausanne, éd. La Concorde, 1921.

9. Fourastié, Jean, *Machinisme et Bien-être, op. cit.*

10. *Revue de l'Institut Solvay,* Université de Bruxelles, oct.–déc. 1937.
11. Prouteau, Gilbert, et Raude, Eugène, *Le Message de Léo Lagrange,* Compagnie du Livre, préface de Léon Blum, 1950.
12. Rottier, Georges, *Loisirs et vacances dans les budgets familiaux,* in *Esprit,* juin 1959.
13. I.F.O.P., *Conditions, attitudes, aspirations des ouvriers, Sondages* n° 2, 1956.
14. Treanton, J.-R., *Le travailleur et son âge,* in *Traité de sociologie du travail,* Paris, Colin 1961.
15. Naville, Pierre, *La Journée de sept heures et la semaine de cinq jours,* in *Tribune marxiste,* n° 8, 1959, Paris.
16. 4e *Plan de modernisation et d'équipement* (rapport sur le).

SOCIAL DETERMINISMS AND LEISURE

1. Lynd, Robert and Helen, *Middletown,* trad. par F. Alter, Paris, éd. du Carrefour, 1931, et *Middletown in Transition,* New York, Harcourt, Brace and Co., 1937.
2. IFOP, *Activités sportives des Français, Sondages,* n° 15, 1948.
3. Lazarsfeld, Paul, et Kendall, Patricia, *Radio Listening in America,* New York, Prentice-Hall, 1948.
4. INSEE, *Une enquête par sondage sur l'auditoire radiophonique,* in *Bulletin mensuel de statistique,* suppl. mars et juillet 1954.
5. Veille, Roger, *La Radio et les Hommes,* Paris, éd. de Minuit, 1952 (coll. *l'Homme et la Machine,* n° 4).
6. Durand, J., *Le Cinéma et son public,* Paris, Sirey, 1958.
7. Cohen-Seat, G., *Problèmes culturels du cinéma,* Cahiers de filmologie, I, II, 1959, PUF.
8. Varagnac, A., *Civilisations traditionnelles et genres de vie, op. cit.*
9. Herskovits, Melville J., *Les Bases de l'anthropologie culturelle,* Paris, Payot, 1952.
10. IFOP, *Sondages,* numéro spécial sur les fêtes, 1er janv. 1949.
11. *Rapport annuel du Conseil supérieur de la chasse et de la pêche,* 1954.
12. Van Gennep, Arnold, *Manuel du folklore français contemporain,* 4 tomes, Paris, éd. Picard (parus entre 1937–1953).
13. Lefebvre, Henri, *Critique de la vie quotidienne,* l'Arche, Paris, 1956.
14. Baquet-Dumazedier, Joffre et Janine, et Magnane, G., *Regards neufs sur les Jeux olympiques,* Paris, éd. du Seuil, 1952.
15. Cassirer, H., *La Télévision dans le monde,* UNESCO, 1957 (cité par).
16. Brams, L., *Signification des contenus de la presse féminine actuelle,* *l'Ecole des Parents* (6), avril 1956, p. 22–38.

17. Bogart, Leo, *"Adult Talk About Newspaper Comics,* in *American Journal of Sociology,* 61, 1, p. 26–30.
18. Enquête sur la télévision et les actes de violence, effectuée en Amérique, 1952–1953.
19. Morin, Edgar, *Les Stars,* Paris, éd. du Seuil, 1957, coll. "Microcosme."

RELATIONSHIPS BETWEEN WORK AND LEISURE

1. Friedmann, Georges, *Le Travail en miettes, op. cit.*
   Friedmann, G., et Naville, P., *Traité de sociologie du Travail,* Paris, Colin, 1961.
2. Gauthier, J., *L'adaptation aux travaux spécialisés dans une entreprise,* in: *Bulletin du Centre d'études et recherches psychotechniques,* 1958, nos 2, 3.
   Gautier, J. et Louchet, P., *la Colombophilie chez les mineurs du Nord,* préface de G. Friedmann, CNRS, 1960.
3. Leplatre, N., et Marenco, C., *Approche sociologique des jeunes ouvriers,* Résultats d'une enquête d'exploration, Paris, Institut des Sciences sociales du travail, 1957.
4. Crozier, Michel, *Les Activités de loisirs et les Attitudes culturelles,* in *Petits fonctionnaires au travail,* Ed. CNRS, Paris, 1955.
5. Varagnac, A., *Civilisations traditionnelles et genres de vie.*
6. Larrue, J., *Loisirs organisés et reactions ouvrières,* in *Journal de psychologie normale et pathologique,* 1958, 1.
7. *Estimations convergentes des dirigeants nationaux des syndicats CFTC et CGT.*
8. Naville, Pierre, *Cristallisation de l'Illusion professionnelle, Journal de psychologie normale et pathologique,* juillet-sept. 1953, PUF.
9. *Peuple & Culture, Journées d'étude de la Culture populaire sur les lieux du travail, Peuple et Culture,* no 35–36 et 37–38, 1956.
10. Riesman, D., *Individualism Reconsidered, op. cit.*
11. Fromm, Erich, *The Sane Society,* London, Routledge and Kegan Paul, 1956.
12. Hekscher, P., and de Grazia, S., *"Executive Leisure," Harvard Business Review,* August, 1959.
13. Havighurst, R., and Frigenbaum, K., *"Leisure and Life-Style," op. cit.*
14. Le Guillant, *La Névrose des teléphonistes,* in: *la Raison,* no 20–21. 1er tr. 1958.
15. Veil, Claude, *Fatigue intellectuelle et organisation du travail, pourcentage de repos,* Thèse de doctorat en médecine, 1952.
16. Pieper, Josef, *Leisure, the Basis of Culture,* New York, Pantheon Books, Inc., 1952.

17. Soule, G., *"The Economics of Leisure,"* in *the Annals*, vol. LXIII, special issue, *Recreation in the Age of Automation*, Sept. 1957.
18. Naville, Pierre, *De l'aliénation à la jouissance*, in *Le Nouveau Léviathan*, Paris, lib. Marcel Rivière, 1957.
19. Benassy-Chauffard, C., et Pelnard, J., *Loisirs des jeunes travailleurs, Enfance*, oct. 1958.
20. Riesman, *The Lonely Crowd, op. cit.*
21. Lipset, S. Martin, Trow, Martin, and Coleman, James S., *Union Democracy*, Glencoe, Illinois, The Free Press, 1956.
22. MacDonald, in *Mass Culture, op. cit.*
23. Touraine, A., *Travail, loisirs et Sociétés*, in *Esprit*, numéro spécial sur les loisirs, juin 1959.
24. Hervé, Solange, *Diplôme d'expert psychologue sur les autodidactes* (dactylographié).
25. Wilensky, H., *Travail, carrière et intégration sociale*, in *Revue internationale des Sciences sociales*, nᵒ spécial 1, *Aspects sociologiques du loisir*, UNESCO, vol. XII, nᵒ 4.
26. Meyerson, I., *Le Travail, fonction psychologique*, in *Journal de psychologie normale et psychologique*, 1952, 52, 1, p. 3–18.
27. Touraine, A., *L'Evolution du travail ouvrier aux Usines Renault*, éd. du CNRS, 1955, travaux du Centre d'études sociologiques.

FAMILY AND LEISURE

1. Dumazedier, J., et Hennion, R., in *Aspects sociologiques du loisir*, Bulletin international des Sciences sociales, UNESCO, déc. 1960.
2. Stoetzel, J., et Girard, A., *Une étude du budget-temps de la femme mariée dans les agglomérations urbaines*, in *Population*, mars 1948, nᵒ 1, oct.-déc. 1958, nᵒ 4, éd. INED.
   Bastide, H., *Le Budget-temps de la femme mariée à la campagne*, in *Population*, avril-juin 1959, nᵒ 2, éd. INED.
3. Daric, J., *La valeur économique du travail de la femme à son foyer*, in *Informations sociales*, supplément 1952.
4. Goode, W., *"Horizons in Family Theory,"* in *Sociology Today*, New York, Basic Books, 1959.
5. Ogburn, W.-F., et Nimkoff Meyer, F., *A Handbook of Sociology*, London, Routledge and Kegan Paul, 2nd ed., 1950.
6. Stoetzel, J., *Changements dans les fonctions familiales*, in *Renouveau des idées sur la famille*, p. 343–369, Paris, 1954.
7. *Consommation, Annales du Centre de recherches et de documentation*, janvier-mars 1958, nᵒ 1, oct.-déc. 1958, Paris.
8. Fourastié, J. et F., *Les Arts ménagers*, Paris, 1947.
9. Naville, P., *La Vie de travail et ses problèmes, Cahiers de la Fondation nationale des Sciences politiques*, Paris, 1951.

10. Fourastié, J., *Machinisme et Bien-être, op. cit.*
11. Chombart de Lauwe, P., *Ménages et catégories sociales dans les habitations nouvelles,* extrait des *Informations sociales,* nº 5, Paris, 1958, éd. de l'UNCAF.
12. *Enquête sur l'équipement ménager des Français,* in *Bulletin hebdomadaire de Statistiques,* INSEE, 12 mai 1956, et INSEE, oct. 1960, Paris.
13. Girard, A., *Situation de la famille contemporaine,* in *Economie et Humanisme,* 16, 103, supplement 1er tr 1957.
14. Le Corbusier, *Les Trois Etablissements humains,* éd. de Minuit, Paris, 1959.
15. Riesman, D., *The Lonely Crowd, op. cit.*
16. Dumazedier, J., et Ripert, A., *Le Loisir et la Ville,* 1er tome: *Loisir et Culture,* Paris, Le Seuil, 1966.
17. *Les Vacances des Français,* in *Etudes et conjonctures,* juillet 1958, PUF, Paris.
18. Giroud, F., *La nouvelle Vague, Portraits de la jeunesse,* Gallimard, Paris, 1958.
19. Lazarsfeld, P., and Katz, E., *Personal Influence,* New York, 1955.
20. Chambre, P., *Enquête sur le travail scolaire à la maison,* in *Courrier de la recherche pédagogique,* Paris, juin 1955.
21. Riesman, D., *The Lonely Crowd, op. cit.*
22. Burgess, Ernest W., and Locke, J. H., *The Family, from Institution to Communionship,* New York, American Book Company, 1945.
23. Meyersohn, R., *"Social Research in Television,"* in *Mass Culture, op. cit.*
24. Scheuch, E. L., *"Family Cohesion in Leisure Time,"* The Sociological Review, 8, 1, July 1960.
25. Fougeyrollas, P., *Prédominance du mari ou de la femme dans le ménage,* in *Population,* janv.-mars 1951, nº 1.

Leisure and Culture

1. Shils, E., *"Mass Society and Its Culture,"* in *Daedalus,* 89, spring 1960.
2. Gorki, M., *A propos de la science* (1933), in *Komsomolskaïa Pravda,* 1951.
3. Lengrand, P., et Rovan, J., in *La Calabre,* ouvrage collectif dirigé par Jean Meyriat, Paris, A. Colin 1960.
4. Riesman, D., *"Work and Leisure in Postindustrial Society,"* in *Mass Leisure, op. cit.*
5. Département du commerce, U.S.A., rapport 1960.

6. Galbraith, J., *The Affluent Society*, Boston, Houghton Mifflin, 1953.
7. Ministère de la Culture, U.R.S.S., *Annuaire statistique sur l'éducation et la culture*, 1960.
8. Prudensky, *Les Loisirs dans la société socialiste*, in *le Kommunist*, oct. 1960, commentaire d'une enquête sur le loisir, dans la ville de Gorki, Novosibirsk, Krasnoiarsk.
9. London, J., *Enquête sur le loisir à Oakland*, 1960 (questionnaire).
10. Wilensky, H., *Travail, carrières et intégration sociale*, in *Bulletin international des Sciences sociales*, UNESCO 1960, déc.
11. Ossipov, C., et Ignatiev, N., *Communisme et problème des loisirs*, in *Esprit*, numéro spécial sur le loisir, juin 1959.
12. Rosenberg, B., and Whyte, in *Mass Culture, op. cit.*
    Larrabee and Meyersohn, in *Mass Leisure, op. cit.*
13. Lowenthal, L., *Un concept à la fois humaniste et sociologique : la culture populaire*, in *Bulletin international des Sciences sociales*, déc. 1960.
14. Daedalus, *Mass Culture and Mass Media, Journal of the American Academy of Arts and Sciences*, 89, Spring 1960.
15. Suchodolsky, B., *La Politique culturelle de la Pologne populaire*, in *Le Régime et les institutions de la République populaire de Pologne*, Bruxelles, Institut Solvay, 1960.

VACATION LEISURE AND TOURIST LEISURE

1. Gounod, B.-Ph., *Les Vacances des Français en 1957, Etudes et conjonctures*, juillet 1958.
2. *Etudes et documents* du Centre de recherches économiques et sociales, 1959.
3. *Les Vacances des Français en 1951, Etudes et conjonctures*, juillet-août 1952.
4. Sorbelli, Sandro, *Le marché touristique : un inconnu, Répertoire des voyages*.
5. Dumazedier, J., *Vers une sociologie du tourisme, Répertoire des voyages*, mai 1958.
6. Hunziker, W., *Le Tourisme social*, TI, AIT, 1951.
7. Association internationale d'experts du Tourisme, *Compte rendu du congrès* 1959.
8. Raymond, H., *Hommes et dieux à Palinuro*, in *Esprit*, juin 1959.
9. Duchet, R., *Le Tourisme à travers les âges*, éditions Vigot, 1949.
10. Boyer, M., *L'Evolution du tourisme dans le sud-est de la France*, sujet de thèse.
11. Enquête orale auprès de la municipalité de Saint-Tropez, effectuée par C. Allo (non publiée), 1960.
12. *Etudes et documents* du Centre de recherches économiques et sociales, fév.-mars 1959.

13. *Trafic au départ des six grandes gares de Paris,* SNCF, direction du Mouvement, 1ère div.
14. The travel market, *A national study,* October 1953, September 1954.
15. Rapport des services de la préfecture de la Seine, 1959.
16. Dainville, Fr. de, *Tourisme social, Etudes,* juillet-août 1956, p. 72-93.
17. Service statistique de l'Union nationale des camps de montagne, 1959.
18. Service statistique du Commissariat au tourisme, 1959.
19. Estimation des services du Haut Commissariat de la Jeunesse et des Sports.
20. Littunen, Y., *Recherches en cours sur les vacances,* Helsinki, 1960.
21. Varagnac, A., *Civilisations traditionnelles et genres de vie, op. cit.*
22. Klineberg, O., *etc., Technique d'évaluation, Bulletin int. Sciences sociales,* mars 1955.

LEISURE AND THE MOVIES
and
LEISURE AND TELEVISION

1. Durand, J., *Le Cinéma et son public,* Paris, Sirey, 1958.
2. Centre national du Cinéma, enquête 1954.
3. Wall, W.-D., *Considérations sur la recherche filmologique,* in *Rapport aux Congrès internationaux de filmologie, Sorbonne,* Paris, 19-23 février 1955.
4. Morin, E., *Le Cinéma ou l'homme imaginaire,* éd. de Minuit, Paris, 1958.
5. Bazin, A., *Qu'est-ce que le cinéma?,* Paris, 1958, Ed. du Cerf.
6. Hoggart, R., *The Uses of Literacy,* Essential Books, Inc., 1957.
7. Huizinga, J., *Homo ludens, op. cit.*
8. Lowenthal, L., *Un concept humaniste et sociologique : la culture populaire, op. cit.*
9. Dumazedier, J., et Sylwan, B., *Télévision et éducation populaire,* Paris, UNESCO, 1955.
10. Bogart, L., *The Age of Television,* New York, Frederik Ungar Publishing Co., 1956.
11. Oulif, S.-M., *Réflexions et expériences. L'Opinion des Téléspectateurs et son approche, Cahiers d'études Radio-Télévision,* no 3, 1954, PUF.
12. Meyersohn, R., *"Social Research in Television,"* in *Mass Culture, op. cit.*
13. Belson, W. A., *Television and the Family: An Effect Study,* London, British Broadcasting Corporation, audience research department, 1959.

14. Barthes, R., *Mythologies*, Parıs, ed. du Seuil, 1957.
15. Adorno, T.-W., *"Television and the Patterns of Mass Culture,"* in *Mass Culture, op. cit.*
16. Anders, G., *"The Phantom World of T.V.,"* in *Mass Culture, op. cit.*
17. Friedmann, G., *Introduction aux aspects sociologiques de radio-télévision,* mimeographed report (une conférence prononcée au CERT, février 1956).
18. Himmelweit, H., Oppeinheim, A. N., Vince, P., *Television and the Child,* London, 1958–1960.
   Schramm, W., Lyle, J., Parker, B., *Television in the Lives of Our Children.* Stanford, 1961.

LEISURE AND BOOKS
and
LEISURE, EDUCATION, AND THE MASSES

1. Berelson, B., *Who Reads What Books and Why?* Glencoe, Free Press, 1957.
2. Varagnac, A., *Civilisations traditionnelles et genres de vie, op. cit.*
3. Delarue, P., *Le Conte populaire français,* éd. Erasme, 1957.
4. Nisard, Ch., *Littérature de colportage, op. cit.*
5. Duveau, G., *La Vie ouvrière sous le second Empire, op. cit.*
6. Perdiguier, A., *Question vitale sur le compagnonnage et la classe ouvrière,* 2e éd., Paris, 1863.
7. Tolain, A., in *Tribune ouvrière,* 18 juin 1956.
8. Barker, E.-R., *Le livre dans le monde,* UNESCO.
9. Monnet, P., *Monographie de l'édition,* Paris, Cercle de la Librairie, 1956.
10. Escarpit, R., *Sociologie de la littérature,* Paris, PUF, 1958.
11. Desplanques, J., *Consommation en 1957,* in *Consommation du CREDOC,* no 1, 1958.
12. Hassenforder, J., *Réflexions sur l'évolution comparée des biblio-thèques publiques en France et en Grande-Bretagne durant la seconde moitié du XIXe siècle,* in *Bulletin de l'Union française des organismes de documentation,* no 4, juill.-août 1956.
13. Levaillant, Mlle, *L'Organisation des bibliothèques d'entreprise, Rapport de la commission "Bibliothèques et clubs de lecture," au XIIe congrès de "Peuple et Culture," 1956,* in *Informations sociales,* 2e année, no 1, janv. 1957.
14. Riberette, P., *Les Clubs du livre,* in *Bulletin des bibliothèques de France,* 1re année, no 6, juin 1956.
15. Enquête auprès des principaux clubs du livre (non publiée).
16. Breillat, P., *La lecture publique et l'école,* in *Lecture publique rurale et urbaine,* 1954.

17. Durand, J., *Le Cinéma et son public, op. cit.*
18. Hassenforder, J., Enquête bibliobus de la Haute-Vienne.
19. Caceres, B., *Comment conduire le livre au lecteur,* in *Informations sociales,* 2e année, n⁰ 1, janv. 1957.
    Caceres, B., *Dans le secteur non commercial quels moyens sont à encourager pour mettre le livre au contact avec le lecteur?* In *Informations sociales,* 2e année, n⁰ 1, janv. 1957.
20. *Ce que lisent Français? IFOP,* in *Réalités,* juillet 1955.
21. Tallandier (Ed. Tallandier) informations orales.
22. Enquête auprès des éditeurs de romans policiers.
23. Fourastié, J., *De la vie traditionnelle à la vie "tertiaire,"* in *Population,* n⁰3 1959.
24. Charensol, G., *Quels enseignements peut-on tirer des chiffres de tirage de la production littéraire actuelle,* in *Informations sociales,* 11e année, n⁰ 1 janvier 1957.

DYNAMIC ATTITUDES AND STYLE OF LIFE

1. Riesman, D., *The Lonely Crowd, op. cit.*
   Havighurst, R., *"Leisure Activities in Middle Age," American Journal of Sociology.*
2. Kaplan, M., *Leisure in America : A Social Inquiry,* New York, J. Wiley, 1960.
3. Lazarsfeld, P., *Personal Influence, op. cit.*
4. *Centre national du Cinéma, enquête 1954, op. cit.*

TENTATIVE CONCLUSIONS

1. Havighurst, R., *"Leisure Activities in Middle Age," American Journal of Sociology, op. cit.*
2. Varagnac, A., *Civilisations traditionnelles et genres de vie, op. cit.*
3. Bell, Daniel, *The End of Ideology,* Glencoe, Free Press, 1960.
4. Wright, C., and Hyman, *"Voluntary Association Memberships of American Adult,* in *Mass Leisure, op. cit.*
5. Glezermann, G.-E., *Le progrès culturel de la société, Etudes soviétiques,* oct. 1953.
6. Marx, K., *Manuscrits inédits de Marx,* in Revue *le Bolchevik,* 1/12/1939.
7. Ossipov, G., et Ignatiev, N., *Communisme et problème des loisirs, op. cit.*
8. Prudensky, *op. cit.*
9. Goricar, *Rapport ronéotypé pour la rencontre de Portoroz* (Yougo-slavie), Groupe International des Sciences sociales du loisir, juin 1960.

Index

abundance, society of, 116
action research, 265–272
action task forces, experimental, 287–288
active leisure, 222; see also leisure
Ader, Clément, 46, 169–170, 172, 255–256
adult education, 238; see also education; self-education
advertising, 20, 64, 136, 238, 253
advertising agencies, 66
Ahtig, Vito, 280
airplanes, 46
alcoholism, 27–28
apartment dwelling, 96
April Fool's Day, 58
archeo-civilization, 73
architecture, 105
Aristotle, 246
Armistice Day, 59
art, 64, 261
Audiganne, A., 36
Augé, Michel, 13
automation, 82
automobile, 8, 48, 101, 127
autonomous man, 221, 259

Bachelard, M., 218
Baden-Powell, Robert S., 38
Baker, R. E., 177 n.
Balzac, Honoré de, 118, 147, 199–200
Bardot, Brigitte, 143
Barrau, P., 36
bars and taverns, 27–28
Barthes, Roland, 168
Bastide, R., 147 n.
Bazin, André, 52, 147, 227
Bell, Daniel, 235
Benassy-Chauffard, C., 83
Benedict, Ruth, 179
Berelson, Bernard R., 253, 256
Bergé, L., 55
Bergson, Henri, 147
Bernard, Claude, 266

Bernard, Jean, 62
bicycle races, 57
Bize, P. R., 15
Blum, Léon, xii
Bogart, Leo, 107, 156, 165–167, 255
Bois, Jules, 46
Bonac, R., 280
book clubs, 187
bookmobiles, 186
book publishing, 176–181
books, 23–24, 63, 119, 173–202; distribution of, 181–193; in homes, 194, 199–200; number of by country, 177–178; readers of, 193–202, 255; taste in, 194–196; television and, 166–168, 201–202
Bookshop Circle, 182
bookstores, 181–183, 189–193
Bouglé, C., 53
Boyer, Marc, 125 n., 126
Boy Scouts, 38
Brams, Lucien, 86
Branly, Édouard, 46
Breillat, P., 192 n.
Buck, Pearl S., 199
Burgess, Edward A., 107

Cacérès, Benigno, 193
cafés, 28
Caillois, Roger, 4, 21, 65
California, University of, 254
camping, 133
capitalism, 8, 260
Cassandra, 64
Catholic Association of French Youth, 38
centralization, x
ceremony, 55
change, resistance to, 53
Chaplin, Charlie, 143–144
Charensol, Georges, 195 n., 197
Chicago, University of, vii
children, leisure and, 103, 106
children's books, 180

301